DIGITAL
STATE

Also by Simon Pont for Kogan Page

THE BETTER MOUSETRAP:
BRAND INVENTION IN A MEDIA DEMOCRACY

From the best-selling author of *The Better Mousetrap: Brand Invention in a Media Democracy*

How the internet is changing everything

Written and Edited by

SIMON PONT

Publisher's note

Every possible effort has been made to ensure that the information contained in this book is accurate at the time of going to press, and the publishers and authors cannot accept responsibility for any errors or omissions, however caused. No responsibility for loss or damage occasioned to any person acting, or refraining from action, as a result of the material in this publication can be accepted by the editor, the publishers or any of the authors.

First published in Great Britain and the United States in 2013 by Kogan Page Limited

120 Pentonville Road
London N1 9JN
United Kingdom
www.koganpage.com

1518 Walnut Street, Suite 1100
Philadelphia PA 19102
USA

4737/23 Ansari Road
Daryaganj
New Delhi 110002
India

Illustrations by Christopher Lockwood.

ISBN 978 0 7494 6885 9
E-ISBN 978 0 7494 6886 6

British Library Cataloguing-in-Publication Data

A CIP record for this book is available from the British Library.

Library of Congress Cataloging-in-Publication Data

Digital state : how the Internet is changing everything / [edited by] Simon Pont.
pages cm
ISBN 978-0-7494-6885-9 – ISBN 978-0-7494-6886-6 (e-isbn) 1. Information technology–Economic aspects. 2. Information technology–Social aspects. 3. Electronic commerce–Social aspects. 4. Internet marketing–Social aspects. 5. Internet–Social aspects. I. Pont, Simon.
HC79.I55D57 2013
303.48'33–dc23

Typeset by Graphicraft Limited, Hong Kong
Print production managed by Jellyfish
Printed and bound in Great Britain by CPI Group (UK) Ltd, Croydon, CR0 4YY

To the Digital Natives, who know no other world but this.
The future is theirs; may they be brilliant with it.

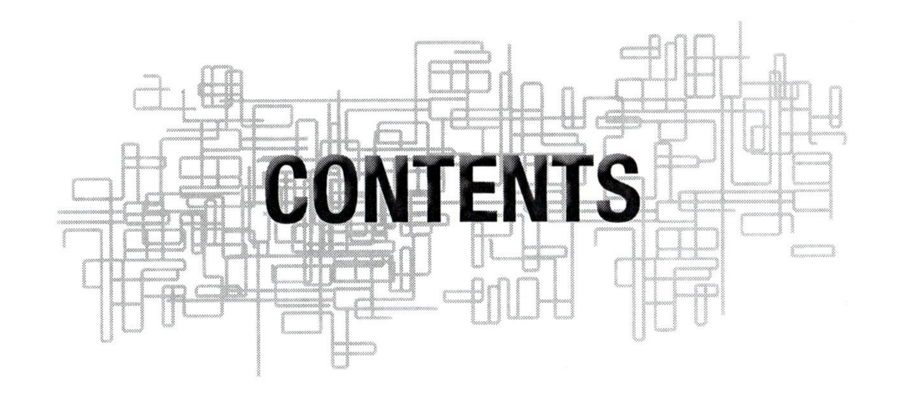
CONTENTS

ABOUT SIMON PONT

SIMON PONT is a writer, commentator and brand-builder. His agency career includes being part of Saatchi & Saatchi and Naked Communications, the pioneers of communications planning. Hollywood movie studios, Icelandic investment banks, British chocolate bars and Middle Eastern airlines figure amongst his time on the inside of Adland. He is chief strategy officer at agency network Vizeum, and an EACA Effies judge. He is the author of *The Better Mousetrap: Brand Invention in a Media Democracy* and *Remember to Breathe*, a novel.

Say hello at **www.simonpont.com**.

© Simon Pont. Photograph by Niklas Maupoix (2013)

PROLOGUE

> Like a squash ball, locked inside an all-glass court, played in a never-ending Sisyphean rally between two invisible and equally able opponents, that's what the *Digital State* first felt like. A descriptor in search of a winning shot, to break the deadlock, to set it free.

I had this idea, not even as much as an idea, more a part-idea, a descriptor, the 'Digital State', a descriptor for something quite real, or soon-to-be-real, that held real significance, an energy and direction for the way in which it feels things are going.

Like a squash ball, locked inside an all-glass court, played in a never-ending Sisyphean rally between two invisible and equally able opponents, that's what the *Digital State* first felt like. A descriptor in search of a winning shot, to break the deadlock, to set it free, unleashing vivid descriptions and Technicolor details.

And set to this creepy little squash match in semantic purgatory, I could hear a soundtrack. I could hear Alicia Keys singing an *Empire State of Mind*... where the streets will inspire you... the bright lights make you feel brand new... where there's nothing you can't do; 'Put your lighters in the air, everybody say yeah, yeah.'

Like I said, all a bit haunting, but captivating too. So very captivating.

The *Digital State*: I felt I was on to something. I felt as though I'd crossed a border, entered a new frontier. And, while I had a good few ideas about the kind of streets and lights ahead, most of all I had questions.

To recycle Hartley's line on *the past* and point it forward, I see *the future* as a foreign country too, where they'll do things differently, remarkably so. And the big challenge with looking forward, with looking through a glass, is that it's likely to be 'darkly'. But let's take that step forward just the same, through the glass, through what has in fact turned out to be a screen, likely HD.

I think there'll be some bright lights ahead, but, just in case, let's get our lighters ready.

SP
London

DIGITAL
STATE

“It was the best of times,
it was the worst of times,
it was the age of wisdom, it
was the age of foolishness,
it was the epoch of belief,
it was the epoch of
incredulity, it was the
season of Light, it was
the season of Darkness, it
was the spring of hope, it
was the winter of despair,
we had everything before us,
we had nothing before us...

Charles Dickens,
A Tale of Two Cities (1859)

The sky above the port was
the color of television,
tuned to a dead channel.

William Gibson,
Neuromancer (1984)

No more secrets.

Sneakers (1992)”

INTRODUCTION

> We're living the polar opposite of splendid isolation. We now celebrate the splendour of feeling and being interconnected, 'on the grid' all of the time... where it's unclear whether we are imprisoning or liberating ourselves, and it's likely we're doing both.

For a time British foreign policy purported that isolation was splendid. Distance from others was healthy. Maybe only an empire, at one point the largest in history, with all the arrogance that comes from presiding over one-fifth of the world's population, could assert such a stance. Such dazzling, reach-for-your-Ray-Bans conceit or, as Cecil Rhodes once put it, 'To be born an Englishman is to win first prize in God's lottery.'

That was all very then. Right here, in our right now, we're living the polar opposite of splendid isolation. We now celebrate the splendour of feeling and being interconnected, 'on the grid' all of the time. We like the idea of living and being part of this world wide web, this matrix, where it's unclear whether we are imprisoning or liberating ourselves, and it's likely we're doing both.

Our quotidian lives are feeling less commonplace because, more and more, that commonly frequented place is cyberspace, a placeless 'space' that sits in between our physical and imagined worlds, where we can feel globally connected. Online, we are all becoming 'citizens of the world', gravitating *towards*, without by extension so quickly recoiling from whatever we are not. The online world is one of 'friends' and 'likes', not of strangers and dislikes. Cyberspace is a cosmopolite's haven.

Take 'living memory', and apply a little stretch. Give contemporary history a timeline that kicks off with the 20th century and a second Industrial Revolution in full swing, and then hurtles forwards with an ever-quickening pulse. The inventions, the achievements, the transformative technologies that race and build along the timeline, each and every one utterly life-changing. Witness: the domestic telephone; radio and television; the aeroplane; the atom bomb; the microchip; the personal computer; lasers and fibre optics; the internet...

The internet: backbone of the Digital Revolution, a revolution in *our* time, which we're living through, witnessing, being so very much part of – technological change continuing to reshape society and steer the human condition. The crossover happened in 2009, when there were suddenly more digitally connected devices littering the planet than there were people. Continue the trend line, and by 2020 connected devices will outnumber people *sevenfold*. In a sheer aggregate sense, the machines *have* taken over. Our 'always on' world has become one of gadget choice, an array of web-linked devices within arm's reach, each a compass by which we continue our cyber-wanderings.

Cisco forecasts that 78 per cent of all web traffic will be video by 2016. YouTube is the most popular desktop home page for people in the UK, a site which now receives 4 billion views from somewhere on the planet every day. 'Every minute 72 hours of video are uploaded to YouTube' (Social Media, 2013). Across 2011, YouTube received 1 trillion views. The numbers – 4 billion, 1 trillion – seem unreal, unrelatable, an abstraction: like Stalin's view of a million deaths, 'a mere statistic'.

In 1982, the movie *Tron* seemed like wonderfully absurd cartoon fiction, but I don't think it's proved so absurdly off the mark. It's just that *Tron*'s depiction of two utterly separate worlds, one physical, one digital, was very literal, too literal, and the reality, *our reality*, is a hybrid, where separate worlds are fusing and augmenting – and this all has quite remarkable implications for what 'reality' is starting to mean to people.

The very idea of 'solid and tangible' is being usurped. DVD box sets are dust-gathering format dinosaurs; films are taking to the clouds, along with our music collections and the contents of our old hard drives.

Now we have *Wikipedia* and an *Encyclopædia Britannica* available only in 'digital format'. On 14 March 2012 *Encyclopædia Britannica* announced it was going 'completely digital', bringing 244 years of hard-copy existence to an ultimate full stop. Jorge Cauz, president of *Encyclopædia Britannica*, declared, 'The end of the print set is something we've foreseen for some time. It's the latest step in our evolution from the print publisher we were, to the creator of digital learning products we are today.' This is significant, I think. Symbolic. All the information online, and only online. On the day of *Britannica*'s press release, a colleague of mine asked, 'If someone somewhere turns off the wrong switch, what happens to all our stuff?'

It's fast approaching a point in time where we can't afford for anyone to accidently flick the wrong switch. And we certainly can't afford for anyone to flick it deliberately. We've uploaded too much, pumped too much of ourselves into cyberspace, to go and lose it all. And the more we invest through our uploads, the more paranoid we become. Cyber-terrorists have become the new bogeymen under the stairs.

And of course there's the obvious irony that we worry so much about the information being gathered on us, by the State, to *protect* us, but then we freely, gladly, pump so much of it out there for 'anyone' consumption. In the UK, protest rings out at a DNA database of 3.1 million people, with 4.2 million CCTV cameras on the streets, rotating on each of us. We want our privacy. And then we chronicle our entire lives through Facebook, provide complete disclosure. But then, too, in the case of *WikiLeaks* and the form of Julian Assange, being a freedom (of information) fighter pursuing a belief in complete disclosure can make you a very wanted person.

Governments are little different to the people they govern; they consist of individuals keen to embrace our digital world, and terrified by its potential reach and influence, should it fall into 'the wrong hands'. Knowing which are the 'right hands' and 'right governments' becomes a point of subjective and biased perspective too. All sides and parties are guilty of wanting to PR-manage and damage-control in the name of 'public interest' and 'the greater good'.

Coming out of the Berkman Center for Internet and Society at Harvard University, the website Herdict (**www.herdict.org**) takes an apolitical, agnostic approach to right and wrong, simply crusading for open access to the web by flagging the real-time blockages. Whether Vietnam or China, the United States or Germany, Herdict names and shames the countries and reports the urls where site access is being slowed or denied.

> *In the interactive world of Web 2.0, the prime mission of some of the technology sector's fastest-growing corporations is to provide cross-border connections. Little wonder that the old-guard officials who dominate repressive regimes see these companies as little more than the arms dealers of the information age.*
>
> ERIC SCHMIDT AND JARED COHEN, THE DIGITAL DISRUPTION, *FOREIGN AFFAIRS* (NOVEMBER/DECEMBER 2010)

OUR NEW STATE

> *STATE*
>
> *(noun) – a particular condition of mind or feeling; a state of being; being in a state of*
>
> *(adjective) – a demarcated, institutionally defined and governed collective*

'State', a double meaning, a defined and governing structure of some kind, and also a condition of *being*: the *state* that we're in, whether as a collective or as individuals, each of us, all of us. What kind of state *are* we in, in both senses of the word? It certainly feels like the cusp, but the cusp of what?

These are fast times, where it feels as though almost anything could happen, and happen in a near-instant. But how should and how do we feel about it all? We fear the sky could come crashing in. We also know that the Digital Revolution could be the beginning of something maybe rather wonderful, which blows the roof off in a very fabulous kind of way. A growing number subscribing to enlightened self-interest? A new age of enlightenment even, grandiose but maybe not over-egging the potential? It all prompts the poser: dare we hope? Should we be thrilled? Or is feeling thrilled just too naive? Is any genuine sense of positivity and optimism just asking for trouble?

I think the Digital Age is opening doors, creating new vistas, new lands to explore and worlds to conquer, on all kinds of levels, real, augmented, virtual, intrinsic, extrinsic. I think it's double-handing in a number of ways too, accelerating opposites, allowing new collectives to rally and shape, but allowing micro-cliques and atomization to spark and run riot. I think it's empowering all kinds of genuine self-expression, and fuelling some borderline-unhealthy levels of self-delusion. It's bringing people together; it's pushing people apart. It's creating new feelings of belonging; it's driving new kinds of estrangement. It's making things happen fast, and it's making things happen too fast.

These are wonderful times; these are overwhelming times. Everyone is speculating. No one knows. But certainly it's a tale of two kinds of cities, make no mistake. And while *no one knows*...

I knew a fair few people had more than a few ideas. In fact, I knew a good few in particular who, guaranteed, had a whole heap of ideas and views and, once you asked the question, the challenge would be getting any of these folk to shut up. That was the ticket, I figured, rallying the kind of firepower who can get a job done, friends of mine, whom I admire for who they are and what they have to say, all crazy smart, where, even when it's only a quick chat, unexpected thoughts can leap and fizz, where the moment can feel heightened and things likely to happen.

Not long after the success of *Pulp Fiction* (1994), I remember watching an interview with Quentin Tarantino where he declared that he wanted to write a 'guys on a mission' movie, a war movie in the style of one of his favourites, *Where Eagles Dare* (1969). Now *Where Eagles Dare* is a goddamn *Boy's Own* classic, Burton and Eastwood taking a weekend out to storm the Schloß Adler, single-handedly beat the Nazis and win the second world war. It only took a Voice, a Squint, some machine-guns, and more machismo between them than a whole German army could counter. Who wouldn't be overcome by that kind of double act, a pairing of Absolute Cool? (Hell, it almost made up for the Cooler Kid getting tangled in the Swiss–German border wire. Almost.)

So in the *Where Eagles Dare* mould of compatible and complementary skill sets, where collaborations can conquer strongholds and best Nazis, I loved the idea of rallying those I knew, maybe an Ocean's Eleven, maybe a Dirty Dozen, maybe as many as a 15-person squad, and to each putting the question: what are we living through and looking at here, this vista before us? Just what's your view of the view? Specifically, what is the Digital State, and what is our Digital State of Mind?

I knew I wouldn't be disappointed by the replies. And I wasn't. What followed is this.

SP
London

1 DIGITAL CURRENTS AND INVISIBLE FUTURES

Faris Yakob

> It wasn't until 'creation' was whittled down to 140 characters and clipped fragments of the web, as with Twitter and Tumblr, that it became obvious that everyone was talking and sharing – and that people were expecting everything else to move in sympathy...
>
> The key thing is for brands to listen to what people are saying *and* then incorporate that into their content and behaviour, thus demonstrating an understanding that media is one system of interoperating parts...
>
> We can entirely reverse the polarity of advertising media. Rather than trickle-down television, we build up from fragments of many conversations, crafting broadcast stories around real people.

I'd like you to meet... Faris Yakob.

Faris Yakob looks quite a lot like a cycle courier. Y'know, kinda wild and crazy-haired and in perpetual motion, zigging and zagging in and out of downtown traffic, playing chicken with taxis and 10-ton trucks, going head to head with the kind of purpose that suggests he'll always come off best, as though he has an inside track on some strand of voodoo physics. Faris looks this way even when he's sitting perfectly still. Maybe it's the dreadlocks, arguably untypical on a short white guy who read English at Lady Margaret Hall, Oxford – and I do confess to having wondered whether those locks possess a kind of latter-day Samson-like strength of intellect.

So maybe Faris's hair is somehow connected to the cosmos; maybe he can metaphysically pass through a steel wall of urban gridlock; maybe his thought patterns do mimic the speed and agility of a Tron light cycle – maybe, just maybe. Speculations aside, what I do know is this. Faris is an original, an original thinker, an original piece of work, because you can divide, define and tag the world in any number of ways but, if you run the dividing line simply between those who have questions and those who attempt the answers, it's not much of a brain-teaser to work out on which side Faris Yakob falls.

*

REM's 'The Great Beyond' was in praise of the late comedian Andy Kaufman, an oddball genius 'looking for answers from the great beyond'. I think Faris Yakob knows a thing or two about the great beyond, and I've always been an applauding fan of the answers he brings back with him. Answers, possibilities, possible futures, that's what Faris's chapter is all about.

Just imagine you're riding pillion on Faris's light cycle, navigating at speed through the inner workings of his brain – because 'Digital currents and invisible futures' fizzes and jumps with thoughts and ideas. It comes at you fast, and merits a double reading. On the first pass, I'd suggest, just roll with it. On the second pass, start wrestling it. 'Media is one system', the 'digital exhaust', the 'invisible web' – to steal a word that Faris is fast making his own, these ideas are pretty *awesome*, and they're both fun and exciting to spend some time with.

It made me think of some kind of organic Swiss watch, where everything is an interconnected and delicate moving part – only, then add a new part, and the watch completely changes in nature, but crucially it still works. The addition of each new part doesn't crunch the mechanism; it just redefines the whole, all the time getting more precise, more intricate, more symbiotic, closer to sentient even – and also, don't let me forget, invisible.

Over to Faris.

THESIS – WELCOME TO THE DIGITAL STATE

The Digital State is social, local, mobile and personal. The future of digital is infinite, invisible, interactive and intelligent. The future of digital marketing is participatory, frictionless, stimulus, solutions, systems and sales. The future is not the present, but is contained therein.

PROSPECTION

Any attempt to look to the future is usually flawed. When we project ourselves forward, the imagined results are always tainted by our present feelings and concerns – we are unable, imaginatively, to feel any different. This has been the case throughout the history of futurology. The bias of presentism ensures that the novelty of the future is always underestimated. And yet, we know this. The economics of cultural production has radically decentralized. This effect is ongoing, as caused by the proliferation of communication and creation technologies. By consequence, the traditional communications and marketing equilibrium is fundamentally unbalanced.

We are all witnesses, and most of us are participants: content *scarcity* has given way to content *overload*, fixed channels of communication have dissolved into fluid and complex networks of information exchange, and once-captive audiences have now become active participants in a largely consumer-driven conversation. This shift requires a new course of action for brands; it demands new marketing imperatives. The answer does not lie in social media alone, or in what social media marketing is purported to be. The solution lies in understanding changing behaviours, patterns of communication and modes of living that the social web merely illuminates. The Digital State is not locked to a screen; it is the redefinition of boundaries between people, institutions and ideas. We must adapt and apply new thinking, skills and methodologies based on these insights.

BECAUSE MEDIA IS A SYSTEM

The Digital State has dissolved the boundaries between channels. Technology has changed the nature, speed and relative scarcity of media. As well as reminding us that media is inherently social, 'social media' has begun to dissolve the delineations that we perceived *between* channels, driving the 'socialization' of mainstream media, and indicating how understanding the mediascape as a system of interoperating real-time parts is the model we need today.

BECAUSE MEDIA IS *ONE* SYSTEM

Kevin Kelly, the founder of *Wired* and author of *What Technology Wants* (2007), has long posited the idea of the 'One Machine'[1] – the next step in the evolution of technology, a single platform, with the web as its initial operating system. Every new device simply provides another window into the One Machine. Media could be understood to follow a similar convergent trajectory.

Digital media strips content from the distribution platform, rendering everything as ones and zeros, which means, as all media inexorably becomes 'digital' media, all media will be platform agnostic – it flows across what we previously thought of as channels, and different parts of the system can effect change in other parts, in as near as makes no difference to real time.

Up until digitization, making things even more confusing, what we called 'media' were themselves assemblages of other things. So 'television' isn't actually a clearly defined thing as such – it's a socio-cultural construct of a typology of content, a distribution platform and a consumption device. Books, magazines and radio all work the same way. A 'book' is a bunch of words printed on paper, with a certain set of culturally defined ideas that float around it.

Up until 'digitalness', you couldn't separate the content from the distribution platform, but in the Digital State 'content' can be unbundled from its distribution platform. When IBM started talking about the brave new 'world of platform agnostic content and the fluid mobility of media experiences'[2] in 2006, we weren't really there yet.

Language, as usual, helps us see where the changes are occurring. When you are watching *30 Rock* on Netflix via your Xbox 360, or on Hulu, on a laptop, screen, projector or iPad, are you watching television? If so, why? If not, why not?

Media companies then face the challenge of redefining themselves in a digital world. Previously, they were defined primarily by their distribution platform – a magazine like *Vogue* is, well, a magazine. In a converged world, *Vogue* may make videos and put them online, or into an iPad experience – then how are they different to other media companies such as a television station or website publisher?

The *Guardian* has long been working around this, redefining itself as the 'World's leading liberal voice', a larger proposition than being a daily liberal newspaper in the UK[3] – replacing a distribution channel with a global community.

But everyone who works with media, including brands, has to face the same challenge. Online, brands have the opportunity to have direct contact with their customers and prospects. The internet is the great disintermediator, connecting everything to everything else. This opportunity comes at a cost – every brand must function like a content company to maintain the ongoing connection.

THE SOCIALIZATION OF MEDIA

All media are inherently social, in the most literal sense – a medium is a conduit for ideas between people – and in the economic sense. Media have the tendency to operate like solidarity goods – a permanent economic class of goods that get more valuable the more they are consumed.

'Social media' – that which is created by the many, rather than the few – has been a long time coming. Henry Jenkins established the blurring of media modalities in 2006:[4] in a digital world of democratized creative tools and access, everyone who consumes can create, and everyone who receives can broadcast. But it wasn't until 'creation' was whittled down to 140 characters and clipped fragments of the web, as with Twitter and Tumblr, that it became obvious that everyone was talking and sharing – and that people were expecting everything else to move in sympathy. In January 2011, Twitter's new CEO nailed the company's long-term vision: 'We want to instantly connect people everywhere to what's most important to them.'[5]

The harbinger of the real-time web did more than drive a change to Google's search and the development of Google Instant. One of the key tenets of the Digital State is that every new channel changes the entire system. So, because YouTube exists, how we think about 'television' has to change. Regardless of whether or not your campaign has a digital component, the world does.

The greatest effect of Twitter to the system has been to bring down cultural latency to almost zero. Cultural latency[6] is a function of the speed of information as it moves through culture. There is a correlation between the amount of time it takes to distribute something and the amount of time it takes for that thing to have an effect and consequently the amount of time that thing stays relevant and interesting. Twitter changes the speed of culture, as information now disseminates so fast: millions of eyes connected to a real-time information network, with a social drive for primacy, are driving cultural latency down to zero. It is this low-latency media system that brands and culture operate within in totality – it is not restricted to Twitter itself. Twitter provides a real-time return path – a low-latency way to interact with other media.

SOCIAL TV

> *I don't know what TV is anymore.*
>
> JAY LENO[7]

As mentioned earlier, 'television' is an assemblage term, one that is only earning more confusion with the newly minted term 'social TV'. What is social TV? Old and new media collide in the living room. The television industry, having defended its closed network thus far, has begun to realize that opening up to the rest of the system provides an opportunity to regain the cultural salience and create more truly shared viewing experiences in real time – the new water cooler effect.[8]

People naturally use social media to find other people to watch and comment on shows with, so inevitably these conversations begin to interact with the content. In fact, contrary to the prevailing discourse, it seems that multi-screen viewing and the ability to connect via the social web are driving an *increase* in television viewing.[9] One of the earliest examples came from MTV show *The Hills* with the Backchannel, which let viewers exchange snarky comments in real time while watching the show.[10] A host of different start-ups have since emerged looking to formalize the grammar, and provide the preferred platform, for social TV. Some, like Starling,[11] are looking to enhance the real-time viewing experience, letting you share short-form comments about what you are watching, which become social objects shared on Facebook or Twitter. Others, like Miso[12] (which Google Ventures invested in) and Philo, export the check-in grammar from Foursquare, letting you check into shows to get points and badges.

Facebook and TV will inevitably hit each other in the future. The electronics programming guide (EPG) is a relic from a former age – scrolling endlessly through thousands of channels simply doesn't work. Google TV was the wrong solution to this problem – you needed to already know what you wanted to find. People 'find' content through social signals and recommendations. Facebook has begun to transform itself into a shared media browser. Inevitably this will lead to a Facebook–connected TV interface, where you find what to consume based on your friends.

This further increases the importance of understanding algorithms. EdgeRank dictates what content surfaces in the newsfeed, and the newsfeed (or something like it) will become the dominant interface for content. EdgeRank penalizes content that is not timely, relevant or engaging, so all content brands create needs to be current and refreshed, and drive elective views, comments and sharing.

INCORPORATE THE 'AUDIENCE'

Reflecting the 'one system' nature of media is increasingly a way to create adaptive content experiences that leverage social content, garnering the authority of the crowd for brands.

Pulling live tweets into digital content is as simple as parsing an XML feed. Banners began to pull in tweets.[13] Trident ran a print ad featuring real tweets.[14] Wheat Thins ran a campaign of YouTube videos, where they tracked down fans who had mentioned them, and then proceeded to have a truckload of Wheat Thins dropped on them. Then Old Spice upped the ante, having the Old Spice Guy *respond* to tweets, creating nearly 200 personal video responses over the course of two days. In the UK, Orange created Singing Tweetgrams, which selected tweets to turn into fragments of song, and followed up with Secret Portraits, which created portraits of influential Twitter users based on their tweets. The Swedish singer Robyn created an online music video that dynamically incorporated tweets that feature the hashtag #killingme in real time.[15]

The former definition of 'audience' is increasingly unhelpful. Previously they, like Victorian children, were seen but not heard, passive receivers of content. Now consumers generate the largest volume of content and are quick to make their feelings known, publicly. If they have no role in the content, they may not pay attention at all.

BEYOND THE TWEET

But this isn't simply all about pulling in tweets. That's just been one of the easiest ways to create dynamic content experiences that react to changes in the system. The larger opportunity comes from understanding that media *is* one system, and that people like it when brands respond to them, publicly.

We can entirely reverse the polarity of advertising media. Rather than trickle-down television, we build up from fragments of many conversations, crafting broadcast stories around real people. The key thing is for brands to listen to what people are saying *and* then incorporate that into their content and behaviour, thus demonstrating an understanding that media is one system of interoperating parts.

TRANSMEDIA ECOSYSTEMS

Digital media do not represent a new channel – they are a proliferating suite of channels, platforms and tactics. For marketers, however, 'social media' or 'mobile' still largely exists within a channel-based marketing paradigm; for many, the Digital State is simply a new channel to chase eyeballs. However, the rise of the Digital State is more than simply the rise of a new 'channel' opportunity. It has signalled a new, complex consumer modality, generating altogether new behaviours and communicative norms in general.

Consumer behaviour is clearly in advance of this, as consumers seamlessly mesh experiences across formerly discrete channels. There is no social or mobile web. The way in which consumers use the web is *social*, and the way they access it is increasingly *mobile*.

'Integrated marketing campaigns' need to do more than simply propagate simple propositions in a variety of places to reach audiences efficiently. Brands and content now exist within participatory systems, defined by the functional interoperation of elements, with a user at the centre, able to graze from infinite sources, with the ability and desire to be empowered, enlightened and entertained.

CONTENT CONSUMPTION, CREATION AND SHARING, AND IDENTITY

Content is now communication. Digital content is ubiquitous, constantly crying out for attention. Millions of digital conversations are orbiting social objects.

In order to prevent overload, users are becoming increasingly selective about what content they consume and engage with. They are becoming more choosy and sophisticated in the way they filter the signal from the noise. They customize, create and propagate content, creating their personality and identity in the process. They carefully edit, refine and control their distributed digital identity across multiple digital platforms. They expect brands to understand them that way, and to do the same.

In order to maintain their close networks and cater to their wider peers, people will broadcast a continuous content stream to their networks to supplement their one-to-one interactions and ensure that they are still 'part of the wider conversation'.

People increasingly rely on recommendations and sharing in order to make informed choices about how best to spend time and money. Some content comes from brands they have befriended, and some is professionally produced, but the majority comes from other people, consciously shared, or from the *digital exhaust*.

DIGITAL EXHAUSTS

Accelerometers and GPS now come as standard inside many of those personal computers we call mobile phones. They are Bruce Sterling's SPIMES – objects that know where they are in SPace and tIME – wagged to life by the trail they create. The digital exhaust of our personal and collective lives, largely invisible through nascent stages of the web and mobile, is revealing itself to be a more natural resource than pollution.

Everything creates data, and now we can give this airy nothing shapes and names. Through applications built to harness it, we can view our lives as we move through our social life (Foursquare), and our real or virtual spaces (Nike+). The mainstream interest in this previously invisible undercurrent of data can be seen through the data visualization explosion. It's changed the narratives of journalism and is painting new pictures of our lives. However, when we go beyond simply painting pretty pictures of our fumes, you begin to realize something athletes (and musicians) have always known – feedback creates loops.

SEEING YOUR BEHAVIOUR... CHANGES YOUR BEHAVIOUR

What starts out as a way to capture what you are doing... begins to change and affect what you are doing... as you look to optimize, to game the system, to compete, to win. Feedback loops are how we learn.[16]

We now mesh our personal exhaust with that aggregated from the world, allowing discovery of new and better ways to navigate our reality as we move through space and time. The Fitbit[17] personal activity monitor and NikeFuel both feed, and feed off, these fumes.

THE LAW OF LARGE NUMBERS

The digital exhaust is not limited to how we can view our individual worlds – it influences how the world sees itself. Human beings don't scale in a linear fashion. A crowd does not behave like a lot of individuals, because the dynamic interactions between individuals create a system with emergent properties. Now that three-quarters of the world's population have a mobile, we can begin to look at some of these emergent behaviours, with a bird's-eye view. This view may provide a greater extension to our collective senses than anything McLuhan dreamt of. 'It is not just about observing what is happening; it is about shaping what is happening', says Dr Johan Bollen, a network scientist at Indiana University. 'The patterns are allowing us to learn how to better manipulate trends, opinions and mass psychology.'[18] Epidemics can be predicted and influencers identified, all from looking at the patterns we are unconsciously creating, in response to patterns unconsciously created by others.

PROXIMITY IS A VIRTUE

Even in a world flattened, things that are nearby are more valuable, useful and important to you most of the time. In the obvious sense this is because, if you want or need something, nearby is usually better. E-commerce, important and convenient as it is, still represents only about 7 per cent of total retail sales in the United States.[19] Most buying is done the old-fashioned way, in shops.

But that's not to say the fingers of digital aren't changing the dynamics of locality and retail. Twenty per cent of all Google searches are local, and that number doubles if you look only at searches from mobile devices.[20] Mapping applications gives us a God's-eye view of the world, one for which we all have Ronald Reagan to thank, as he insisted that GPS satellites would be made available for civilian and corporate use back in the 1980s.

Sometimes, though, standard maps are quite enough. Point Inside[21] is a mobile app that provides maps of indoor destinations so you never need get lost in an airport or shopping mall again. Neighborgoods.net[22] lets you save money and resources by sharing your stuff with your friends around you. Whipcar.com[23] lets you utilize the untapped capacity of your car (cars spend 90-plus per cent of their life parked) by renting your car to people around you. Zaarly[24] takes this idea one step further, enabling you to buy and sell goods with people around you. The rise of collaborative consumption presents opportunities and threats.

People are less and less likely to keep buying, upgrading and replacing things that work. Brands have a role in rewarding these kinds of behaviours in ways that drive commercial value, providing platforms to facilitate them, increasing brand loyalty and engagement.

LOCATION AS A PLATFORM

Foursquare is, of course, the biggest proponent of proximity, and it is used as the location platform for lots of other ideas thanks to its open application programming interface (API). Donteat.at[25] is a web app that automatically mashes public data from the New York City Department of Health and your Foursquare data to send an SMS alert if the restaurant at which you just checked in, no matter how gilded, is dirty under the surface. These kinds of invisible services, patched into personal data, will increasingly become marketing.

Our digital exhaust becomes a remote control for the physical world. Data that confirm where we are and who we know can actually unlock doors, as apartm.net did for its New Year's Eve party.[26]

Location-based reminders such as Geo-Reminder[27] prompt you to complete an errand when you happen to be in the right area, letting your exhaust engage with its own time-shifted self.

A networked crowd, connected to the cloud, would create tighter feedback loops, more visibility, and the possibility of creating significant positive externalities for the proximate. If you have an hour to spare and want to volunteer, there hasn't really been a way to act on that altruistic impulse, but location-based services can help. Groundcrew.us[28] taps into the surplus the network can show us. The platform utilizes geo-location and messaging to help people find and participate in volunteer projects based on where they are.

CONTEXT IS EVERYTHING

Proximity is a virtue for marketers because what's around you can tell brands a lot about you. Experian has long traded in data that profile consumers based on where they live. Proximity is a hugely influential driver of behaviour and decision making.

The biggest influences on you are the people you spend the most time with – usually the people you work with. Behaviour is socially contagious[29] within certain parameters. A Harvard study analysed 50 years of lifestyle data to uncover the fact that things like obesity and happiness spread through association, so choose your friends and colleagues wisely; in the Digital State behaviour is visible and it spreads. The environment you are in is itself both a powerful driver of influence and a good indicator of context, and being a customer is a kind of context.

There are, fundamentally, two different kinds of marketing: 1) customer relationship marketing, where you engage with specific people; and 2) everything else, where you don't. For the majority of marketing, it may be better to not think of customers as people.

CUSTOMERS ARE TO PEOPLE WHAT WAVES ARE TO WATER

'Customers' are a repeating pattern of behaviour that expresses itself in people. From the point of view of a company, it doesn't really matter who those people are when they walk into a store. Throughout the marketing process we spend a lot of time trying to understand the kind of people who are most likely to buy, but behavioural economics and decision research all suggest that *where* and *what* and *when* are at least as important as *who*. So we can look to market to contexts, instead of people, now that we have access to proximity and intention data that can suggest context.

The Social Currency[30] application from American Express does just that. It establishes location and intention, by encouraging you to check in (the application is built on top of Foursquare) with retailers, and share what you bought and what you want with your social network. So now we know where you are and what you want to buy – very useful context to market to. The American Express/Foursquare partnership extends further. They recently rolled out a national programme that allows you to connect your card to your Foursquare account, so when you check in to certain retailers you can now receive kick-back offers on certain purchases, where the savings are automatically credited to your account. These kinds of seamless experiences, built on top of APIs and existing behaviour, will become increasingly important to all marketing.

PROXIMITY PAYMENTS

NFC is all about proximity – it stands for 'near field communication'. It goes beyond payment. You could use NFC to interact with objects around you – tapping a billboard to get a digital coupon.

GPS-enabled devices have allowed us to track our own behaviour through space, and associated services append context to that digital exhaust, allowing it to interact with itself and the world. But instant, frictionless payments change the dynamics of the purchase process, collapsing consideration periods. Stimulus is verified via social reviews, price compared and purchase carried out in a few instants through a single device interaction.

For people, business and the behaviour that is customers, it's not just where you're at that's important; it's what's around you.

A PORTRAIT OF THE FUTURE DIGITAL CONSUMER: THE INVISIBLE WEB

> *We tend to overestimate the effect of a technology in the short run and underestimate the effect in the long run.*
>
> ROY AMARA, PAST PRESIDENT, INSTITUTE FOR THE FUTURE

Or, to put it another way, you ain't seen nothing yet. The true extent of the social and cultural impact of technology is only felt when it becomes invisible.

The philosopher Martin Heidegger provides us with the best-known example of invisible technology: a blind person's cane. The cane becomes more than a tool that the blind person uses to navigate; it becomes an extension of the person's arm. It goes from being part of the external environment and becomes part of you, a part of you that has specific influences on your experience of the world.

Although we are living in technologically accelerated times, the social impact of the web will become evident only when it is pervasive, ubiquitous and invisible, a tool used so intuitively by the generation that grows up with it that it is no longer a tool, but an extension of the self. Once it has vanished, we will know that the web has become central to how we live in and experience the world.

The beginning of the web's disappearance is the convergence of a number of different technologies that will integrate data into the real world, an idea known as augmented reality. At the moment we still think of the internet as something that sits behind the browser on a computer. Hence we refer to the 'mobile' internet, because the modifier is needed. Relatively soon, that will no longer be the case.

Forget about the mobile internet and consider a Digital State, with data integrated into every element of your existence. GPS is the first component. Geo-location on your mobile phone enables *geo-tility*: making things useful for where you are. The basic element of this has been mapped out: you never get lost. Now add in temporal awareness – your phone knows where and when it is. The mobile is the first device that allows you to access augmented reality. As a SPIME it can begin to offer you services and, of course, advertising – offers based on when and where you are, direct to your phone.

Beyond location-based advertising, whole new types of insight and ideas can be built on SPIMES. MIT's 'reality mining' project uses the technology to study 'computational epidemiology' and model the spread of disease through populations, or how civil unrest in Kenya changes movement and interpersonal communication. How we move as a species becomes visible. Geo-location begins to change the nature of privacy. Kevin Kelly points out that the cost of true personalization is absolute transparency, at least to the (one) machine.

Now take your SPIME and make it socially aware, so it has access to your social network. Loopt, the social mapping service, turns your phone into a 'social compass', alerting you when your friends are nearby. MIT's 'serendipity' experiment takes it a stage further, connecting location-aware devices to user profiles, involving everything from your Amazon profile to where you hang out to an inference engine that guesses who your friends are, using the social graph in the same way that Facebook does to suggest people you may know. The result: a real-time, real-world network that connects like-minded people in close proximity.

Proximity is important. At the moment, to use our phones to interact with the world, we have to snap a QR code or text a number, but that is unnecessary once all phones know where they are and what they are near, using another component technology – radio frequency identification (RFID).

Nokia and O2 have already run a pilot project on the London Underground that uses NFC chips in your phone as a contactless Oyster card. The same technology will allow your handset to interact with the world in manifold ways, pulling data from a poster or paying for cinema tickets. Google Wallet is already accepted in Duane Reade pharmacies.

RFID can connect everything, every product, place and piece of clothing, to the network. Everything becomes a SPIME, and objects begin to host the capacity for intelligence alongside an IP address.

Take GPS and RFID and add in accelerometers, devices such as those in the iPhone and Wii controller that tells the device which way up it is and which way it is moving. Now things are getting interesting. Now you have a device that can point and click on the real world. Japanese company GeoVector have a platform that allows you to point and click on 700,000 buildings, shops and local landmarks in Japan to instantly retrieve information at whatever your phone is pointing.

Now take the same technology and add in the camera, the screen on your phone, and image-based search technology. You just point your camera at the building in question and it overlays the geo-tagged data on to the image on your screen, blending data with the world itself. Take a picture of a tree and discover what it is. Facial recognition, mapped to social networks, turns a crowd into a community.

Mobile broadband IP connections mean you are now always connected to the web; the idea of 'being online' or 'being offline' will no longer make sense. Everything will be connected at all times to the One Machine, with the web as its operating system.

How does marketing function here? In two primary ways: as stimulus and solution systems.

What we understand as traditional advertising will, having transformed into content or social objects to prevent being filtered, trigger behaviours. Seamless solutions will capitalize on electively shared personal data and contextually derived inference data to achieve the apotheosis of marketing – sufficiently relevant, timely, solicited communication that consumers perceive as *news*.

Imagine walking to work. Intelligent agent software is constantly tracking your behaviour and preferences across all platforms and beginning to make intelligent inferences about what you will want. It will be incredibly, sometimes hauntingly, accurate. So, as you walk to work, the agent will pull in location and contextually relevant data, looking for patterns. It finds an author is giving a reading in a bookstore a few blocks from your route later that week. You have never bought anything by this author, but Amazon's collaborative filtering algorithm indicates people with your profile have often bought books by her. It checks your social network to see if you have any proximate friends with similar reading habits. It checks reviews and mentions of the author's talks in social media. It checks your calendar to see if you are free when the reading is. It interfaces with a vast number of APIs, seamlessly blending data sets to extract relevance. It applies a Bayesian probability algorithm to weight its decisions, and decides to act. Finally, it suggests the event, explains why you might like it, suggests friends to invite, and offers to invite them and create a reminder event and map for you. It then suggests places for dinner or drinks afterwards, based on OpenTable profile data and Zagat reviews. It notifies you of offers at some of the restaurants, pulled from Foursquare and other sources.

Now imagine all that and take away the phone. The screen is sitting inside a pair of glasses, or projected on to your retina by contact lenses, or delivered directly into your occipital lobe, stimulating your brain to see what the machine sees. Instead of a handset, you control the data stream by gesticulation; the accelerometers in your hand know exactly what you want. Suddenly the web is invisible, because suddenly it is everywhere, all the time. No longer a tool, in the Digital State it is an extension of you, just like the blind person's cane: it is functionally part of how you experience the world.

FY
New York City

NOTES

1 http://www.kk.org/thetechnium/archives/2007/11/dimensions_of_t.php
2 https://www-935.ibm.com/services/uk/index.wss/ibvstudy/bcs/a1024186?cntxt=a1006904
3 http://farisyakob.typepad.com/blog/2007/01/what_is_a_media.html
4 Henry Jenkins, *Convergence Culture* (New York University Press, New York, 2006).
5 http://mashable.com/2011/01/10/twitters-new-ceo-finally-nails-down-the-companys-long-term-vision/
6 http://www.fastcompany.com/blog/faris-yakob/technology-strategy/cultural-latency
7 http://articles.latimes.com/2009/sep/14/entertainment/et-leno14
8 http://www.nytimes.com/2010/02/24/business/media/24cooler.html?_r=1
9 http://2-screen.com/
10 http://www.mtv.com/ontv/backchannel/the_hills/
11 http://starling.tv/
12 http://gomiso.com/
13 http://www.adweek.com/aw/content_display/news/digital/e3i76ad91ab65e65f6dce9330b714e37851
14 http://mashable.com/2009/12/18/trident-layers-twitter-ad/
15 http://www.robyn.com/killingme/
16 http://www.wired.com/magazine/2011/06/ff_feedbackloop/
17 http://www.fitbit.com/
18 http://www.psychologytoday.com/blog/digital-pandemic/201106/has-the-era-big-brother-finally-arrived-1
19 http://techcrunch.com/2010/03/08/forrester-forecast-online-retail-sales-will-grow-to-250-billion-by-2014/

20 http://blog.kelseygroup.com/index.php/2011/05/25/20-of-google-searches-are-local-40-on-mobile/

21 http://pointinside.com/

22 http://neighborgoods.net/

23 http://www.whipcar.com/

24 http://www.zaarly.com/

25 http://donteat.at/

26 http://www.fastcompany.com/1709781/foursquare-door-guys-say-they-might-start-selling-their-system

27 http://itunes.apple.com/us/app/georeminder/id398922761?mt=8

28 http://groundcrew.us/

29 http://www.wired.com/medtech/health/magazine/17-10/ff_christakis

30 http://aboutfoursquare.com/social-currency/

2 UTOPIA, DYSTOPIA. DISCUSS

Simon Pont

“The one-word consequence of the Digital Revolution for me: liberation, and all the good – and bad – that can ride shotgun with it, because liberation can of course also mean freedom to *not* conform or ‘fit in’, to be a ‘minority interest’, a deviant, a bad-ass. And this is made all the easier when you can hide behind avatars and pseudonyms of dark purpose...

There are those who fear a chumming-up with technology is going to bring on our inevitable damnation, because it’s tantamount to shaking hands with the devil, where the devil is a robot, a cyborg, maybe the Terminator...

What ‘Digital’ really means is that we all now have the means to show our true selves and true colours...

Like any utopia, like any dystopia, it is ours to make. We are free to form our wings or our shackles.”

All at once, everything changed. At least, that's how it felt, that all at once everything had changed, as if, from out of nowhere but clearly heaven-sent, a mean-looking anvil or seriously weighty baby-grand piano had motored south and zeroed in, and all anyone had expected was maybe a little light rain.

I remember it very clearly – 8 October 2008, a Wednesday. From Iceland: 'Your prime minister, he just cut us off at the knees.' The phone line was crystal clear, the fate of the global economy as murky as the grey skies outside my office window. In London, it was just drizzling, but systems, bigger and more brooding than the weather, had taken dark and spectral forms.

No one knew how it was going to play. Pretty much everyone had a foreboding sense of 'bad', as though someone had just distributed Fisher-Price 'My First Uzis' in a kindergarten free-play session. Because all at once, everything *had* changed, with no former points of familiar reference. This was a new set of dynamics, a paradigm shift that felt like an unkindly shaped proctological probe. *This... was binary*. Too fast out of the blocks, too quick on the trigger.

I'd worked with Kaupthing Bank, my client, an Icelandic investment bank, for close to two years. I'd helped build their brand, define their brand, their look, feel, created the glossy-brochure wrapping that helped make it feel as if it was a tangible *something*, though it all belied the practices of maverick and cavalier trading, unchecked practices playing fast, loose and reckless across the surface of the global economy, Vikings cutting deals up, down and diagonally, and working to the crazy-casual principle that things 'will only keep going up'.

The share traders and deal makers the world over had long since forgotten to heed the small print. They'd happily started buying and drinking their own mezzanine-tranche Kool-Aid. 'Subprime' had become the latest entry of jabberwocky gibberish, keeping company with the likes of 'near miss' and 'friendly fire'.

Kaupthing Bank, standing in a long line with the more usual suspects, was bankrolling genesis and universe expansion with other people's money. Who knew that what Tom Wolfe had once labelled an inevitable 'Bonfire of the Vanities' had transpired to be no more than an opening act?[1] The Icelanders had been bitten by the same bug of excess, ego and immortality that had befallen 1980s Wall Street, only they'd upgraded it. Forget 'good'. Greed had become God, and Wolfe's yesteryear 'Masters of the Universe' had gone all-the-way God-complex, turned 'Manipulators of the Markets', 'manipulation' netting out at 'fraud and embezzlement'.

Fast-forward five years to the here and now, and I'm the ad guy with a couple of former clients who remain wanted by Interpol for crimes against the good name of Capitalism. Either in jail or on the run and looking nervously over their shoulders for once-convivial, now considerably less so, Russian 'family' types (formerly investors, latterly aggrieved), the Icelandic bankers who once took what they wanted continue to pay for it.

But back to 'your prime minister', he being Gordon Brown. His act was to use the anti-terror laws, in an attempt to recoup the money UK savers, from grannies to local authorities, had hoarded in the Icelandic operation Landsbanki, specifically its show-stopping high-interest account Icesave. Gordon had frozen Landsbanki's UK assets to the tune of £4 billion, as offset to £4.6 billion that had gone into some 300,000 savings accounts.

No question, Gordon had called in the biggest legislative big gun available in international law, and aimed it at the Icelanders' knees. Certainly, he'd cut them off all right, and he'd used a double barrel to do it. Few beyond the 320,000 people living in Iceland had any real issue with it, were happy to watch the dominoes fall, because everything *was* moving too fast anyway, and everyone's understanding of what might be going down was playing dim-witted catch-up – because the money was moving, had already moved, and the balance sheet was suddenly, instantly, so far below the zero line that it had to be wrong, must be wrong. Only it wasn't. All the money had gone, all at once, scarier than any stunt Keyser Söze could pull. Yes, this was our new world: outcome unknown, with consequences unknowable. This was what binary *felt* like.

I looked out again on a lightly spitting London Town, the occasional pedestrian erring on the side of umbrella and high-collar, while 1,100 miles away, outside my client Helga's office, Reykjavik had taken to the streets, angry, bewildered, confused, holding not umbrellas but placards, some sporting balaclavas and wide eyes, looking for answers as to how a group of bankers and fellow countrypeople had somehow so betrayed them, had made their króna worthless, had suddenly dragged them all back to the Dark Ages. The Barbarians at the Gate now had their own barbarians to contend with.[2]

This, *then*, was the moment I *really* realized that 'Digital' was the biggest kind of big deal.

ONE WORD, THREE BEATS

As we depart Iceland and the 'opening scene', let me just stress: I'm not saying the Digital Revolution had anything to do with subprime, avarice or the global economic meltdown, but I *am* suggesting it had a lot to do with the *speed* at which some of those events played out. The actions and over-reactions in response to that speed, and the very sudden dawning at how fast events can now move, *this* was digital's contribution. Digital is flux. It's the accelerant in our two-speed world. The planet turns as it always did, but life now plays out on a much faster setting.

I liked the idea of starting in Iceland, in wrestling this beast of a question, but where I really have to go and what I really have to start with is fear. Digital represents radical change, and it enables change to unfold at radical speed. And radical change *at pace* brings palpable fear, all kinds of knee-jerk anxieties in reaction to the unknown, especially when it's fast unfolding.

The internet happened, is with us. We can't unlearn or 'un-invent' it, but we have to learn how best to deal with it, and harness it. It's a matter of how we manage and best react to this changing set of circumstances, where technology is fusing ever deeper into society. The fear is that we won't cope well, that we'll even succumb to the Dark Side.

The more I've thought about all of this, the more I keep landing back on the same word, 'liberation', with maybe three beats:

1. liberation from social mores;
2. liberation from fixed identity;
3. liberation from feeling limited.

'Liberation' sounds pretty good, right? To be released, to be set free – from oppression, from dictators, heavy lids so evolved to ably blink away their own curling cigar smoke. Forgive the caricatured digression; back to my point. The one-word consequence of the Digital Revolution for me: liberation, and all the good – and bad – that can ride shotgun with it, because liberation can of course also mean freedom to *not* conform or 'fit in', to be a 'minority interest', a deviant, a bad-ass. And this is made all the easier when you can hide behind avatars and pseudonyms of dark purpose.

You manage a society, '*care*-take' it maybe, by walking a fine line on policies (while ideally not sitting on the fence), and 'the internet' is forever throwing hand grenades into the debating chambers. Permissive societies are just great, so long as they don't give permission to bigots and creeps. One person's 'freedom of speech' is another's dissemination of propaganda, one person's... you get the idea. The internet can open trapdoors for abuse and exploitation all over the place.

So let's start with the bad stuff, try to get that out the way, where particularly liberation from social mores and fixed identity can take us in some unacceptable directions.

SWEATING THE BIG AND BAD STUFF: THE LOWEST COMMON DENOMINATOR AND THE TERMINATOR

Society needs structures, many structures, to maintain its well-oiled and stay-on-the-tracks function. Without structures, society collapses, gets real feral really quickly, complete breakdown, disintegration, where society eats itself, and most likely even the vegan-eating members start eating each other.

Consider zombies. Yes, I said zombies. Even zombies have subtext. I take zombie movies to be a very un-Disney cartoon analogy for society in breakdown. Zombies are an over-the-top metaphor: the loss of all humanity and our descent into cannibalism as 'society' goes south, where we all lose control and become mindless.

The 'fear' is that the internet will somehow turn us feral, will bring out the rebel yell and zombie in all of us, because it represents some kind of anti-establishment and deconstructive force. In the more conservative bedrooms of the world, night sweats are likely to follow the thought of 'the internet' as an unregulated, unchecked and invisible force, allowing society to express and in a kind of way start *rebuilding* itself 'bottom up' – because the panic is that people can't be trusted, that the outcome will be ugly, will be the Dorian Gray (un)preserved in the frame, where the lowest common denominator and most base appetites prevail. The fear with a free-wheeling and laissez-faire society is that it'll be a sinister one, bestowing all the dry-mouth charm of being greeted by a clown in the moonlight.

In mid-2012, Habbo Hotel stepped up as a vivid cautionary tale. Social network Habbo Hotel temporarily suspended its chat function in June 2012, following a two-month investigation by UK broadcaster Channel 4. Channel 4 News described 'the world's largest social game and online community for teenagers' as 'a children's brothel', not jam-packed just with avatars and roaming ponies, but also with roaming paedophiles looking to groom victims, drawing them into 'cyber-sex' and inviting them to take their chats offline and on to Skype. Habbo Hotel is aimed at children aged 13 and upwards, played by children as young as nine, and has 250 million members worldwide. Some tweets later made light of Channel 4's parent-shivering exposé. 'Habbo Hotel has always been full of paedophiles. Avoiding them was part of the game', tweeted one. Debate followed, rally exchanges from the baseline, self-regulation versus the need for light moderation versus policing as a moral imperative. When Habbo turned the chat back on, it did so in phases, sound-biting that it would be 'a new era of protected democracy', that the site would be 'a regulated environment that protects free speech, as well as the safety and interests, of the legitimate user community'.

Moving on from under-age cyber-sex, we have a further and just-as-thick layer of bad stuff still to go, namely Angry Robots. There are many angsty quarters (probably in those conservative bedrooms) that fear a chumming-up with technology is going to bring on our inevitable damnation, because it's tantamount to shaking hands with the devil, where the devil is a robot, a cyborg, maybe the Terminator. (Not everyone loves sci-fi.)

Moore's law (1965) plots a curve where the number of transistors that can be placed on a microchip doubles every two years. This trend has remained uncannily accurate for nearly half a century, closely linking to the broader leaps in computer technology as they evolve at rates more exponential, the curve inclining to the vertical. Some line-drawers suggest there have to be logical limits to all of this, an inevitable ceiling, rather than technology ascending directly north, non-stop and heaven-bound.

Now the story-makers embrace the dire hyperbole of artificial intelligence getting smarter and smarter, ultimately evil-smart, a HAL 9000 ('Hello, Dave'), a Skynet, a Matrix, a taking over, taking control, machines crushing their former masters, turning them into slaves, corpses, maybe biological batteries. All gorgeously vivid, gruesome stuff. Humans, too smart for their own good. Technology, human-made, human-ending. Nice ironies, with salivating smiles.

Thinkers like Francis Fukuyama do very well from prescient-sounding texts like *The End of History and the Last Man*.[3] Despite actually purporting a genuinely cheerful theory that our liberal democracy in the West marks a potential evolutionary apex, a title like *The End...* deftly wrong-foots, with the kind of very terminal, very final-sounding themes that tend to grab headlines, sell books and get you invited on to TV talk panels. And, of course, Fukuyama's riding a long-standing evocation.

Orwell's *1984*[4] and *Animal Farm*[5], *Lord of the Flies*[6], *Brave New World*[7], movies like Gilliam's *Brazil* and Ridley Scott's *Blade Runner*, they all revel in depicting the utopian opposite, as if the sour, curdled, dystopian view is almost inevitable, that original sin and apple-eating mean that creating hell-in-a-handbasket is all we can ever muster, that it doesn't pan out for us, doesn't end well, we don't in the final analysis play nicely together but instead raise sticks, see red, and incline to some mutually agreed bludgeoning. Bleak, noirish, nihilistic, we are all damned because we just and damned well can't help ourselves. Fade-to-black is our destiny.

And, yes, there is something darkly seductive and rather hypnotic about looking into the abyss, but we also need to draw a line between the stuff of fanboy fiction and decisions over our collective fate, because tightrope-walking stops being a buzz the minute your balance gives, and indeed what's required is balance in every sense, the balance of reasoned discourse, the appreciation that there's a dark *and* a sunny side to most streets. So let's cross over, put the bogeymen 'hacktivists', the Terminator, and moonlit clowns out of our mind for a while. Let's instead talk of the 'liberation from feeling limited'. Let's talk of the world changers and reach for our shades.

FROM MOORE'S LAW TO THOMAS MORE

> *Progress is impossible without change, and those who cannot change their minds cannot change anything.*
>
> GEORGE BERNARD SHAW

Turning towards the light is who we are too, by instinct, by nature. Even in the wintriest light, we turn towards an outline of the Sun. I think being human is about holding on to hope, believing the impossible can sometimes be made possible. I think it's about liking the idea of there being a better tomorrow, and believing we might be able to make it so. I think we are mostly romantics. An arcadia, a Shangri-la, a Schlaraffenland, an Eden: we are hopeful, aspiring, wish for our heaven-on-earth.

> *[The island of Utopia is] two hundred miles across in the middle part, where it is widest, and nowhere much narrower than this except towards the two ends, where it gradually tapers. These*

> *ends, curved round as if completing a circle five hundred miles in circumference, make the island crescent-shaped, like a new moon.*
>
> THOMAS MORE, *UTOPIA*, 1516[8]

Thomas More set his fictitious island of Utopia, like the fresh night of a new moon (with no clowns), in the New World, Atlantic-side (if you were wondering), somewhere off the coast of Brazil. Think: elected monarchs, freedom of choice and movement, zero ownership; a democracy, but where no one actually 'owns' anything, all goods are fairly distributed, and everyone simply 'gets on'. Yes, More's 'Happy Place' was made of all the right stuff, a heavy dose of socialism here, a sprinkling of democracy there, all in the kind of genuine, sanguine and good times that maybe only come with the right kind of island life.

And, while More made no direct reference to wi-fi, I'm guessing Utopia would be a very connected and convergent place, because in many ways its founding values echo those of the internet: open source; the fair (because affordable) distribution of technology, enabling instant access, and empowering all to explore and self-express, to demonstrate who they are and what they can do; and the devaluing of 'ownership', because digital consumption is not about materialism or shiny objects you can polish and covet and envy your neighbours for.

And I certainly believe 'digital' is subverting what it is to 'possess', subverting the idea of physical things and ownership. Consider our once very physical music and movie collections, which we'd proudly scan in their very physical, perhaps alphabetized rows, and which now 'exist' in a very intangible cloud, to be spirited forth and streamed upon our beck and call, 'digi' replacing 'physi'(cal), playing havoc with Marx's idea of commodity fetishism, but playing *into* the themes of More's *Utopia*.

FROM CYBORGS TO SETH GODIN

Forget serpents and apples. I incline to think original sin is 'giving up', no longer trying, that sin is lethargy, apathy and resignation to 'how it is'. The Digital State is a riposte to this kind of original sin, an open invitation for people to shape the world as they want to reshape it. I believe the Digital State makes it that bit easier for world changers to start the changing. To this belief, I'll finish with three exhibits, businesses where our Digital State has made the formerly impossible *possible*. Ladies and gentlemen of the jury, I give you...

Exhibit 1: MOFILM (www.mofilm.com)

MOFILM runs with the by-line: 'Inspiring filmmakers to create videos for big brands and social causes'.

To my mind, MOFILM wholly reflects the sense of burgeoning empowerment that 'digital' has brought to the table. In an analogue world, MOFILM would not have been possible, would have been a pipe-dream notion kept forever out in the cold, far beyond the film and ad industry's castle keep.

In a post-analogue world, MOFILM is an exemplar for how conventional industry models are being subverted and the former intermediaries deftly assassinated. In their own words, 'Our revolutionary new process is transforming the video creation industry by connecting brands more directly with film-makers and eliminating multiple layers of bureaucracy and administration which waters down creativity and inflates costs in traditional processes' (**www.mofilm.com**).

Very simply, MOFILM runs open competitions, inviting anyone with an idea and a camera to submit their efforts. And there's the thing: 'anyone with a digital camera' is pretty much everyone these days, so anyone can take on the top ad agencies and show them what a 'TV ad' should really look like.

Exhibit 2: the Domino Project (www.thedominoproject.com)

The Domino Project sees best-selling author and marketing guru Seth Godin join forces with Amazon. Their mission: 'to change the way books are built, sold and spread'. Seth is a huge fan of ideas being like viruses, spreading, and being like dominoes, toppling, all the time gaining momentum and mass. Like MOFILM, the Domino Project aims to be a rule-breaker, to be a 'publishing house organized around a new distribution channel, one that wasn't even a fantasy when most publishers began'.

For me, the Domino Project is a great neon-lit illustration of how digital is providing the *means*, inviting people to 'have a go', where before they'd have been frozen out of the game, the very thought of being granted such an opportunity being a thing of fantasy.

As far as Seth Godin's concerned, the only thing fine in life is trying, trying and then trying some more. Seth looks on failure as that simple road to eventual success, the only thought reprehensible to him being to stop walking that road. With the Domino Project, he's encouraging and making it a little bit easier for everyone to walk that road-to-somewhere with him.

Exhibit 3: RockCorps (www.rockcorps.com)

My third and final 'exhibit' is wrapped up in one of those very positive kinds of positive thoughts. Ready? Think: 'internet' as an input, 'social responsibility' as an outcome.

I believe a more (technologically and therefore immediately) connected society is able to develop a more intimate sense of being a collective, and this collective awareness naturally helps breed a greater sense of social consciousness. I believe a company like RockCorps, while not a 'digital business', is hugely indicative of living on a digital planet, proof that sometimes it really *is* 'all good'.

> *RockCorps is a pro-social production company that uses music to inspire people to volunteer and get involved in their community. To date, over 80,000 volunteers have attended more than 30 live concert events. The company launched in the US in 2005, in the UK in 2008, France in 2009 and Israel in 2010. RockCorps' principal idea is 'Got 2 Give to Get (US), Give, Get Given (UK). Tagline: Moving a Generation to Change the World.*
>
> WIKIPEDIA

This business model is built on 'enlightened self-interest', pure and simple. RockCorps is bank-rolling 'social currency pay-back', based on a pay-it-forward karma-credit, the pay-back taking the form of *exclusive* concert experiences featuring big names like Lady Gaga, Razorlight, Snoop Dogg, Mark Ronson and Plan B. To get to see these kinds of headline acts, you have to give up four hours of your time, rock up at a RockCorps-organized volunteer event, and roll up your sleeves. RockCorps concerts invariably generate 5,000 volunteers a time, banking 20,000 hours of do-gooding.

It's a shrewd acknowledgement of what social commentators and marketers have commented on and acknowledged since teens began (a truth that extends to almost all of us, in fact). We part-build our self-esteem through bragging rights, whether it's experience-based or simply being able to say we know about something first. And most of us are happy to pitch in with some light-to-heavy(ish) lifting to earn those rights.

I was keen to ask RockCorps' COO, Grady Lee, how it all came about, from the seed of an idea to the will to make it happen:

> *We believe youth are just one experience away from changing the world. Youth want to engage in their community, in civic life, but often don't know how or where to begin. We bridge that gap. Our insight is that nothing mobilizes younger generations more than music. By combining an authentic trusted passion for music with a new experience, volunteering, RockCorps helps youth discover their true power. The thought that you can do great things is a reasonable one. It's not a crazy thought! It is just that sometimes you need to be shown how reasonable it is, and we love doing that around the world. To date, we've generated more than 500,000 hours of work in the US, Israel, UK, France, Venezuela, Colombia and Mexico. We use digital tools to generate physical results and provide transformative experiences.*
>
> GRADY LEE, COO, ROCKCORPS

Digital is how RockCorps can reach its audience, mobilize them, bring people together and bring about some tangible good. It's about kindness, crowd-sourced, with digital being used a tool, little different from and alongside the use of a spade or a rake. Whether physical or digital in form, a tool can empower.

If God really did give rock 'n' roll to us, I think he'd approve of what's being done with it.

DIGITAL BECOMES US

The boil-it-right-down question in all this might simply be whether the internet is unleashing the good or bad in us. And, of course, the answer is neither black nor white, but rather many compelling and telling shades of grey. Yet, in spite of much varied grey, the 'exhibits', the Habbos and the RockCorps, illuminate the opposites, this tale of twos, a world of dualities, yins and yangs, the great digital discourse of:

- self versus collective;
- empowerment versus limitation;
- expression versus delusion;
- connection versus alienation;
- same versus different;
- utopia versus dystopia;
- good versus evil.

This is what 'the internet' is *ultimately* doing, I think: it's highlighting and amplifying our 'opposites'.

Now the German philosopher Hegel (1770–1831) was heavily into opposites, conceiving a system for understanding ('absolute idealism' being Hegel's ultimate goal) based on the notion of harmonious contradictions. I think Hegel would have enjoyed taking on the Digital Age and its implications. I think the internet is forging a very Hegelian world, where thesis and antithesis chip along and happily take chunks out of each other, before swinging around to an agreed resolution. Hegel argued that *becoming* is born of *being* and *nothing*, is the synthesis of these two apparent contradictions. (The very word Utopia itself, in the original Greek, packs two meanings: a 'good place' and 'no place'.) Being and nothing, for me, is the Digital State's definition and its future – that *it*, and our *becoming*, is bound up in the discursive resolution of so many opposites.

What is our 'Digital State', our 'Digital State of Mind', as the question asked? Well, paranoia, uncertainty, some fear – yes to all, but also hope, opportunity and, maybe most of all, *liberation*. What 'Digital' really means is that we all now have the means to show our true selves and true colours. If there's talent in the mix, it will rise up. If there's something darkly unpleasant and writhing, it's going to reach the surface too. With 'the internet', society is more than ever wearing its truth, its soul, on its sleeve, to be watched on a screen of our choice.

I'm a big believer in visualization and self-fulfilling prophecies. Set yourself up to win, and you're loading your hand in all the right ways. See yourself failing, and you're likely as not going to trip over your feet. 'The internet' is a decision. Yes, in so many ways a 'state of mind'. It's a case of perspective, of how we choose to view it, how we choose to use it, how we let it liberate us, so we may fulfil its potential and ours. Like any utopia, like any dystopia, it is ours to make. We are free to form our wings or our shackles. This liberation is ours to make of what we will.

I believe the Digital State can be a techno-shaped arcadia, a place with few limits and much personal exploration, a utopia in that it can be a good and healthy place, but like any wilderness it can bite back, turn nasty if treated with naivety. Let's not be naive or stumble. Let us, with hope, look to the light.

SP
London

NOTES

1 Tom Wolfe, *Bonfire of the Vanities* (Farrar Straus Giroux, New York, 1987)

2 Bryan Burrough and John Heylar, *Barbarians at the Gate: The fall of RJR Nabisco* (Harper & Row, New York, 1990)

3 Francis Fukuyama, *The End of History and the Last Man* (Free Press, New York, 1992)

4 George Orwell, *Animal Farm: A fairy story* (Secker and Warburg, London, 1945)

5 George Orwell, *Nineteen Eighty-Four* (Secker and Warburg, London, 1949)

6 William Golding, *Lord of the Flies* (Faber and Faber, London, 1954)

7 Aldous Huxley, *Brave New World* (Chatto & Windus, London, 1932)

8 Thomas More, *Utopia*, (More, 1516)

3 HOW THE DIGITAL STATE CAN CURE MODERN MARKETING

Judd Labarthe

> I imagine my little manifesto is nestled among chapters extolling the wonders of digital technology, their authors having written with intelligence, wit and passion about instantaneousness, the inevitability of mobile, the inescapability of 'social', the power of data and, possibly, the implications of all that for real-time marketing. And these are all important facets to discuss – but none of this is what excites me about the Digital State...
>
> For all the technological brilliance of the Digital State, what really excites me is the *emotional* intelligence we can observe there: the values or principles that shape how we use that technology, integrate it into our routine and watch it inform and inspire new expectations in our wider lives.

I'd like you to meet... Judd Labarthe

Judd Labarthe's written more industry award papers, and walked off with more silverware, than just about anyone I know. And I mention industry awards, because I first met Judd through sitting next to him on a judging panel. The awards were the Euro Effies. The room was the kind of hotel conference room decor that only the best and blandest inter-continental hotels can muster. It was right by the international arrivals gate, a Hilton airport hotel, not so much preventing you from feeling 'Welcome to Brussels' as ensuring you felt sufficiently dislocated to feel nothing at all.

Now sitting on jury panels, judging awards submissions, is an ever-so-slightly odd business. Unless it's a regular gig, you invariably rock up and know everyone about as much as they know you, which is not at all. Some people smile at each other. Other people don't smile at each other. Everyone has a fat lever-binder full of written awards entries. You read one at a time. Then there's an open discussion. Then you vote.

When the facilitator threw it out across the large rectangular table, inviting comment from the 15 or so esteemed invitees gathered, it was clear to me within about the first 15 seconds Judd Labarthe was going to walk away from the day clutching a 'Smartest Guy in the Room' T-shirt. Listening to Judd dissect, damn or discern a campaign entry is a professional pleasure. Judd knows brands; he's as *au fait* with the art and science of how to build them as he is with the back of his hand, and after being on the industry front line for closing in on a quarter of a century he's become a kind of bad-ass cross between Mr Miyagi and Blade, with a bullshit detector that counters on a phaser-to-kill setting.

*

Inviting people to join me in *Digital State* was asking everyone to take a leap of faith – certainly, maybe a small one as leaps go, but still a leap. For me, it meant that every time a chapter contribution landed in my inbox it came with a double-whammy slam of excitement and apprehension. I had every faith in who I'd asked, but there were no guarantees with how anyone was going to cut it up, what they'd say, how they'd say it.

Post that first attachment double-click, it commonly took about two sentences for a smile to start playing across my lips. And from there the smile invariably went wide. In slight contrast, I was kinda banking that Judd was going to nail it before I had to reach the two-sentence marker. Just occasionally, it's not dangerous to assume; for me, Judd's chapter is a real treat.

I think Judd has really zeroed in on the heart of the matter. Not to give anything away, but to maybe tease just a little, Judd sets out a kind of roadmap for how the discipline of marketing should, in fact *must*, evolve. He signposts how the biggest possible upside to the Digital State is how its influence can transcend, and that to truly grasp the opportunities presented by 'digital' there's but one thing that we must all bring to the table. And it's not a tech thing. It is our humanity.

Over to Judd.

I love Google. Specifically, I love being able to learn instantly how many millions of stories are floating around making the argument, say, that the internet is making us stupid (66 million) or that it's making us crazy (109 million) or that it's evil (a whopping 490 million). It certainly can seem that much of the activity with which internet junkies fill our time *is* driven by the darker sides of our nature: by lust and envy; by loneliness and status anxiety; by closed-mindedness and manufactured outrage and the triumph of opinion over argument. There's much more to it than that, of course, but let's stick with darkness for a minute, because I'm a big fan of 'the dark side'. In fact, I'm convinced that, if more brands were in touch with their own dark sides, they'd be more honest about their limitations and as a result have a better handle on their real strengths. Armed with this new-found focus, they'd demand that their marketing become a lot more useful, or at least a lot less annoying, to the people they aim to serve. I say all this as a practitioner, one coming up on a quarter-century in this business, and one who's become convinced that marketing needs a major reboot. Consumers don't trust it; most CEOs don't respect it; business as usual – *our* business – isn't working.

Proof is all around us. Only one in six trade promotions shows a profit. Only one in 10 new products survives its first year. Most consumer packaged-goods campaigns return only 54 cents on the dollar, and advertising ROI in general hovers around only 4 per cent. And consumers perceive little or no difference among brands in 40 of 46 categories. No wonder that, at just 22 months, the average CMO's tenure is less than half as long as that of the CEO who hired him or her.[1] (Data on the number of fired CMOs who drag their CEO down with them are apparently harder to come by.) And it's not as if marketing's failings are hidden away in the professional literature. The whole world seems to be watching: I recently googled *marketing mistakes*, *marketing myths* and *marketing blunders* and came up with around 63 million combined hits – against around only 11 million for *most effective marketing campaigns. I hate advertising* yields 1 billion stories. Dark, indeed.

Why is it so? Too many me-too products; 'brands' expressing no personality, point of view or purpose; 'new and improved' offers that are neither; campaigns that try to argue their audiences into liking the brand or, worse, to dupe them into accepting the brand's offers; a misplaced emphasis on refining product communication at the expense of improving the product experience, in the belief that people cultivate deep, advertising-driven emotional bonds with the brands they buy despite ample evidence to the contrary; short-term thinking and the concomitant loss in our ability to measure and understand marketing's longer-term effects; and a persistent and fallacious tendency to manage brands as if marketing were warfare (as opposed to storytelling, its much more natural cousin).

We've traded credibility for cynicism, and our desperation is showing. And yet, if we look in the right places, we can see reason to hope.

Now, I imagine my little manifesto is probably nestled among many chapters extolling the wonders of digital technology, their authors having written with intelligence, wit and passion about instantaneousness, the inevitability of mobile, the inescapability of 'social', the power of data and, possibly, the implications of all that for real-time marketing. And these are all important facets to discuss – but none of this is what excites me about the Digital State.

Born too soon to be a digital native, this digital immigrant could easily be mistaken for a Luddite. It's true I've never been the first on my block to own the latest whatever. I did eventually get around to buying an iPhone, but actively use probably less than 5 per cent of its capability. I seldom post, and almost never check in. I even use a mouse to navigate my MacBook. Not only can I not keep abreast of digital technology, but I'm hardly tempted to try.

No, for all the technological brilliance of the Digital State, what really excites me is the *emotional* intelligence we can observe there: the values or principles that shape how we use that technology, integrate it into our routines and watch it inform and inspire new expectations in our wider lives.[2] It's witnessing experiences that originated in the digital space making the leap beyond that space, and coming to provide new frames of reference for everyday life. This is the genius of the system, the ethos of the Digital State.

In sociological terms, ethos is *the fundamental character or spirit of a culture*, the underlying sentiment that informs the beliefs, customs or practices of a group or society. In literary terms, ethos is *the moral element that determines a character's action*. Both senses are relevant to this piece, for if you believe as I do that marketing is the search for the intersection of brand promise and consumer desire then we as marketers and managers of brands must develop a better understanding of both 1) what people are hoping to find at this intersection and 2) how brands need to behave when they meet the people waiting there.

Why focus on emotions? Because while science has been great at making 'digital' faster, more powerful, and more accessible, it has yet to invent a new emotion. The Digital State may be a recent phenomenon, but the fundamental emotional drivers at its core have been here all along. Our search for understanding, for belonging, for purpose: these are the same things that were motivating Bill Bernbach's 'unchanging man' way back in the 1960s (and of course long before then as well).[3]

These needs have over time found various outlets for expression as well as diverse sources of fulfilment, but I'd suggest that, for the purpose of cleaning up marketing, the genius of the Digital State lies in its offering us three interlocked emotional values in particular with which to pursue our own search for meaning: empathy, generosity and collaboration.[4]

It's neither accident nor coincidence that these values tend to be encountered in combination with and experienced as building on each other – as I'll show in a minute, it's a lot easier to get people to collaborate with you if you've established a bona fide invitation (via empathy) and offered a meaningful incentive (via generosity) – and together they constitute the core of an emerging digital ethos whose growing success in the Digital State holds powerful implications for those of us trying to help marketing recapture its own sense of purpose.

Empathy, generosity and collaboration? OK, you may say, but there are plenty of other emotional drivers at play in the Digital State, too – all that lust, envy, loneliness, greed... the 'dark' stuff I mentioned earlier. With the Digital State still maturing, and the game far from settled, what gives me confidence that the ethos I'm identifying here is the right one to cure marketing of its cynicism and irrelevance?

Evolution. In his book *Nonzero: The Logic of Human Destiny*,[5] the journalist and bloggingheads.tv co-founder Robert Wright argues convincingly that the development of human civilization has followed an evolutionary path strikingly similar to and as inevitable as that of human biology: the strongest cultural organisms (or 'memes') win out over time. His analogy makes intuitive sense, but there's a twist – 'strength' is here determined not by a meme's tendency to consume or destroy competing ideas, but rather by its tendency to promote cooperation within the culture in which it arises. Essentially, Wright is saying that the ideas that have tended to win out across time are those that have most helped our civilization become and stay, well, more civil.

'Becoming and staying more civil' – if we're seeking a mission for tomorrow's marketing, we could do a lot worse than this! Indeed, there's a growing body of evidence that brands that adopt this empathy/generosity/collaboration ethos will improve their chances to succeed – not in some fictive 'lovemarks' sweepstakes, and not just as social or cultural organisms, but also in the hard financial terms CEOs and shareholders demand.

Now empathy, generosity and collaboration seem pretty clearly to fall from the same tree as cooperation. They differ from it, though, in subtle but important ways. These merit examination and, since collaboration is the endgame, let's work backwards from there to build a model of purpose for tomorrow's marketing.

COLLABORATION

As I'm using it here, *collaboration* means a more active, more directed form of engagement than just *cooperation* (which, after all, can sometimes mean two parties simply agreeing to do nothing). It is creative, iterative, even sometimes playfully improvisational. It is call-and-response, a series of 'offers' and 'yes, and...' counter-offers, where (as in most areas of life) the clearer the brief, the better the answer. Collaboration has become a driving force in creative problem solving; film studio Pixar's offices were even designed to foster 'collisions', to get different types of thinkers from different departments to literally bump into each other. And we know now that the success of any 'brainstorming' exercise depends on the degree to which it encourages participants not to accept but to revise and build on the ideas generated there. Many examples could help illustrate the attractiveness and prevalence of collaboration in the Digital State; here are two of the giants.

In the technology space, we see collaboration manifested in the global open-source movement. Linux software was the original 'name brand' here, but open-source is also being practised even in companies better known for zealous (some would say fanatically unfair) defence of their intellectual property. Take Apple's App Store, a virtuous ecosystem in which all players profit. Talk about non-zero: users of Apple products get access to almost 700,000 tools and toys that enhance their usage experience, for an average price of under $2 a pop; Apple developers get access to a market of tens of millions of Apple customers worldwide, and a non-trivial cut of the revenues these customers generate; and Apple, with heroically minimal effort, creates ever greater customer stickiness.[6] Much imitated but not even close to being duplicated, the App Store, which opened in July 2008, went from zero to 100 million downloads in just two months, and hit an astounding 10 billion in January 2011. Now *that* is a winning meme.

And in the knowledge space there's *Wikipedia*, the largest-scale intellectual-collaboration experiment in history. Though far from perfect, this once-quirky project in collecting and curating the wisdom of crowds has quickly become the go-to resource for half a billion unique users worldwide, one whose 10 billion page views every month make it the planet's sixth-most-visited website, all on the strength of articles, edits and updates contributed by some 36 million volunteers working in 285 languages.

Now, in the part of the world in which I grew up, Encyclopædia Britannica was the last word in knowledge, and certainly no one-person project. And today's Britannica (yes, it still exists) proudly lists among its thousands of contributors 'more than a hundred Nobel laureates, four presidents of the United States, countless Pulitzer Prize winners and others of international renown'. In contrast, those millions of Wikipedians seem happy to toil in anonymity. Why would anybody do this?

According to *Wikipedia* itself, the top reasons are that it's fun, it's a way to support the ideology that knowledge should be free, and it's altruistic, which helps to put a new gloss on a notion much abused in the Digital State – 'connection'. Since the dawn of the Digital Age, a desire for greater 'connectedness' has often been cited as a prime motivator of all kinds of behaviour in the digital space. And yet, as the above examples of collaboration suggest, at least some of the time what we want to be 'connected' to is neither other people nor our expensive devices, but rather something *larger* than ourselves – a project, a principle, a purpose. (A good time to pose a question: 'Which purpose, Mr and Ms Marketer, are *you* proposing to users and would-be users of your brand?') The human search for purpose is of course anything other than new, but, fuelled by technology, this desire is finding new momentum in the Digital State, where collaboration is helping us combine our own instincts and intellect with the information we glean from our friends and peers to find and in many cases create authorities we can trust more instinctively than, say, institutions or brands.

The opportunity for marketing, and for brands whose own authority is rapidly draining away, seems clear enough – we've got to get better at inviting brand users to participate in the lives of our brands, from product development to product communication.[7] When we apply brand users' input intelligently (meaning, keenly aware of the potential outcomes) *and* capitalize on these users' reach, we'll help our brands meet their objectives more effectively. More specifically: if you're a marketer, collaboration means the chance to dramatically expand your brand's reach by getting your product naturally into the bloodstream of popular culture – to get people talking not about ads or funny videos, but about their own experience with your product.

Now, most readers of this book will be working in mature markets, where growth in market share comes almost exclusively through growth in penetration, that is, popularity. That means marketers must focus on more or less continuously generating trial. So becoming more popular isn't just a nice thing to do; it's a must.[8] Seeming to be talked about more and more is one way to build perceptions of popularity. Actually *being* talked about more and more is even better. A not-yet-published analysis by Millward Brown of Effie winners in North America comes to a similar conclusion – among other findings, the study notes that, compared to Effie entrants in general, Effie winners' success was more likely to have had a strong consumer collaboration component, ranging from word of mouth to various forms of interaction, including with the product itself, not just with its communication.[9]

I'm not surprised by any of this, and you probably aren't either. What is surprising, perhaps, is how many brands get collaboration wrong. Sometimes they simply fail to put the consumer's ball back in play – responding inadequately to the consumer's response violates the rules, and can end the game quickly. Quite often they miss by focusing primarily on developing deeper relationships with only a small handful of hard-core fans or heavy category users, instead of going broad. Naturally, a self-professed brand fan is more likely than a very casual brand user to engage with a collaboration offer from that brand – but the point is to win the lighter user *with* the collaboration, not *for* it. A wealth of evidence shows that it's breadth of appeal, not depth of appeal, that fuels brand growth – so brands should always be aiming to establish casual relationships with a wide swathe of category users.[10] And, since people naturally take less interest in what brands do than in what other people do, the more a brand's conversation is carried on by these other people, the further it'll be carried. Collaboration with a few should always yield conversation among the many.

(You may remember the 90/9/1 rule from the dawn of the Web 2.0 era – as in, of all the people who see your brand doing stuff, 90 per cent will passively watch, 9 per cent will talk about it and only 1 per cent will react more concretely. But over time I've come to believe we've been looking through the wrong end of the telescope: if engaging 1 per cent of category users in collaboration with my brand means another 9 per cent will talk about the collaboration and the remaining 90 per cent will get at least a glimpse of what's going on, I like that arithmetic quite a lot. Any marketer should.[11])

GENEROSITY

About 10 years ago I started thinking that maybe the first rule of marketing should be: 'Give something away, and see what people do with it.' Now, after almost five years of leading the planning group at one of Germany's top digital agencies, I *know* it should be – especially if you're trying to spark collaboration.

The question is: which flavours of generosity are likely to motivate somebody to participate with a brand? Many companies have guessed wrong here, and we've all learnt that an open channel alone doesn't constitute a gift. Since there are several crucial dimensions to consider, and citizens of the Digital State are coming to expect such gifts, an acronym may help to make the various possibilities stickier – so meet the 'FACES' principle. Each letter stands for a specific type of gift, with a specific value, and as with gifting in general there is much to be gained by mixing them, either sequentially or simultaneously.[12] Indeed, in the most effective campaigns it's sometimes hard to tease out where one gift ends and the next begins:

F stands for *freebie*: an actual gift with legitimate material value – a voucher, a product sample, a sweepstake with a truly exciting first prize. Anything that's free is usually of relevance. Crispin's much-awarded Whopper Sacrifice on Facebook is a good example. A personal favourite of mine is the office-supply store Staples' campaign to announce its new name in Norway: instead of the typically dull 'We're now called...' routine, Staples created 'Norway's best-paid job' by offering a half-million kroner to the person who most correctly pronounced the company's new, decidedly un-Norwegian name.[13]

A stands for *amusement*, or the gift of diversion (which can, but doesn't have to, be funny in the classical sense). Any fulfilling distraction will do. Content quality is really essential here; lots of would-be 'virals' never pass this barrier, but lots of branded games manage to – if it's easy and fun, I'll ask someone else to play, too. A terrific amusement case is the micro-budget 'Samsung Shakedown' campaign from Sweden. Marketed exclusively via brand members' own Facebook profiles, the effort invited people to play with the product remotely; a successful demonstration of the main product proposition resulted in the player winning the phone. Brilliantly non-zero, and extremely talkable.

C stands for *contribution*, or the gift of letting me offer meaningful input to the brand. 'Meaningful' lies of course in the eye of the beholder, but experience shows there's a wide spectrum of possibility: from voting on the introduction of a new flavour, new package design or new colour (eg M&Ms' colour vote) to pitching in product- or service-improvement suggestions (eg Dell's idea storm and MyStarbucksIdea) to participating in the development of new products via open-innovation initiatives (eg the Nestlé Marktplatz, a social-commerce platform developed and launched by my former agency, argonautenG2).

E stands for *empowerment*, or the gift of a platform where I can become a better version of myself. The internet can't make me funny, or sexy, or creative if I'm not – any more than it can help brands and companies mask crappy products or services – but can dial up whatever positives I've got. The right gift here can make me a more creative person, a funnier person, a person who's less shy in starting a communication with a stranger, a person who's able to promote a better picture of himself in the social web (as numerous 'create and post' efforts have shown, including my own former agency's Havana Club Remixer and Replay Fragrances Watercolorator) or a person whose literary opinions are worth paying special attention to (as an Amazon top reviewer).

S stands for *service*, or the gift of making things easier. Help me pick the right book for example, or the right new computer, or the right hotel, and I'm likely to want to help you in return. This can be a matter of offering useful and timely information – Amazon's collective-intelligence- and collaboration-based social shopping features are an excellent example of the power of 'service' (again, a very non-zero proposition); Best Buy's 'Twelpforce' shows how a retailer can offer valuable assistance for purchase decisions via Twitter. Service can also be powerfully delivered via privileged access (eg to new products, or to discontinued styles, or to 'sneak previews' of a brand's work-in-progress). Telling or showing me something I didn't already know about and had no other way to discover is a good way to make me feel special. And that's a story I'll gladly spread around.

Freebie, Amusement, Contribution, Empowerment, Service: give something away that encourages natural interaction with your brand, and then see who responds, and how they do it, keeping in mind that each response is a counter-offer, one that puts the ball squarely back in your court.

EMPATHY

Collaboration that increases my brand's reach and popularity is the goal; *generosity* provides incentives for people to accept my invitation to collaborate. But, if these two memes aren't built on a platform of *empathy*, the game can be over before it's even started.

While sympathy means literally 'feeling with' – compassion for or commiseration with another person – empathy is 'feeling into'. You feel empathy when you've 'been there' and sympathy when you haven't. So, for brands looking to grow in the Digital State, it's clear which is more useful. But I'd suggest that in addition to being clear on this distinction there are also three equally important but very different ways of creating empathy, and brands need to understand these equally well.

One: simply being human – meaning admitting weakness, owning up to mistakes, being seen to listen and learn, explaining apparent flaws. Partly, it's charming. Partly, it shows your brand has been in touch with its own dark side. Mostly, it fulfils what citizens of the Digital State expect from the brands they choose to do business with. And, yes, you'd think that by now this would all be simply table stakes, but the shitstorms that erupt when companies fail here – think BP, or pretty much any US airline – suggest some of us are still learning where corporate 'transparency' ends and real empathy begins. 'Show me more, and I'll trust you more' – this is the gist.

Two: conveying the sense that 'somebody knows how I feel'. Now I'm certainly not suggesting that people seek affirmation or understanding from a brand at a personal level – quite the contrary, that's what their friends and families are for, after all, and I imagine I'm not the only person who finds it pathetic and slightly creepy when brands encroach too closely on my personal space. So, while it's essential for a brand's audience to get the sense that 'somebody knows how I feel', I see this functioning not so much at the 'me'-level but rather the 'us'-level. If I get the sense that the brand has understood the lives and needs of people *like* me, and has identified real problems and developed real solutions for me and others *like* me, then I'll also get the sense of a brand operating at an appropriate emotional level. The implication for marketing: if you want to help your brand grow, find something concrete to fix. If you're not sure what's really bothering or exciting people about your category, the Digital State offers plenty of technologies for observing people's fascinations. But simply going after Brand X isn't cutting it any more; the world wants marketing that responds to its real needs, and it wants it now.

And three: clearly defining the conflict at the heart of your brand's story. 'Conflict' may seem like an odd thing to mention in a discussion of empathy, but you can't build empathy without it, because, when we identify with a story's hero and root for the hero's desires, we're rooting for our own, according to Robert McKee, arguably the world's leading authority on storytelling. So properly identifying the conflict driving your brand's story is centrally important – to you, for it gives the brand focus and energy, and to your audience, for it gives them the most essential clue they'll need to decide whether or not to give your brand their allegiance. (Of course, this allegiance must be cemented via satisfying, if not downright excellent, product experience.)

There are many types of conflict, but I'd suggest these three cover most of the normal range of marketing experience:

- *Brand versus brand.* A relational conflict, ie a struggle for category or thought leadership, like Mac versus PC, or McDonald's versus Subway, or Airbus versus Boeing. Of course, a brand can be driven by a conflict with a 'strategic competitor' that's never explicitly mentioned in advertising or other external communications but nonetheless provides essential impetus to its opposite.
- *Brand versus itself.* An internal conflict within the brand, ie a struggle for identity or clarity, like British Petroleum rebranding as BP (or any 'repositioning' exercise for that matter); or Marmite (which has very cleverly turned its 'love us or hate us' taste experience into a winning

brand proposition); or even my client Nestlé here in Germany, a company long esteemed as a nutrition expert but insufficiently acknowledged for making wholesome, tasty foods.

- *Brand versus culture.* A social conflict with a specific group of people, ie a struggle against misperception, prejudice or other 'incorrect' beliefs, like Dove taking on conventional attitudes toward depictions of feminine beauty (a conflict that has been worth over $1.3 billion in sales for Dove, according to one of their Effie-winning cases); or Omo/Persil detergent asserting that 'dirt is good' (a conflict that Unilever finds magnetic enough to use as a recruiting mechanism at the corporate level); or the US 'green clean' brand Method, whose conflict is driven less by its specific competitors than by the beliefs those brands have drummed into us over the years, namely that household cleaning products have to be harsh and even dangerous to be effective. 'People Against Dirty' has not just de-positioned a whole category of FMCG Goliaths; it's also helped Method grow from zero to $200 million in sales in its first 10 years.

Essentially, empathy is about creating space – much as a good storyteller knows what to leave out so that listeners can complete the story in their own minds, an empathetic brand leaves room for category users to come to their own conclusions regarding that brand's purpose, intentions and motivations. And, if a good story leaves room for the audience to participate, a great one invites them straight in, so a pretty good test of your brand's empathy is this: how easily can you imagine people wanting to participate in your brand's story? How much would they want to join your cause? How eager would they be to turn its promise into a movement? How much would you yourself?

THE GENIUS OF THE SYSTEM

The Digital State is a restless place, one where dark energy abounds, but shining through all that is a hope-filled character, a driving spirit gaining in strength, an increasingly popular ethos – a triple meme that is 'winning out' on a global level and, better yet, starting to make a dent in contemporary marketing. Some years ago, Dan Packard (of Hewlett-Packard) presciently opined that 'Marketing is too important to be left to the marketing people.'

He was wishing, I suspect, for more involvement from product developers and R&D people; today, he'd be demanding input from an even wider range of players. I share his sentiment and would add that marketing is also too important to be left simply to wither on the vine.

The good news: inspiring examples of how to do it better are multiplying, the changes we need to make are not that difficult, and the rewards for making them are quite rich. Applying the ethos of the Digital State – its defining spirit of collaboration, generosity and empathy – will not only help us 'become and stay more civil' as a profession, but also increase our effectiveness as a business. By inspiring a kind of marketing that people feel invited into, naturally want to connect with, and increasingly expect, it'll also create a more meaningful role for marketing itself. And, by giving deeply rooted human values a seat at the marketing table, it'll put some 'genius' back into a 'system' that sorely needs it.

JL
Berlin

NOTES

1. All this according to Peter Krieg of Copernicus Marketing Consulting, in warc.com.
2. Think of the ways in which, to take just one example, Amazon's pioneering use of customer reviews and collective as well as contextual intelligence ('people who looked at X also looked at Y') has fundamentally and irrevocably altered how we shop – both online and off.
3. If you're under 40: Bill Bernbach was one of the authors of advertising's creative revolution, and the B in DDB.
4. Don't get hung up on my labelling these 'values' here – think of them as attributes or benefits if that's more helpful.
5. Robert Wright, *Nonzero: The Logic of Human Destiny* (Pantheon, New York, 2000).
6. I'm well aware of the irony inherent in citing the App Store in a paragraph about open-source – but to me the success of this venture, despite valid counterarguments about Apple's lack of openness in other areas, simply proves how powerful this meme truly is.
7. Just to be clear, my emphasis here is on *participation in, not direction of, the life of the brand*. I shudder every time I read about a marketer 'putting the brand in the hands of the consumer'. Don't get me wrong: I love consumers,

and they can serve up treasure – but they've got no real stake in a brand's success and are therefore in no position to guide a brand's objective-setting. Collaboration is not about getting consumers to do our job, it's about working in ways that yield better, more fulfilling results for brand stakeholders and brand users alike.

8 Previous brand purchase behaviour is still the best predictor of future brand purchase, but as DDB's Brand Capital Study, among others, has shown, the extent to which we believe a brand is becoming more popular strongly influences our interest in trying a brand in the first place.

9 Thanks to Effie Worldwide for giving me access to this material.

10 If you're interested in consulting this evidence, one good source is the University of South Australia's Ehrenberg-Bass Institute: www.marketingscience.info

11 I've seen it suggested that the influence figure is even higher, perhaps as high as 62 units of conversation sparked by a single unit of advocacy, according to Steve Barton in a piece titled 'Word-of-Mouth Marketing' on http://warc.com

12 Thanks and kudos to my former colleague and planning partner Elisabeth Unverricht for identifying and codifying these 'gifts'.

13 I'm not able to include every case URL, but this one is really worth it: http://awards.mediafront.no/cresta/2010/staples/video/Staples_presentasjon_h264.mov.

4 THUNK

Bettina Sherick

> When I find myself saying something like 'I don't get Twitter; it seems so silly' (which I did say), I just as quickly ask myself, 'What is it I don't know? What is it that drives people to use this shiny new thing? Will it change the way we think, work, communicate, experience? Am I dismissing it because it doesn't fit into my perception of how the world works?'
>
> I no longer think Twitter is silly. Once I heard myself say those questioning words, I set up an account and started using it. Sure, it was silly. At first. But then, as I started following interesting and relevant Twitter accounts, and connected with people in both the digital and entertainment industries that were actively posting and sharing info, I found it to be a very engaging, useful way of connecting and staying up to date.

I'd like you to meet... Bettina Sherick

I've met some big personalities, and Bettina Sherick is up there in that top drawer. Whether around a boardroom table or dinner table, whether in a meeting or living room, Bettina is a larger-than-life, energized, vocal presence. She could never be a spy. I don't consider 'inconspicuous' is among her many gifts – but then, unless you actually are a spy, who'd want 'inconspicuous' in their repertoire of skills anyway? And I think, more than anything, that big personalities are born of one thing: big hearts.

Bettina has a big heart, has a sincerity, openness and generosity of spirit that is very evident, very... *conspicuous*. She probably couldn't hide it if she wanted to, but I can't imagine why she would want to. It makes Bettina who she is, betrays only that she has that brand of genuine confidence where she speaks her mind and lets her feelings be known. There's a line from the Bible (Proverbs 23:7), 'As he thinketh in his heart, so he is.' He, *she*, the principle applies across the gender divide. Big personality, ergo: big heart.

No, Bettina would not make a very subtle spy, but I imagine her rather a lot like a gunslinger, a quick mind and fast draw fighting the good fight in today's still wild Digital West.

*

It feels very fitting that Bettina Sherick is based in Los Angeles, that her view of the Digital State is a West Coast one, with Silicon Valley a couple of hours up the road, and the state of California originally built by frontiers(wo)men who carved a wagon trail towards the unknown, but in hope of something better. I know, I maybe sound a little romantic, but I like the parallels, like wagon wheel grooves in the dry dirt, those first pioneers making one line, and the late-20th-century dot-com explorers the other, tracks and timelines that tell a story, a history, on repeat. And I very much like the fact that Bettina Sherick is one of those latter-day (digital) pioneers, that she was there in the early days, when it was all a lot wild, unlawful and unwritten. And this is the story that she tells, of her digital journey 'out West', back in the day, when the days were the late 1990s, which at once was not so long ago but also actually a whole other epoch ago.

It was over a taste-bud-assaulting lunch (in a good way) that Bettina and I first discussed 'digital history', a thought I found as gently marvellous as our restaurant's menu, which had also become famous for successfully matching contradictions. We all tend to talk about 'digital' in an 'on-the-cusp' way where we think *forward*, but of course 'digital' has already been around long enough to have a past, and a past we can learn from, just as we can learn a lot from Bettina Sherick.

Over to Bettina.

T*hunk*. That was the sound of my digital awakening. It was the end of 1996, and the average person was just learning about this 'world wide web' or the 'information superhighway'. There were many new sounds being introduced to those of us who early on embraced this new way of connecting with the world: the hissing noise of the dial-up modem connecting through telephone lines to the internet; the voice of Elwood Edwards, AOL's 'You've Got Mail!' guy, and Wylie Gustafson, the yodelling Yahoo! guy.

That sound, *thunk*, was the sound of a simple box, dropped by a delivery person on to the doorstep of my apartment. I was in graduate school then, taking evening courses towards my MBA while working full time in the buying office of a chain of linen retail stores. I needed a certain textbook that had sold out of the student bookstore and was on back order. A fellow student suggested I try ordering from this 'online site' called Amazon that claimed to be 'the world's largest bookstore'. I did indeed check out this online bookstore, and there was the book I needed. I will admit it took me at least two full days to be brave enough to send my personal details and credit card information through this website, but order I did. And, a few days later, *thunk*. I opened the box, and in a flash I thought, 'My God. This is going to change everything.'

It took many years before everything changed. But, at that moment, my curiosity was piqued, and my interest both personally and professionally became focused on just what this new form of connectivity would create.

Of course, there were many people who did not share in my sense of vision. The retailer for which I worked had a website up with the name and mail-order phone number, in 16-point Times New Roman font. My first target was that website. Armed with nothing more than passion and Microsoft FrontPage 97 I set out to make a real online brand site for the company. Up until then, my technical expertise was limited to Word and Excel, with a thrilling foray into Access to build a contact database. So, armed with some Microsoft tricks and blind ignorance, I taught myself how to use the software, and through much trial and error I eventually launched the company's first real website.

Brochureware, however, was not enough to satisfy my burgeoning digital curiosity. I wanted someone to experience the joy of ordering from our online store. Thus I found myself standing in the executive boardroom, a room that up until that point had been a mystery to me. I'd convinced the executive team to allow me to give a presentation to them about this world wide web and pitch the idea of opening a store online. I spent weeks learning about search engines, Boolean syntax, e-commerce virtual shopping malls, online shopping carts... I analysed the competition for our particular retail vertical (bedding and bath products)... I knew how much of the business was coming from mail order, and I had my projections of what could be migrated and then expanded upon through an online storefront.

The CEO walked in, took his seat at the head of the table, and announced, 'OK, young lady. I may be the only person in America who cancelled my AOL account because I don't get what the big deal is. What are *you* going to tell me?' Two hours later, I walked out with the remit to come back and present to the executive committee our plan to harness this 'world wide web' for the benefit of the company.

In addition to grad school studies, and my day job at the company, I dived into my special project. I met with USWeb (which became MarchFirst before becoming a dot-bomb casualty), iCat, blue suits from IBM pitching their WebSphere solution, consulting companies, tech companies, other e-commerce companies... and a few months later I presented a plan to the executive committee. Although companies were spending millions during these heady dot-com boom days, I had a plan to launch an online store for a mere US$300,000.

The plan sat on the desk of the CEO for several weeks before I was called in for his final answer. The good news: I would be promoted to marketing director. The bad news: I would not get the funding for my online store.

It was about that time that I became reacquainted with a college friend, who was employee number 76 at Yahoo! It was also about that time that Yahoo! purchased a software company that would soon become Yahoo! Shopping. They were looking for bricks-and-mortar retailers to populate what would be their online mall. With one phone call, I was back in the game.

I gathered a team that included a dedicated resource from the Yahoo! Shopping team, the services of Pasadena Advertising (an award-winning retail advertising agency) and an intern from Pepperdine University. Together we launched a fully functioning website offering 2,000 SKUs of merchandise. The orders were processed through mail-order services operating in the back room of one of the larger retail locations. The final cost of launching our online store? US$30,000. We launched the store in May 1998. Within a month, the online store was making as much in sales as one of the smaller bricks-and-mortar stores – with a fraction of the overhead.

For almost a year I toiled away on the website – merchandising new products, setting up an e-mail program using freeware to build customer retention, dealing with credit card fraud, upgrading the front end of the website, improving search results, experimenting with banner ads. There came a time, however, when I realized that the old company culture would not embrace a new digital reality. In 1999 I left the retailer that was my employer of seven years. Battling the influx of big-box retailers and e-commerce competition, the company closed its doors for good in 2003.

*

10 January 2000
6.30 am
My phone rang. 'I think you should turn on the news.' I turned on CNN to see Gerald Levin, Dick Parsons and Steve Case announcing their merger between old and new media. The new company was to be called AOL Time Warner. The merger was valued at $350 billion.

After leaving the linens company, I struck out to find my place in this brave new digital world. After all, it was the dot-boom period, and anyone with a working understanding of the web was in demand. What followed was more like 'brave alternative reality'... and a series of very interesting interviews with various dot-coms and tech companies in various stages of funding with questions such as 'If a plane landed on your front lawn, how would you measure the depth of the divot it creates without using a yard-stick?' or 'You're a NASCAR driver, but you're not the best driver. You need to increase your fans. What do you do?' and my favourite: 'What is more important, revenue or eyeballs?' (For the record, the correct answer was 'eyeballs'.)

However, practicality outweighed my appetite for risk, and instead of going to a 'pure play', as the dot-com companies were called back then, or a tech company, I signed on with Warner Bros Studio Store. I was the director of marketing for the Warner Bros e-commerce business. At the time the online store was affiliated with the bricks-and-mortar chain of stores, part of Warner Bros Consumer Products. For a year I worked on establishing an e-mail marketing programme, an affiliate marketing programme, marketing our stores on Entertaindom, an early effort to organize an entertainment experience around a single branded hub, and even an AOL store. I sat through meetings with companies who told me 'I didn't get it' because their business model made no sense to me. I sat in meetings with old-school retailers that were clearly non-believers in the future of e-commerce.

Then, that morning, with the big AOL announcement, I became an employee of what was then the biggest company merger in US history. I was now officially in the brave new-media world – for at least a few months.

Somewhere in boardrooms far away from the warehouse where we merchandised our online store, new media decided that the retail business didn't fit their vision of the digital future. Soon I found myself in front of the Warner Bros Studio Store executive team, signing my walking papers. The e-commerce store was to close, the team was to be laid off, and shortly after the bricks-and-mortar stores were shuttered.

As they say, when one door closes another opens. That door happened to be at Twentieth Century Fox International, where I have been a digital marketing executive since December 2000.

*

Much has happened in the digital world since 1997. I feel fortunate to have had a unique vantage point in which to be both a witness and a participant of the Digital Revolution.

In 1996 I discovered and became strangely drawn to sites like Angelfire, Geocities and Tripod. The idea of connecting with other internet users with similar interests, the ability to share pictures, even my résumé, was intriguing and exciting. Of course, the number of people willing to do so was limited, and the need to know rudimentary HTML was limiting. Fast-forward to MySpace, and now Facebook, and you have the grown-up versions of what were started as early website services, with better UI and way more people willing to share pictures and personal info – and a lot of pictures of food.

I learnt my first HTML codes from a stranger via ICQ, an early messaging program. Eventually AOL, MSN and Yahoo! all introduced much more user-friendly messaging services, complete with downloadable themes. Messaging used to require that a user be logged into the service via a computer. Imagine that! Of course, now we carry around messaging devices in our pockets. Services like WhatsApp have enabled free texting, and now Facebook has opened up its messaging platform for mobile-to-mobile messaging.

I used to have a screensaver that pushed news and information live from the internet to my PC when I was connected to the internet. It was run by a company called PointCast. While certainly novel, it often caused my computer to freeze and crash. But the idea fuelled my desire to get live news that was refreshed frequently, which led to RSS Readers and then Google Alerts. Now, every morning, I check my Twitter feed for the latest news around the world.

The very first 'privacy policy' I ever posted to a website was created using a form editor on a free website. Back then, privacy policies and terms and conditions were considered optional, a nice thing to have. Now, I wouldn't consider launching a business website without legal counsel. Privacy is a critical condition to a website's commercial success. Today's consumers are becoming more and more savvy, and demand certain protections around their personally identifiable information (PII). Every move by Facebook, Instagram, Zynga or any other popular place where consumers hand over PII is scrutinized by press and social media. It took me two days to be brave enough to enter my credit card information into the shopping card on Amazon.com, but there are many sites online today with a lot more info on me, that's for sure!

*

After I'd launched that first e-commerce store, an executive of the linens company called me into his office and said, 'Bettina, how do we get on the web?'

Perplexed I replied, 'Well, we are on the web. We have secured three URLs, which all point to our e-commerce store. We are on the web.'

He rolled his eyes at me. 'I mean On. The. Web. So everyone can see us.'

'I'm confused; we are on the web, sir. Do you need me to give you the web store address again?'

'I know the web address!' he sputtered in frustration, his voice raised. 'I want to be ON. THE. WEB.'

This 'who's on first' conversation continued, both of us getting more and more frustrated than the other, until it hit me. I walked over to his computer, typed in **www.msn.com**, pointed to the banner at the top of the start page, and asked, 'Do you mean this page? How do we get on this page of the internet?'

He looked at me and shouted, 'Yes! Exactly! On the web. How do we get there?' This executive, a tough, old-school retailer, looked at me as if I were an idiot and said, 'I want us to be *there*. What would it take?'

'A million dollars', I replied.

You see, back then companies like AOL and MSN were building what were called 'carriage deals' – retailers like Pets.com, eToys and other companies that were building up their e-commerce businesses were paying crazy money to have their brands featured on the home pages of popular portal sites. MSN was the default start page for Internet Explorer, and thus was considered to be prime internet real estate.

'I think you're full of shit', he growled. And, with that, I knew my time at the linen retailer had to come to an end.

I bring up this story partially because I still get a chuckle from it, but mostly because it taught me something that I still try to remember today. Digital has changed and will continue to change business as we know it. Digital will force business rules to change. The idea that a tiny 468- by 60-pixel ad on a computer screen would be worth $1 million was ludicrous to a man who'd built his career buying ads in newspapers. He couldn't be bothered to learn about these new business models. Indeed, when I tried to suggest that we reach out to Idealab, a Southern California-based venture capital company that was incubating some popular e-commerce sites at the time, I was told, 'We don't reach out; we get introductions.' Once we finally did get that introduction, we found out that a couple of Harvard MBAs had already pitched and received funding for an online linen business. Once I quit my job with the retailer to seek out my new digital adventure, I never had contact with that executive again. I am sure he celebrated a bit of *schadenfreude* during the dot-bust.

But change was already in progress. The dot-com pioneers may have failed, but they started a change. Each one of those companies helped move us into the Digital Revolution. So, when I find myself saying something like 'I don't get Twitter; it seems so silly' (which I did say), I remind myself of that conversation about the MSN start page with that executive and I just as quickly ask myself, 'What is it I don't know? What is it that drives people to use this shiny new thing? Will it change the way we think, work, communicate, experience? Am I dismissing it because it doesn't fit into my perception of how the world works?' Certainly there are those new businesses that come along and there's no there *there*, but often there is a lesson to be learnt.

I no longer think Twitter is silly. Once I heard myself say those questioning words, I set up an account and started using it. Sure, it was silly. At first. But then, as I started following interesting and relevant Twitter accounts, and connected with people in both the digital and entertainment industries who were actively posting and sharing info, I found it to be a very engaging, useful way of connecting and staying up to date.

The next time you want to dismiss something new, stop and ask yourself why. Then challenge yourself to be open. Be curious. Be brave... Be digital. As for me, I'm anxiously waiting for my next big *thunk*.

BRS
Los Angeles

5 TEENAGE KICKS

Austen Kay

“Facebook in particular and social networking in general have introduced an extra layer of teenage angst. What you wear, what you listen to and who you hang out with are no longer your sole concerns. Now you need to curate your lifestyle online. Putting it more succinctly, what you *share* says more about you than ever before...

Teenagers should be encouraged to post anonymously online, and to view the social web as a sandbox where they can experiment with different styles of expression without risk of being held to account by the playground. In short, they should be allowed the time and space to develop their social confidence through real-life engagement with small groups (as my generation did) or anonymously with large groups, not with 500-plus connected ‘friends’ who know your name, where you live and your favourite type of pizza.

I'd like you to meet... Austen Kay

I first met Austen in December 1990. Just typing 1990 makes me smile, and feel a little old, and make the point I really want to make. Austen and I met when we were kids – kids trying to work out what kind of grown-ups we might go on to be, and what kind of students. Against the pseudo-serious backdrop of college and faculty interviews, attended by a pseudo-sophisticate collective of posturing teenagers hoping to progress their studies at Oxford, Austen and I spent two days acting as if we'd already been given our university places, drinking pints, playing pool and trying to impress girls. It was representative enough of how university life would eventually play out.

And I continue to smile at how our lives have continued to run in parallel: each with the same number of children, similar ages, following the same gender roll-call; a helter-skelter career through advertising and media agencies; and a current thrill and fascination in the direction our digital world is progressing, and a want to positively contribute to that progress.

Austen, once more based in his home town of Manchester, continues to march to the beat of his own drum, and I've always liked the fact that Austen's march is more of a groove and a swagger. I was really thrilled when Austen, a very clever guy from a very analogue kind of past, said yes to writing a chapter about our very digital present.

*

It was over a mid-December pint (a warm bitter on a very frosty evening), where Austen had just submitted his chapter, that he offered (quite sincerely between sips), 'I don't have all the answers.' It was true, of course – Austen, along with everyone else. No one does. But I think that's always the point, that, whether as adults or as children, we're all on that same path, looking for answers, learning a little more as we go, through trial and error. Now as adults we should be better equipped to absorb the knocks and take our mistakes on the chin, but as children we almost all have a glass jaw. It's why everyone's rites of passage should be about making a few mistakes, and getting away with it – like Ferris Bueller.

But, while growing up is tough enough, imagine never getting any breaks, where your every action, deed, word has a potential comeback. Like wearing a leather jacket too much like Ferris Bueller's, and the photo evidence floating through cyberspace for ever.

In 'Teenage kicks', Austen posits that 'digitalness' has made every digital native's growing up tougher, because our digital identities expose our impulses and follies. They become points of exhibited, trackable and permanent (public) record. And so, if you happen to be a kid right now, that's being cut no slack at all, you're being set up to inevitably fall, because the whole point of growing up is that you're 'not yet formed', you're trying on identities and looking in the mirror to see how they fit. Everyone's youthful trek over the semi-savage ground of self-discovery should come with the air-cover of at least some anonymity. Austen might not have all the answers, but, his humility aside, he has more than a few very fine suggestions.

Over to Austen.

> *Our economy is moving into a new phase – the social economy – whereby young people seek to define themselves not only by what they own or what they do but primarily by their ability to connect, to share and to broadcast.*
>
> *THE TRUTH ABOUT YOUTH*, MCCANN WORLDGROUP (MAY 2011)

It's tough being a kid. You want to fit in. In my day, as a teenager growing up in suburban Manchester through the 1980s and early 1990s, your tribe was dictated by your musical tastes. Were you an indie kid or a raver? Or maybe (God help you) a goth or a rocker? These tribes came with their own unspoken rules. Fashion often boiled itself down to your footwear: Filas for ravers, Doc Martens for goths. Your outward demeanour was also determined by association. Goths were sad. Ravers were happy. Although in reality the ravers were drug bores while the goths were a good laugh (maybe it was the cider). Still, as a teenager you were obsessed about this stuff. Hanging out in the right places and latching on to the right crowd were crucial elements in determining your nascent identity. Even though you probably didn't realize it, you were building the foundations of your social confidence.

These rites of passage continue to be relevant for teenagers the world over. However, as developments in technology create new outlets for people to communicate, the challenges facing today's youth become broader and arguably more difficult. The rules of the game haven't necessarily changed, but playing it has become a lot harder.

We now live in a 24/7 connected society. Facebook in particular and social networking in general have introduced an extra layer of teenage angst. What you wear, what you listen to and who you hang out with are no longer your sole concerns. Now you need to curate your lifestyle online. Putting it more succinctly, what you *share* says more about you than ever before.

> *You can't take something off the internet; that's like trying to take pee out of a swimming pool. Once it's in there, it's in there.*
>
> JOE GARRELLI, *NEWSRADIO*

In 2011, McCann Worldgroup[1] interviewed 7,000 young people across the globe to try to understand what made them different to the generations before them. Given a list of things (including cosmetics, their car, their passport, their phone and their sense of smell) and told they could save only two, 53 per cent of 16- to 22-year-olds admitted they would give up their own sense of smell if it meant they could keep an item of technology. Pretty drastic, don't you think? McCann concluded that, 'for young people, technology is more than a useful tool or enabler. It is truly their fifth sense.'

According to TGI data,[2] in the UK the proportion of young people who use social networking sites climbs steadily from 36 per cent of seven-year-olds to 95 per cent of 17-year-olds. As a member of the advertising industry, you might find me rubbing my hands with glee as our future consumers become wedded to a communication infrastructure that is far more accessible, accountable and malleable than the old media bedrocks of the 20th century. Allen Gannett, in an article for *The Next Web* in 2012, suggested 'The Facebook of 2022 will look a lot more like a data warehouse; that is, a utility providing users and web developers an easy way to store and access personal information.'[3]

However, it's not our future privacy vis-à-vis advertisers than concerns me as a parent. I gave up that battle a long time ago. Of far more importance to me is how we, and our children in particular, manage privacy amongst *ourselves*. Our kids are truly at the vanguard of this experiment. Collectively as parents we have very little control or even understanding. A 2011 study by Ofcom in the UK reported that 70 per cent of parents with children aged 12–15 who use the internet at home think they know less about the internet than their children do. Less than 40 per cent of parents have set internet parental controls at home.[4]

I've worked with many websites written for and by youth audiences, and I'm struck by the degree to which today's generation gap is digital. Digital natives have created their own rules, mannerisms and even language. Some of these elements bubble up to the mainstream with occasional unfortunate results, for instance when David Cameron notoriously mistook 'lol' for 'lots of love'.[5] Most of it remains a fiercely protected sphere, though, where coded language and semi-secret communities purposely keep parents at arm's length.

One key generational shift is the degree to which young adults are completely redefining the concepts of friendship, intimacy and sharing. McCann suggested that 'once upon a time teenagers had a small group of friends (typically 4–7 people)... nowadays things are more complex. Using social media, a typical teenager is likely to manage and maintain multiple, intersecting groups of friends.' They refer to a friends' arms race, where these 'stranger' or 'disposable' friends are sought and maintained to make you look popular, to spy on or to show off to. Pew Internet reported that American teenagers have an average of 201 Facebook friends.[6]

The dangers here are obvious: a teenage generation growing up instinctively wedded to technology, with their parents unwilling to monitor them or incapable of doing so; and peer group pressure leading these young, impressionable adults to harbour a vast and frankly unmanageable network of 'friends'. As a parent it really makes me worry. If you pee in the swimming pool, you can't take it back.

> *Technology and social networking has absorbed some of my close friendships, and they've dwindled. I miss the times where we could just go hang out and laugh.*
>
> 16-YEAR-OLD TEENAGER, QUOTED IN *SOCIAL MEDIA, SOCIAL LIFE: HOW TEENS VIEW THEIR DIGITAL LIVES*, COMMON SENSE MEDIA'S PROGRAM FOR THE STUDY OF CHILDREN AND MEDIA (2012)

OK, I admit it. In case you hadn't noticed I'm a paranoid parent. I have three young kids, aged seven and under. I wonder whether they'll grow up suffocated by their social graph, doomed to a dysfunctional adulthood where friendships are commodities to be traded like Panini stickers, hyper-connected but essentially lonely. Or, in my more considered moments, I wonder if they'll experience a social evolution, an advancement of our innate social skills, enriched by technology. Will they become sophisticated social schemers, mastering multiple communication channels with nonchalant ease, like a Dire Straits keyboard player for the modern era? If you're old enough to get that reference you're old enough to worry about this subject.

The answer as always is probably somewhere in between. There's certainly an undercurrent of anxiety attached to an always-on social media profile. McCann report a trend among youth who fear 'missing out' because they worry that a lack of presence, even temporarily, can affect their social status. The need for approval is tangible – as a teenager in the UK said, 'When you've put up a status that you've put a lot of effort into you want someone to comment on it.' Young people describe sitting in front of the laptop continuously hitting refresh, waiting for someone somewhere to hit 'like'. They conclude that 'the flipside to mass self-expression and connectivity is the ability to continuously measure your own life achievements against those within your network. Never before have young people found it easier to benchmark their successes (or lack of). As the social economy increases its reach, could we find an entire generation impacted by social status anxiety?'

In contrast, however, research in the United States by Common Sense Media[7] revealed that teens are much more likely to report that using social media has a positive impact on their social and emotional lives rather than a negative one. Only 4 per cent of teens in this study claimed that, on balance, using social media has had a negative effect on their relationships with their friends, while 52 per cent say it has mainly helped those relationships. In a nod to the positive aspects of social media, more than one in four teens said that social networking made them feel less shy (29 per cent) and more outgoing (28 per cent). In contrast, only 5 per cent said social networking made them feel less outgoing, 4 per cent felt worse about themselves, less confident and less popular after using their social networking site, and 3 per cent felt shyer.

So where does the truth lie? In its carefully worded conclusion, Common Sense Media suggested that:

> *None of this means that there's nothing to worry about when it comes to teens and social media. The concerns are real: about privacy, bullying, hate speech, body image, and over-sharing, to name a few. And we won't know for a long time how the immediacy of digital communication may be shaping interpersonal relationships and social skills. But the results of this survey do help put the challenges and pitfalls of social media into a broader perspective and offer reassurance that, for the most part, the kids are all right.*

As a paranoid parent, I admit that does reassure me a little, but the responsibility we have as parents to manage and nurture our children's online presence does not change regardless of which side of the fence we sit. I want to go beyond passively monitoring my children's usage. I want to go further than simply reacting to their social media faux pas. I want to give them a roadmap for the future.

> *We're moving towards persistent identity. We're moving towards a lack of privacy.*
>
> CHRISTOPHER POOLE, TED (2010)

In 2003 Christopher Poole, or 'moot' as he is known online, was 15 years old and still at high school. His fondness for Japanese animation led him to an image-board forum called 2chan. The code for 2chan was publicly available, so he translated it from Japanese to English using Altavista's BabelFish, threw it up on the web and sent it out to 20 people: 4chan was born.

I'm not quite sure he realized what he'd created. Now 4chan is the largest active forum in the United States. In 2010, Christopher told TED that 4chan receives over 7 million unique visitors and 700 million page views every month. It is notorious for many things. Its /b/ random board has been described by Gawker as a place where people try to shock, entertain and coax free porn from each other. It's the originator of countless memes, including Lolcats and my personal favourite, Rickrolls. The 4chan community has also been behind some of the most notorious internet pranks and hacks of recent years. As I write this, 4chan users have collaborated to place North Korean leader Kim Jong-un top of the *Time* magazine person of the year poll. The 4chan community has also been responsible for hacking Sarah Palin's e-mail, and causing Apple's stock to fall after posting a hoax story claiming Steve Jobs had suffered a major heart attack. Perhaps most famously, it is widely recognized as the originator of the hacktivist Anonymous movement.

You might fairly wonder what this has to do with protecting teenagers online – particularly when you consider much of the content across 4chan is dubious at best, illegal at worst. I saw Christopher Poole at an SXSW keynote speech in 2011, where he stole a few headlines by going up against Facebook's founder and cause célèbre Mark Zuckerberg. In his speech, an adaptation of his TED talk in 2010, he vehemently argued against Facebook's approach to social media.[8]

At the core of this dispute is the notion of authenticity. Mark Zuckerberg believes Facebook is truly authentic. People have to log on as themselves. They have to represent their true identity. Of course, it's not impossible to create a fake identity, but you will be doing so in contravention of Facebook's user policy,[9] which you sign up to when you create an account: you will not provide any false personal information on Facebook, or create an account for anyone other than yourself without permission; and you will not create more than one personal account. This represents the philosophy of persistent online identity, where your (verified) online identity exists across the social web. It's at the heart of Facebook Connect, which allows developers to enable sign-in to third-party websites using your Facebook profile.

Now, we all have our gripes with Facebook privacy. I recently bought tickets to a gig at Joshua Brooks in Manchester via a local ticketing site called Skiddle. To save time, I logged in using my Facebook details rather than signing up from scratch, and as a result Joshua Brooks is now listed on my profile as a 'favourite venue'. It isn't. But that's just one example of Facebook posting information you'd rather it didn't.

However, even without Facebook apps posting trivial information on our behalf, the philosophy of persistent online identity across the social web encourages us to share the very minutiae of our lives. As Christopher Poole stated in an interview with CNN in 2010, 'if someone called you up on the phone and asked you all of these things [that people post online] you'd say "hell no" and hang up. But now we're flooding the Internet with information about ourselves and I think that's scary. So I would like to see people push back.'[10]

Poole argues, successfully I believe, that being forced to represent your true self online runs counter to authenticity. You're constrained by social mores and convention. Posts and conversations become sterile. Anonymity online frees you from these constraints and allows you to post in a 'completely unvarnished, unfiltered, raw way'.

His comments regarding the innocence of youth really strike a chord. In an interview with the *New York Times*, he said:

> *As kids, we say stupid things, and because there's not a record of it, nobody is going to give you a hard time at 30 years old about something you said or did when you were 8 years old. Online, you have all these social networks that are moving to a state of persistent identity, and in turn, we're sacrificing the ability to be youthful. In 10 years, everything you say and do will be visible online, and I think it's really unfortunate.*[11]

The case for 'authenticity' is important, but of more importance, particularly in relation to teenagers developing their social skills in this brave new world, is the case for *protection*. The minimum eligible age for a Facebook account is 13. I'm a libertarian at heart but when it comes to children I take a different view. In my opinion, 13 is too young to fully understand or appreciate the dangers of persistent online identity. Teenagers should be encouraged to post anonymously online, and to view the social web as a sandbox where they can experiment with different styles of expression without risk of being held to account by the playground. In short, they should be allowed the time and space to develop their social confidence through real-life engagement with small groups (as my generation did) or anonymously with large groups, not with 500-plus connected 'friends' who know your name, where you live and your favourite type of pizza.

For the record, I'm not suggesting 4chan is the answer. There's too much unfettered filth on 4chan to make it suitable for most law-abiding adults, never mind children! But moot has a point (pun intended). Anonymity has its advantages, and it shouldn't be cast aside in the race to marry our real and virtual lives.

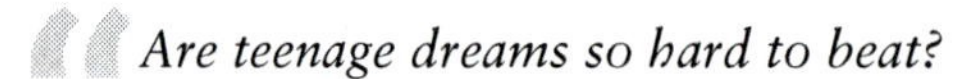

> *Are teenage dreams so hard to beat?*
>
> THE UNDERTONES, 'TEENAGE KICKS'

I know parents who grew up in the late 1970s and are completely bemused by social media. Computing and mobile technology didn't exist until well into their adult lives. While Facebook might have grabbed the attention of mums, the dads have no need or desire to gather online. Their mobile phone is really just a phone. By consequence, they have little or no capacity to monitor or advise their daughter regarding her social media activity.

In the end, the kids are probably going to have to work most of it out for themselves. At present, there's a rush to Facebook and persistent identity. Contrary to some of my more polemic comments above, I have no issue with a considered approach to true-identity social media. As noted, there is evidence to suggest that in general the positives outweigh the negatives.

However, I'd like to see more checks in place to verify friends for under-18s, thereby encouraging teenagers to maintain a virtual social 'graph' that truly reflects their real-life friendships. Common sense should dictate that your friends who know you are more likely to respect your feelings (although I acknowledge that's not always the case). I'd like to see children actively encouraged to join moderated, virtual worlds with anonymous or cloaked identities where they can treat the social web as a sandbox. Currently, MMORPGs (massively multiplayer online role playing games) such as RuneScape fulfil this function for many teens, but I think there's a need for something a little bit closer to the real world, without the social pressure and real-life consequences true user identity brings.

I'm afraid I don't have all the answers. I've used this piece to posit some theories and offer some suggestions. My knowledge and opinions are gleaned from my experience in youth marketing but also more pertinently from my concern as a parent. I'm sure a sociologist or child psychologist could rip massive holes in my arguments. However, what led me to write this piece was the tragic story of Amanda Todd, a sweet yet vulnerable teenager from British Columbia who committed suicide in October 2012 as a direct result of cyber-bullying via Facebook.[12]

So, whether you agree or disagree with my conclusions, one overriding point should hold firm. Our society is undergoing a revolution in communication and technology, and its effect on children is uncertain. As parents we need to understand the benefits and hazards of this revolution. If we do not, we are not fulfilling our duty to our children.

AK
Manchester

NOTES

1 http://www.iab.net/media/file/TheTruthAboutYouthMcCannWorldgroup.pdf

2 TGI, as cited by MediaTel, July 2010.

3 http://thenextweb.com/facebook/2012/08/05/what-will-facebook-look-like-in-2022/

4 http://consumers.ofcom.org.uk/2011/04/half-of-parents-know-less-about-the-internet-than-their-children/

5 http://www.bbc.co.uk/news/uk-politics-18032027

6 *Social Media and Young Adults*, February 2010, Pew Internet & American Life Project

7 http://www.commonsensemedia.org/research/social-media-social-life

8 http://www.ted.com/talks/christopher_m00t_poole_the_case_for_anonymity_online.html

9 http://www.facebook.com/legal/terms

10 http://scitech.blogs.cnn.com/2010/02/12/4chan-founder-anonymous-speech-is-endangered/

11 http://bits.blogs.nytimes.com/2010/03/19/one-on-one-christopher-poole-founder-of-4chan/

12 http://en.wikipedia.org/wiki/Suicide_of_Amanda_Todd

6 STORIES INTO ACTION

How storytelling and digital platforms will make our world a better place

Christian Johnsen

> Meaningful change won't come from governments alone, and it won't come from brands. It will come from people – people who are feeling increasingly empowered to take matters into their own hands and for the first time in history, as a consequence of the Digital Revolution, have the platforms that allow them to do so. All they need now is the spark, the unavoidable trigger, that will thrust them into action. I believe that this spark is anchored in an art form as old as humanity itself: a story. No: a great story...
>
> My father once told me that the purpose of life was to live your story, share it and hope others could become better for it.

I'd like you to meet... Christian Johnsen

Christian Johnsen wants to change the world. Don't hold it against him. He's an idealist, an optimist, a glass-half-full, 'Let's wake up today and take on the bad guys' kinda guy. I love that about Christian.

A lot probably stems from his upbringing (as it does for most of us): y'know, the parental examples, the early influences, the particular nurture–nature cocktail. And trust me that it's easier if you don't go asking Christian Johnsen about his nationality. 'Where he's from' is a story that starts with dramatic pause, and plays like the lineage of a 007-inspired criminal mastermind. He's part Norwegian (father's side), part Portuguese (mother's side), fluent in both languages, though speaks English with the kind of mid-Atlantic tell-tale that can only come from US schooling – though he spent a portion of his upbringing in Mozambique, before his family started challenging how things got done and it all got a bit tricky with the ruling powers of the day.

I met Christian when I joined Aegis, in London, before he later asked if I could help him transfer to the New York office. I didn't take it personally, just harboured the feeling that he's never liked, and never will like, the idea of sitting still for too long, which is a thought that reflects how his mind works too; it moves around fast, wanders off into some really (I think) compelling places, takes real delight in thinking about what it, everything *and anything* can, should, might all mean.

Not asking Christian to share his view on the Digital State would have been like visiting Disneyland with him and then refusing that he hop on any rides.

*

What is a weapon? Reflexive mental images tend to conjure up traditional items that are sharp, stabby, maybe use gunpowder, or go *boom* on arrival. The spectre of cyber-terrorism, of those with ill intent able to bring the world to the brink with a laptop, is intoxicating – because it subverts the convention, feels so paradoxical. But a laptop, and the digital tools to which it links, *can* change the world.

But park cyber-terrorists for a moment, cast them from your mind, and consider instead cyber-Samaritans. Consider digital tools, like any revolutionary tools, as the means for change, but think about them 'in a good way', a bloodless and cheerful way, facilitating change 'for the better'. And then consider what sits behind the impetus for change, any change, in any age, how 'passions and actions' are a demonstrative response to a sense of 'cause'. And then consider how any cause truly takes hold:

through the power of narrative – whether as a sentence or an epic, either way it is the story of an injustice. This is what Christian Johnsen has been considering – because, yes, he's an idealist, and because he believes 'story' is the ultimate spark to light the touchpaper and have us all jumping from our armchairs.

Over to CJ.

What do these three moments in history have in common?

1. The 'Kony 2012' movement.
2. President Obama's election campaign.
3. The Egyptian revolution.

If you guessed some worldwide conspiracy theory you are, unfortunately, wrong. It is much simpler than that. The commonality is that they all, deliberately or not, tapped into one concept: that a (great) story can fundamentally create a tremendous amount of energy, and in today's digital world we have platforms that can put that energy into *action*. This concept is especially relevant when it comes to a project, any project, that seeks change.

However, there is often an imbalance between 'the story' and 'the action'; sometimes there is a powerful story with no platform for action and other times plenty of opportunity for action with little story. Additionally, when action is required in projects seeking change, critics are often quick to point out that a 'simple tweet will not change the world' and that for change to happen it requires 'greater action/risk'.

With this chapter I want to lay the foundation for finding an ideal intersection between story and action, proposing that there is a broader, more powerful approach to action within the digital space. Ultimately, if applied correctly, this model may provide an opportunity for people, brands, organizations and even governments to make change happen and shape the world we live in. Most importantly it could help address some of the greatest collective challenges that we face across the globe. Yes, I am being ambitious.

IF YOU WANT SOMETHING DONE, DO IT YOURSELF (AND THEN GET OTHERS TO DO IT WITH YOU)

For change to happen it often needs some sort of activism. According to Stanford sociologist Doug McAdam, activism can be plotted on a spectrum that ranges from 'high-risk' activism to 'low-risk' activism. Perhaps unsurprisingly, high-risk activism requires a deep involvement that generally has a high personal cost of action, ie your life could be threatened. McAdam refers to the case of Freedom Summer during the US civil rights movement, a campaign that attempted to register as many African-American voters as possible in Mississippi. The campaign involved an incredible amount of high-risk activism, and by the end of its 10-week period several people had been killed, hundreds beaten and thousands arrested, and several buildings belonging to African-American communities had been burnt to the ground.

On the flip side, 'low-risk' activism is something that many of us have probably participated in at some point in our lifetime, eg a 'Save the dolphins' campaign or 'Stop animal cruelty'. In fact, it could be argued that many of the world's challenges could result in change through 'low-risk', collective (and it needs to be collective) activism – if we all just decided to engage and put our minds to it. To employ 'high-risk' action in these cases would only be disproportionate, inappropriate and ultimately detrimental to their cause.

Consider climate change for a moment. It is an issue often caught in extremes, often misused and mostly misunderstood, but nonetheless an issue that will only become more of an acute reality as time progresses. Unfortunately, for many, climate change has become so politicized that it has transformed into an ideological war, whilst others simply perceive it to be so distant and daunting that the easiest response is apathy. And this isn't true just for climate change, but for numerous other global issues, such as resource depletion, global poverty and mass extinction.

Apathy and politicization are by far the two biggest barriers that need to be overcome in order instead to start solving. The solution is not going to come from one or two or 200 people taking a 'high-risk' action, eg a group of people sabotaging an oil refinery. Instead what is needed is global consensus, a consensus to make change happen collectively at a 'low-risk' level, eg millions of people cutting carbon emissions.

In 2009, in an effort to address these barriers, I, along with two good friends, put together ThisPlace09. The world was six months away from the Copenhagen Climate Conference (COP15) and, because of the politicization of the topic and broad public apathy, the chances of a positive outcome were very low. ThisPlace09 encouraged people to think of how climate change could affect them on a local level, and hoped to make COP15 delegates realize that, in the end, everybody in the world wants the same thing. Our request was simple and 'low-risk': we asked people around the world to tweet an answer to a simple question: 'What's Worth Saving in #ThisPlace?' Each tweet, whilst limited to 140 characters, had its own story, which told us that people of course did care about the world around them. The tweets were many, and many were notable:

- 'My entire city of Bombay.'
- '#Thisplace will start sinking once water levels start rising. That's 17 million people affected right there.'
- 'Franz Joseph glacier – 1 of most amazing/beautiful things I've ever seen – want it to be there when my kids & their kids grow up.'

The shortlisted tweets were then complemented with illustrations by various artists and illustrators invited to react visually to the tweets they read. The tweets, alongside the artworks, were finally compiled into a small book and delivered by hand to the delegates of COP15.

The ThisPlace09 project was a success in regard to the response from people who 'took action', but COP15 as a conference was declared a failure. At the end of the day, delegates weren't able to agree, and the media often portrayed the conference as a battle between serious people in suits and a bunch of outraged hippies.

Sadly, the delegates' stalemate and the media's portrayal masked a stark reality: the fact that the vast majority of people sit somewhere in the middle, and yet increasingly there is a sense of urgency amongst this unrepresented middle ground to solve the big social and environmental issues that have emerged in a globalized, industrialized world.

This sense of urgency isn't surprising. As industrialization and consumption-based economic growth accelerate throughout the world, our societies and planet will come under an increasing amount of stress. To put things into perspective, if Asia was to consume as the West does, the production of steel, cars and paper would have to double, we would have to produce an additional 20 million barrels of oil per day, and the consumption of poultry in Asia would increase from 16 billion to 120 billion a year.[1] Additionally, in a continuous race for profit, companies will continue to push for human efficiencies, laying people off whilst taking the environment and raw materials for granted. There are of course many businesses and brands out there that are trying to bring about change, and they can be a very powerful tool.

A great example of this is Chipotle with its 'Back to the Start' campaign. During a commercial break in the 2012 Grammy awards Chipotle aired a two-minute animated story that had as its protagonist a small farmer. As the farmer's ambitions grew, so did his farm, and before he knew it he had gone from having a couple of happy piglets to a monstrous 'factory farm' where animals were mistreated, injected with hormones and systematically slaughtered. At the end of the video the farmer had a change of heart, destroyed the factory and went 'back to the start'. As its soundtrack, the story had a Willie Nelson cover of Coldplay's 'The Scientist', which could be purchased on iTunes, with its proceeds going to the Cultivate Foundation and Farm Aid.

The campaign was a hit. Twitter was inundated with tweets like 'Um, so the Chipotle commercial made me tear up. Tell me I'm not alone', and the track was catapulted to the number one downloaded track spot on iTunes. Part of its success was because Chipotle as a storyteller had some level of credibility. Unfortunately, in a world where 'greenwashing' is prevalent amongst the corporate world, Chipotle is more the exception than the norm.

As Chandran Nair argued in his book *Consumptionomics* (2011), when it comes to brands and corporations 'Father Greed' will ultimately stand in the way of the kind of change that 'Mother Nature' truly needs. The statement might come across as cynical, but the truth is that, for every corporate success story, there are numerous failures. Ultimately, when the story told does not align with the storyteller's actions, backlash and disillusion are inevitable.

Given the ineffectiveness of government and corporations at creating change, it is hard not to feel negative, disappointed, helpless and cynical even – but, if there is one thing that ThisPlace09 taught me, it is that meaningful change won't come from governments alone, and it won't come from brands. It will come from people – people who are feeling increasingly empowered to take matters into their own hands and for the first time in history, as a consequence of the Digital Revolution, have the platforms that allow them to do so. All they need now is the spark, the unavoidable trigger, that will thrust them into action. I believe that this spark is anchored in an art form as old as humanity itself: a story. No: a great story. I believe that every successful initiative for change has to start with a fundamental truth: a great story can create a tremendous, potentially untold amount of energy.

THE POWER OF A GOOD STORY

My father once told me that the purpose of life was to live your story, share it and hope others could become better for it. Within that statement he managed to encapsulate my deep passion for film, and any other storytelling vehicle, for that matter.

I remember when I first watched Richard Attenborough's *Gandhi* in 2004. As the end credits rolled, I felt inspired, I felt empowered and I felt as though I could change the world. I was brimming with energy, as were those who had watched it with me. We all felt as though we could change the world.

This collective impact is, of course, not unique to the movie *Gandhi*, but rather a by-product of a compelling, deeply engaging story. As Jonathan Gottschall lays out in *The Storytelling Animal*,[2] the world does not lack anecdotal evidence of how stories have shaped individuals and cultures, from Harriet Beecher Stowe's *Uncle Tom's Cabin*, which was widely credited for rousing the North's abolitionist sympathies in the prelude to the American Civil War,[3] to books like Dickens's *A Christmas Carol*, Orwell's *1984* and Lee's *To Kill a Mockingbird*.

It is only recently, however, that society has begun to understand how some of the changes that stories make are, in fact, predictable and systematic. Fiction has proven to be much more 'effective at changing beliefs than non-fiction'. As Gottschall explains, this has been demonstrated by showing, amongst other things, how racial attitudes have a positive shift when white viewers watch a show that positively portrays black family life, such as in *The Cosby Show*. Gottschall writes, 'When we read non-fiction, we read with our shields up. We are critical and sceptical. But when we are absorbed in a story, we drop our intellectual guard. We are moved emotionally, and this seems to leave us defenceless.'

It is that ability of making people empathize, of shifting people's attitudes and so sparking action, that is the true potential of great storytelling. Consider this: during the course of a week we might be bombarded with images of pot-bellied starving children surrounded by flies in Somalia. We can easily block *these* images out. They have little to no emotional impact, and the reality is that we are not likely to act based on them. Now imagine a movie, even something as commercially obvious (and successful) as Edward Zwick's *Blood Diamond* (2006). You are much more likely to feel for those characters and their circumstances.

Richard Attenborough and Edward Zwick, despite their movies being very different, instinctively know this, what all great storytellers know. Their movies succeeded by telling a highly immersive story and creating enough energy for people to want to participate in change. However, in each case, there was no conduit, no platform that allowed people to convert that energy into action, and therein lies the opportunity in today's world, an opportunity that has come to be as a result of the Digital Revolution, namely digital platforms that can unleash the potential and creativity of millions of people around the world.

An example of a story that did take a narrative experience into action is *Kony 2012*. From a content and format perspective it couldn't be further removed from the epic three-hour cinema experience of *Gandhi*. *Kony* was in fact a 30-minute YouTube video. However, they were both deeply engaging stories in their own right.

The *Kony 2012* video/campaign was an expertly produced and well-crafted story about the Ugandan warlord Joseph Kony. The 'story' is narrated by an American, Jason Russell, who, after learning about the atrocities being committed by Joseph Kony in Uganda, dedicated 10 years of his life to an attempt to change the status quo. This campaign was his way of doing so, and at the end of the video there was a clear call to action urging people all around the world to use social platforms in order to 'make Kony famous' – and not in a good way. Viewers were left in shock by the atrocities committed by Joseph Kony, and were in awe of Jason Russell's drive and desire for change. It was a great story that created high emotional energy and made people a promise that was irresistible at that moment in time: 'With the click of a share button, become part of this and change the course of history by stopping a very evil man.'

In less than 72 hours *Kony 2012* went from 7 million initial views to over 43 million views. Social media streams were flooded with shares and tweets from 'OMG this is sooo inspiring' to 'Dear Joseph Kony, I'm Gonna help Make you FAMOUS!!!! We will stop YOU #stopKONY!'[4] People's attentions were diverted from the Kardashians to a country that most people couldn't point out on a map, and in the process it got the attention of the mainstream media and of arguably the most powerful government in the world, the US government.

However, just as quickly as it rose, it fell. After the initial 72-hour frenzy people began criticizing the campaign for oversimplifying the issue, questioning Jason Russell's own agenda and back-story, and ultimately damning *Kony 2012* as reaching the apex of armchair activism. *Kony 2012* fell short of its potential in a big way. Today it's not uncommon to hear the words 'I was a victim of Kony' come from the mouths of young Americans.

Armchair activism is the source of much criticism for any cause-related campaign that uses digital platforms as a tool. The argument is that something as simple as a 'like' or a 'retweet' isn't going to change the world, but might give people the illusion that they have done enough and can go back to their daily lives. That criticism, however, is short-sighted. A 'like' or a 'retweet' is only the most basic step of 'low-risk' activism that these platforms can serve. The tools themselves are powerful, but for their full potential to be unlocked we must look at them differently and expand our ambition.

There are three potential steps within every cause-related action. As you climb the ladder, the more motivation and passion for action need to be evoked, arguably suggesting more immersive and engaging stories are needed. Those steps are:

1. *Ignite.* Generate mass awareness through media platforms.
2. *Unite.* Bring people together for a specific action and tap into their ability to create change, individually and/or as a group.
3. *Revolutionize.* Reimagine the world, and come up with new solutions and/or business models to address a cause.

Kony 2012 ultimately delivered on the ignite step and was on track to unite people before its downfall. Part of the problem was that the steps it asked people to take proved too limited of an action for solving a very complex issue (aside from all the other negative elements). Even with mass awareness, the impact that millions of people in the Western world could have on a very local topic in Uganda was always going to be limited. Instead, Russell and his team could have endeavoured to understand where the most impact could be achieved, eg if it had been uncovered that Kony's militia was indirectly financed by the West (it wasn't), and designed a campaign that made people aware and asked them to take action by demanding more government transparency.

A campaign that did get the balance between story and action right was Barack Obama's 2008 presidential campaign. It also succeeded in taking action one step further than achieved by *Kony 2012*. After eight years of a Bush presidency, two deeply unpopular wars, and an explosive first chapter of the financial crisis, people (especially young people) felt powerless and wanted to get on a different track. Barack Obama's story of hope and change tapped into all those feelings, and generated an unprecedented amount of optimism and energy. That energy was so great that people were not only sharing, liking and tweeting, but creating content to help ignite change.[5]

Even more significant was how the campaign took things to the point of 'unite'. Taking advantage of all the energy, Barack Obama's campaign was able to successfully use digital platforms to engage one of the most historically politically apathetic constituencies, namely youth. It resulted in probably the greatest grassroots movement the world has yet seen, giving people digital tools to 'get the vote out', and allowing people to use digital platforms as a fund-raising and campaign-financing tool.

It is worth noting that, during the 2012 campaign, the Obama machine once again used the power of story to lead to digital action. *The Story of Us* is a goosebump-inducing, four-minute video housed on YouTube that looked at Obama's journey, and concisely laid out all that his presidency had accomplished thus far. As a viewer it is hard not to feel a *personal* sense of accomplishment, and the Obama campaign used that energy into action with a not-so-subtle yet masterfully crafted call to action sitting right next to the video: 'Watch the video that looks back on this improbable journey. Then, please make a donation so we can finish what we started. Donate Now.'

In 2008 there was the desire, and the will, to truly revolutionize Washington, and digital platforms would have played a fundamental role in that revolution, eg redefining the role of people and youth in government by allowing people to have their say through social media, and making any follow-up action by politicians transparent and visible. What Obama started in 2008, he now has the opportunity to finish. With his return to the White House in 2012, my hope is that he may be able to take that crucial third step, to convert collective passion into demonstrable momentum: to *revolutionize*.

BY THE PEOPLE, FOR THE PEOPLE

What about things that don't have a story, and yet have the potential for action? The truth is that there aren't many examples that come easily to mind. One example could be *Good*, an online and print magazine, which addresses a series of topics surrounding sustainability. In 2012 they announced that they would be evolving to a platform that 'helps you make Good things happen' – essentially, a digital action platform for projects... for good. The projects vary in scope, but mostly fall under the 'revolutionize' step. However, I think it will be interesting to see whether in the long run, without any story, the platform can attract enough participation for it to be viable. Without the emotional energy that a story generates, there is a tendency to be too easily forgotten and left behind.

In today's connected world it is easy to focus on digital platforms as the solution, rather than a tool that will simply aid the cause. Of course, a change-maker's mode of operation is revealing, and does pass comment on them. According to Malcolm Gladwell, 'Where activists were once defined by their causes, they are now defined by their tools.'[6] However, the tools do not define the artisan. More so, artisans self-define through their tools.

I witnessed this first hand at a talk I attended in March 2011, at the Frontline Club in London, named 'Protest, technology and the end of fear'. As the name suggested, the purpose of the talk was to understand the role that technology had played in recent revolutions, specifically the Egyptian revolution. The panellists included Alaa Abd El-Fattah, the prominent Egyptian blogger and digital activist who (according to the Egyptian newspaper *Al-Ahram Weekly*) was 'in many ways synonymous with Egypt's 25th of January revolution'.[7]

From my seat at the Frontline Club, I had a very clear view, and I remember the moment clearly. With each question asked, the frustration felt by Alaa Abd El-Fattah and his comrades noticeably grew. 'What was the role of Twitter?' 'What was the role of Facebook?' 'What was the role of technology?' They did not want to talk about Twitter, or Facebook, or even technology. Alaa Abd El-Fattah and his comrades wanted to talk about their people, their country, the challenges they still faced and what their future held. All the while, a giant screen strategically placed behind them streamed real-time tweets of the evening's discussion.

Their frustration and responses made it very clear to the audience that, despite the Western headlines, this was *not* the Twitter revolution, and it was *not* Facebook's revolution. It was *Egypt's* revolution. Too much emphasis was being continuously (mis)placed on the platforms; of course they were important, but the revolution would have happened without them. It might not have happened at the exact moment that it did, and it might not have spread as quickly, but the platforms should not take away from the fact that it was the courage and desire for change that came from the people of Egypt that truly created that change.

They were absolutely right. Fundamentally, digital platforms purely enhance the power and passions that people have. Their potential is only as great as the human spirit itself. Within this chapter the beginnings of a framework are laid out, a framework that helps increase our understanding of the interrelationship between human behaviour, society, and the potential of our newly acquired digital tools. One day, in the near future, they will stop being tools that are solely about status updates, check-ins and daily tweets, but powerful tools driven by stories that will help to address societal needs and fuel change for good – but only if we have the ambition and desire to make it so. I believe we do.

CJ
New York City

NOTES

1. Chandran Nair, *Consumptionomics* (Infinite Ideas, Oxford, 2011); Jonathan Watts, *When a Billion Chinese Jump* (Faber and Faber, London, 2010).
2. Jonathan Gottschall, *The Storytelling Animal* (Houghton Mifflin Harcourt, New York, 2012).
3. In fact it got so much credit that, as Gottschall writes, 'When President Abraham Lincoln met Harriet Beecher Stowe, he famously said, "So you're the little woman who wrote the book that made this great war."'
4. This was amongst several other celebrity tweets, this one coming from P Diddy's account @iamdiddy.
5. Prominent examples are Will.I.Am's 'Yes We Can', and Obama Girl's 'Crush on Obama'.
6. Malcolm Gladwell, 'Small change: why the revolution will not be tweeted', *New Yorker*, 4 October 2010.
7. Even since Mubarak's fall Alaa Abd El-Fattah has been a continuous supporter of the Egyptian revolution and the drive for freedom of speech in Egypt. In October 2011 he grabbed international headlines when he was arrested for protesting against the Supreme Council of the Armed Forces that took control after Mubarak's fall and was eventually released on 25 December 2011 after tremendous worldwide pressure.

7 EVERYTHING CHANGES, EXCEPT ME

Hans Andersson

> Since the very first day that kings, governments and churches started to tax us, we have been identified by a simple chain of information to assess our ability to pay up: our name, our address, our gender, our age, our family status, our profession, our income, later our religion, even later our education. Ever since that day, demographics has been the means of power and control for any prince above us.
>
> This information serves as the basis for an abundance of society's institutions and supporting systems. It's the basis for governments' budgets and the main source of political debates. Miles and miles of research use it to underpin the statistical significance of any conclusion.

I'd like you to meet... Hans Andersson

Hans Andersson is an ad man, a damn fine one. Even better than that. It runs through him, comes out of him in elegant, softly spoken, impassioned eulogies, the kind you could never fake, even if you've been RADA or method trained. I see Hans as a kind of Madison Avenue throw-forward, a senior partner of one of the hottest ad agency hot-shops on the planet, which is not based on Madison, but above a department store in Gothenburg.

For me, Hans is the real deal, in that he loves what he does, and couldn't care more about doing it better and trying every time for a whole yard beyond the measured nine. He's also enormously good company over a tidy glass of French red, seems to have cheated time by an easy 10 years, and might be Sweden's closest thing to George Clooney. And, while this last sentence may be pure parenthesis, it's never bad to have even a half-measure of someone if you're going on to read 3,000 or so of their words.

*

In the chapter that follows, Hans addresses a fundamental question and how it's become the giant elephant in the boardroom, a well-fed one trumpeting away, mocking those present, but baffled as to why all those seated crane their necks and turn cheek and ear the other way.

If successful advertising is anything, it's the simple act of delivering the right message to the right person. But there's nothing very simple in understanding the 'right'. How is it the 'right message'? Who is the 'right person'? This thickest of broths reduces down to the most tricksy of questions: how do we go about *understanding* people? How do and how should we *define* people?

And that's what brings in the elephant. 'Demographics' has quite the legacy, a dawning on Day One of modern civilization, a perspective proven to have all the well-built staying power of a Roman road. But the (defining) 'labels' we try to stick on folk aren't so clearly defining any more. They are becoming arbitrary, analogue conceived, past their shelf-life; they fall so far short as to arguably be (at best) bland generic descriptors. They therefore fail to do the only thing asked of them: to help explain and define us. The Digital State, more than ever before, now challenges us to redefine how we define ourselves.

Over to Hans.

I hate 9 o'clock meetings. Have to get some coffee first, and this time round I think we're going to need it. OK, here we go again...

Some trouble with the connection from his laptop. Oh, he's got the presentation on a stick. Smart move. Now we're rolling. OK, let's see. No news on the product or the offer.

The target group is... men, 36–45, income above average, family, car owners, interested in news and sports, living in major cities, and presently using Competitor X.

I would never buy it myself. My wife might buy it for me, though.

How on earth am I going to make this sound useful to the creatives?

Oh, this takes... for ever.

Come on, it's the same group we had in the last campaign?! And we had an 0.08 clickrate. I don't get it. We posted that campaign all over the place, posted it everywhere the media people directed us. And it was a fair offer, wasn't it? Just like this one? But it had an 0.08 per cent click rate. And they say that's pretty OK?! The market average. But really, how do they know? Surely the decimal place has to be in the wrong place for anyone to be satisfied?

Still, nice PowerPoint. Wonder if they will serve lunch?

*

A couple of years ago one of my sons, 13 at the time, began to play *World of Warcraft*. I didn't particularly like it, but I figured that if he played for just an hour now and then it wouldn't be all bad. When he couldn't get up in the morning and started to skip classes, we had a memorable clash. It turned out that, after we'd all gone to sleep, he would sneak up in the middle of the night and play for hours and hours. Although angry, I was yet fascinated with the fact that this game could get this usually slow and tired teenager out of bed in the small hours. It couldn't just be the slashing of make-believe monsters, could it?

I joined the game with him, on a weekend of course, and it was pretty obvious that there was a completely different story to it. He played with a group. The group made appointments to meet at a certain time, at a certain place within the game, where they together could take on the vile creatures and giant bosses that none of them would be able to defeat on their own. It was an interesting gang. Most of them were quite a bit older than he was. One turned out to be a middle-aged German engineer, another was a housewife from northern Sweden, somewhere near Sundsvall maybe. The group came from both genders, from all ages, from different countries, and ordinarily did different things during their daylight hours. And I was the only one who cared about their 'true identity'.

That was the point, of course. To them, my son wasn't the adolescent with big feet that I knew. He was nothing more (or less) than the character he became online, and he was measured and judged only on how that character behaved and where he appeared. If identity play was ever big with teenagers, this was one very real opportunity to be someone you liked better than yourself. For my own part, I realized I had learnt something that I felt was somehow profoundly important, only I just didn't know yet what to do with it.

A few years later I was closing in on 50 – time for an age crisis. And surely enough, having spent a sizeable portion of my career in a creative agency, I had been exposed to all kinds of age deceptions. Young, cool colleagues, rumbling music, ready-trashed ('distressed', as they say) jeans, anything else that could keep me in sneakers; but I hadn't really fallen for it. I wasn't young; I knew that. I had some wrinkles and quite a few grey hairs, and had been catapulted out of the agency's football team.

But on the inside I felt the same. Only, I also didn't. I soon had to admit that, as much as I could relate to and liked to work with young people, some things were better in the 'old days'. I had changed in many ways, and become a pretty responsible father of five, with a house and a car and all the trimmings. So what fooled me at first? Was it just the fear of ageing and the desire to hang on to life? Or did young people just seem to have more fun?

Looking at myself (something I can recommend all communication execs do, as at least then you will know at least one person in your target group), I realized that what I interpreted as being the same on the inside as when I was young was rather that many of my deepest interests, values, views and preferences had been shaped a long time ago. Certainly, I had added a few on the way, but the core self was still my core self, and those basic passions had remained. And as, to quote Anatole France, 'our passions are ourselves', it was obvious that ageing, both physically and mentally, didn't really mean I had become someone else. Hence I, myself, was not really defined only by my age or by my circumstances and the situations I had stumbled through in life.

I struggled a lot with these findings (and still wrestle with quite a few others) in my daily work, and it wasn't until one Christmas that it came to me in its full, terrifying splendour: 'In those days Caesar Augustus issued a decree that a census should be taken of the entire Roman world. [This was the first census that took place while Quirinius was governor of Syria.] And everyone went to their own town to register' (Luke 2:1–3, New International

Version). Since the very first day that kings, governments and churches started to tax us, we have been identified by a simple chain of information to assess our ability to pay up: our name, our address, our gender, our age, our family status, our profession, our income, later our religion, even later our education. Ever since that day, demographics has been the means of power and control for any prince above us.

This information serves as the basis for an abundance of society's institutions and supporting systems. It's the basis for governments' budgets and the main source of political debates. Miles and miles of research use it to underpin the statistical significance of any conclusion.

Come to think of it, most of the amassed knowledge about our world is empirical, and based on statistical evidence that takes its standing point from demographics. 'Counting people', and dividing us all into little boxes, is quite simply one of the things that makes it possible to direct and understand our society. Or rather, it gives us that soothing feeling of comprehension. Demographic mastery gives anyone with some sort of power the impression of control, and that is absolutely essential to the functionality of conventional leadership.

My own line of trade, the communication industry, couldn't exist without it; it's practically founded on demographics. It's the very bloodstream and the genes of it. That's how it all started, with the voice of kings: 'I have this message. I want to send it out to as many people as possible, because they must hear it.' In those days, because no one has ever welcomed intrusion or cared to listen, the king would send a drummer along (they're nowadays called creatives) to raise attention.

The entire advertising industry is founded on a centrally produced message reaching a decided part of the masses. (If they answer us back, we call it relationship marketing.) Like a garden hose, the message can be pointed in any chosen direction and, applied with the correct sprinkle, it will efficiently distribute the holy water (of conviction and persuasion) to all the chosen plants below. If the water is scarce, then we distribute it in the most judicious and measured manner so that the most beautiful specimens may flourish.

In response to media channels that proliferated and fragmented, media assuming so many new forms, with so many competing commercial messages, we simply spent more money. As long as we could show a return on investment that was better than not doing anything at all, everyone was fine, so the industry and its clients designed systems to project a possible return on investment, based of course on empirical information, and most of the billing systems, research methods and media planning supports were built from the same principle.

Over time, methods to dissect target groups have been refined infinitely, to the point that, given detailed enough information, we can actually identify selected individuals. Breaking it down, shredding the onion layer by layer, there is soon only one person left to fit the description – and that's you, dear reader. But does that mean we actually know you? Of course not. Don't worry. By shredding the onion we know everything that you're not. And any onion layer is only as good as the information it's built upon. We may know where you are, in body, but we can still only guess how you will react. However, we harbour some very clear hopes. We want you to hear our message, and we want you to react to it in the way we desire. Today you have a mind of your own and the right to say: 'No thanks'. In those early days, a king's word was law. If his people heard his command, he felt certain they would heed it. If not, he would simply send out a bunch of guys with big swords (quite like the kind my son used to slay those vile creatures in *WoW*).

Not too differently, the same model of one-way communication with reasonable effect was the guiding principle of the analogue media world, where streams of commercial messages flowed from a central source to all those open and blossoming recipients.

Why not apply the same guiding communications principles and beliefs to the internet? I mean, we have this whole industry, all these people with all this training, all the media planning and programming systems, all the business models. A web page looks a little bit like a newspaper page, doesn't it? With ads and stuff. Everybody seems comfortable with that, so let's just carry on.

Only, in his digital life, my teenage son wasn't a man, 12–19, family, student, interested in (depressing) music and waiting for his father to buy him his first razor. He was only what he did out there, and where he appeared. Judging by his father, who still has a hard time predicting his own reactions to things, he might be just as hard to figure out on the inside 40 years from now.

Now, none of this is really new, you might say. True, the internet is full of unsavoury ways of tracking your behaviour, cookies, cache probes, you name it. And what the likes of Google and Facebook will use all our footprints for remains to be seen. Still, all the possible imperfections of tracking might make the results dubious anyway, which is good. Individuals don't like their every move to be logged, many do what they can to avoid it, and luckily some governments agree that there should be such a thing as personal integrity.

No, as Homer might have put it (not Simpson, but the Greek guy), this is that 'bitter cup to drain': we can no longer have faith in quantitative, demographic information. It doesn't work in the Digital State. As actors online we cannot effectively or insightfully be understood by age, gender, income and religious belief. A 2,000-year-old system has come to a dead end.

Now I'm convinced that many people have known this for quite some time. They just don't talk about it very much, and they are perhaps right not to. There are many good reasons to hold your tongue. If you're a wise media owner, you should put all your efforts into finding a new business model, because that's what all successful digital start-ups consist of. Don't tell anyone until you're done, because you will be copied instantly.

If you're a marketing executive, you must start to make demands on results that come in at a clickrate a lot higher than 0.08 per cent. You must push your agencies to go where nobody has gone before, and you must push while maintaining the illusion of a world-class ROI on your conventional advertising or else your CEO might consider sending a bunch of guys with swords after you.

If you're in a media agency, you have to protect all your knowledge and all your systems for as long as you possibly can, while you spend nights and weekends trying to find out what on earth to do instead, because every system you have, or build now, comes with a built-in expiration date.

If you're in a research company, instead of hoping for a future of quantitative quick-fix web queries, you might consider hiring a bunch of social anthropologists to help your clients find out not what people say they do in their lives but what they actually do.

But if you, like me, work in a creative agency, there are no excuses. This is your time. There's a brief chink in the iron curtain where you, if you're really smart and work hard, can break the rules. It's an exploitable chink that we haven't seen since the creative revolution in the 1960s.

I remember an old comic strip from those days. A couple of men studying the impressive creations of metal and rubber in a Cadillac showroom and, at the exit, a basket filled with small, ugly VW Beetles with a sign saying 'Take one'. This was the context in which Bill Bernbach and friends decided to make history by headlining a Beetle ad 'Lemon'. I bet they couldn't have cared less for demographics.

Our agency, F&B, has had more than its fair share of creative success in the digital field, one reason, no doubt, being that our creatives were really good at doing newspaper ads, billboards and TVCs, before they then fell in love with digital. However, we constantly struggle not to be infatuated with the ever new technology and the heaps of market information flooding our mailboxes. Many of our award-winning ideas have a tendency to be more complicated than they have to, just because we can.

Certainly, the latest technological advances can be fascinating, and sometimes they have enabled us to create a totally new user experience. That's good. But first and foremost they are the latest, which means that, when you see them for the first time, they are the future, but when you've seen them a couple of times they are yesterday. New technology is at its best as an enabler or a presenter of the idea, more seldom as an idea on top of the idea.

To remind me of why the best ideas are often simple and true to insights on the human character, I occasionally pull up a banner we once did for the Salvation Army: a tiny pop-up shows a group of soldiers in a shopping mall thrashing away on their guitars, and you hear them, ahem, 'singing' at the top of their lungs. When you click to close the banner, it just pops up in a new place, and again, until a sign comes up saying 'Give us money, and we'll stop playing', followed by a giro number. Not much research there, but plenty of insight, and everything stripped away from anything but the bare necessities and naked truths.

No, I haven't changed all that much. I don't believe people change all that much. From Homer to Shakespeare to Anatole France. Technology does, and context. All the time. But the disparate and unpredictable ways we all react to events remain, thank heavens, something of a riddle. For many other professionals in the communication business, that's a reason for denial or for bad sleep. For a creative mind, it's kind of blessing.

For those entering the communications business in this new age of digital, I can confidently say this. It will be a tough journey where you will have to think for yourself. Many people will oppose and ridicule you. Trust yourself. Go back to the basics. Look really close by, next door, to your family and friends. Ask yourself, why should anybody want to buy this thing you're keen to sell? What kind of people would be the most likely actually to like it or buy it? How are they thinking and acting? As best you can, put yourself in their shoes and inside their mind and, whilst occupying those shoes and that head-space, simply ask yourself the 'million-dollar question': why should they want you, and how will they find you?

HA
Gothenburg

8 MY DIGITAL STATE

Christopher Lockwood

> “What excites me more than most other things about these developments in science and technology and the empowerment of the everyday ‘you and me’ is that it breeds, possibly more strongly than at any other time in the entire history of humanity, a ‘nothing to lose’ or ‘get up and have a go’ culture, where little experimentation is prohibited by cost, and in the truest sense there is no stigma attached to failure – more likely a kudos for trying, and appreciation of the knock-on benefits for those who pick up where you left off... Technology has levelled the field. The tools for development are no longer afforded simply by the few... Small garage businesses and lone teenagers can compete on a world stage against the behemoths, get noticed, and quickly, and win.”

I'd like you to meet... Christopher Lockwood

In 1996 I walked into my first agency as an employee. I'd spent nearly six months walking through the doors of agencies across London, asking if they'd like to give me a job. Eventually one did. Earning 12 grand a year, I landed a graduate programme as one of five who made the cut. Christopher Lockwood was another. When we later went our separate ways, me to Saatchi & Saatchi, Christopher into magazine publishing, we both kept in touch and kept bumping into each other. I don't think it's necessarily so much a small world as an intertwining one. There are some folk who share life paths set to cross and keep crossing. Whatever our personal journey, I think someone's perhaps taken care of the casting. And whoever my Cosmic Casting Agent is, I rate them, because I really delight in Christopher and I having kept in touch, and in him being able to join me on this particular adventure.

In the Introduction I mention *Where Eagles Dare*, the war movie, and how *Digital State* felt like a project that could only be bested through 'compatible and complimentary skill-sets, where collaborations can conquer strongholds'. I still feel that way. If I was literally going to storm a Nazi-occupied mountain top, I'd fancy having Christopher on my side, because he looks physically capable and has a rather rakish 'matinee idol' look going on. And while I don't really know how tidy Christopher is with a machine gun, I know he can handle himself as an artist; a talent you can see for yourself in each of the 16 illustrations that gives *Digital State* its 'visual thread'. To conquer strongholds, you need people like Christopher.

*

When I first read Christopher's chapter, over Sunday morning coffee, sitting in the late summer sunshine, I was really delighted at how I could hear Christopher coming through. Caffeine and Vit D are my kind of stimulants at any kind of time, but I still really enjoyed how Christopher had chewed on the theme, ranged wide, and kept it personal. It was all very clearly him, and the points he makes come through just as loud and just as clear. Because while Christopher might be happiest thinking in pictures, I found that the words of his chapter construct a picture equally as vivid as his very brilliant illustrations. His is a personal journey, a chronicled introduction and a practical, emotional and creative response to 'technology'.

With the eye of a publisher, an editor's perspective, and an artist's self-expression, quality control and intellectual property all fall under the spotlight of Christopher's discourse: his self-acknowledged aesthetic snobbery; his embracing of social media on his terms; how too much digital content is produced by too few; how his early, really quite pioneering endeavours into the grey fug of content *curation* sit in jarring contrast to what the likes of Pinterest are now openly 'getting away with'.

Christopher Lockwood lives in a Digital State, and like the rest of us he's trying to figure out the angles and implications. His take is thought-provokingly honest and candid.

Over to Christopher.

THE 'NEAR' DISTANT PAST

Simon and I actually started our first real jobs together, at the same London agency, on precisely the same day, back in the mid-1990s. Apart from the fact that it was a difficult job market and our new masters revealed that we had just pipped some 2,000 other graduate applicants to the five available posts, there was actually very little that was unusual about our situation, when compared to that of any of the thousands of other bright-eyed 20-somethings hitting the job market in a wide variety of industries and professions that autumn. Within the context of the subject of this book, however, it may as well have been the Dark Ages.

Although just over 15 years ago, the irony (and one entirely wasted on my children, neither of whom is quite yet 10) is that, 'technologically speaking', so much advancement *has* taken place in this short time that it *was* in fact another era.

In 1996 no one in the media industry had a mobile phone (a few chief executives and chairmen had car phones, but not actual mobiles); they simply weren't around, and in the space between your desk phone and your home phone there was, well, peace and quiet. A hundred per cent of your mail arrived in the form of real letters on your doorstep between Mondays and Saturdays, and had invariably taken between one and five days to reach you. Voicemail, 'answering machines' as we then called them, were tape-based and needed to be turned on and off in the same way that we now use 'out of office'. The small tapes that were recorded and re-recorded over and over again distorted and damaged very easily, making messages difficult to decipher, and were in a lot of people's minds more trouble than they were worth. More commonly, in your absence, someone (generally the colleagues who sat at desks to either side of yours) would lean across and physically answer your desk phone, take a message on your behalf, then write it down and leave it amongst the deep piles of paperwork festooned across your desk. They might, if you were lucky, have used a Post-it note – but they too were fairly new and regarded as somewhat of an extravagance – so it was more likely to be on a scrap of torn notebook, or across the middle of an important document that you had deliberately left in clear view, so reminding you to fax it to your client, before it was defaced. Now and again of course there was a genuine drama that needed to be dealt with in your absence, but most of the time the instigator of the call would simply say, 'Oh, OK then, I'll try again tomorrow.'

In spite of my generation's exposure to early home computers such as the beloved ZX Spectrum and Commodore 64, they were really little more than the precursors to games consoles, and had done little to prepare us for the burgeoning computing needs of the late 1990s office. Very few of us owned our own 'real computers', and certainly I don't remember anyone having them in our shabby, shared young professional flats.

Only in my last year at university had it become compulsory to 'word-process' essays as opposed to writing everything by hand, and you did that with slow two-fingered typing in suites of impossibly rubbish PCs sporting front-loading floppy disks. A few of the keener mature students on my course had clumsily been experimenting with a new-fangled presentation programme called PowerPoint, but I had staunchly resisted it in favour of beautifully hand-illustrated OHP (overhead projector) acetates. Although it seems funny to write this as a reasonably technologically savvy 39-year-old, I have to admit that, when Simon and I started that year at CIA Medianetwork, the mountain that was Microsoft Office's Word, Excel and PowerPoint (and other rudimentary media planning and buying software) provided by far the steepest learning curve compared to anything else we were exposed to as young graduates.

My memory fails me now as to which department Simon joined back then, but I was assigned for my first six months to the press buying department, and as the most junior member of the team was responsible for the 'team' e-mail account. This was a time that predated personal e-mail accounts (even individual professional ones), and I remember thinking, as I sat at the unique computer terminal that had been set up solely for this purpose, just how farcical the whole affair was, not least because I didn't know how to use e-mail, and because neither did any of our clients, so I very rarely actually received one. On the rare occasion that I did, no one yet trusted the new technology anyway, so they would send a hard copy of the same thing through the traditional post or by fax. And, even by the end of 1997 (as e-mail became commonplace), *that* pretty much remained the extent of our 'digital world'. If you wanted to buy something you still went to a shop; if you wanted to find a flat or a job you looked in the classified pages of daily newspapers or trade magazines; and if you needed contact details for someone you looked at your Rolodex of business cards or in a three-inch-thick copy of the London telephone directory (which was rarely more than arm's reach away in the office). Most other enquiries were generally solved by colleagues, neighbours and family members, or by going to the local library.

TECHTOPIA

I share the aforementioned memories, not to be nostalgic (it was after all not so long ago), nor to pretend for a second that I belong to a generation that hasn't welcomed technology with open arms, or even to prove in some way that life was better before the internet – it wasn't – but simply to make the point that, even before the onset of middle age, I have the benefit of remembering a time when none of the things that my children take utterly for granted had been invented or, in a lot of cases, even considered. We were quite happy *without* the internet and frankly hadn't worked out yet that we needed it.

My personal journey through technology has been a privileged one – being forced to look after that e-mail account before anyone else, and being then at the right level as I grew up through the private sector to benefit from the first round of mobile phones, then laptops and BlackBerries, then smarter iPhones, and later still tablets. I feel lucky to have been just the right age to have comfortably learnt the technology as I have grown, and at no point ever felt too far behind (or for that matter ahead of) the crowd.

As a young family we have multiple Macs, iPhones, iPads, an Xbox with Kinect, a Sky+ box, a digital radio and a number of top-flight digital cameras, and a large number of these devices can already communicate with my car. Between us we keep the wheels turning at Google, Club Penguin, Tumblr, Miniclip, Pinterest, Moshi Monsters and Facebook, to name but a few, and our primary content consumption habits are moving fast away from scheduled and networked TV in favour of Lovefilm, YouTube and iPlayer. If my kids do ever find a show playing out in real time, they instinctively put it immediately on pause and do something else for five minutes, so that when they eventually sit down they can fast-forward through any ads (I certainly didn't teach them this – it's been advertising that has after all put food on our table for most of their lives!).

I love the fact that my children don't even really see the technology that they use all day long, and use it naturally and intuitively, as an extension of their own brains and as if their fingertips constantly and reliably possess magic powers. I like the fact that my car recognizes me when I get into it – that the music on the car radio is *my music*, and the numbers in the phone are mine, that it remembers places I have visited, and so cleverly monitors its own parts and pragmatically tells me what's wrong and what to do about it such that I feel like an F1 engineer rather than the mechanically useless creative mind that I really am.

Whether you personally love or hate the legacy of Steve Jobs, I am firmly in the camp of the 1970s creatively talented kids who had been advised by their parents away from the 'impossible dream' of becoming artists and had, with frustration, followed alternative routes until the emancipation created by Apple, Sony, HP and Adobe, which allowed us to do in our back bedrooms what before had only been possible by professional photographers and retouchers, music producers, film studios, enormous after-effect specialists and post-production houses. I know it sounds so ridiculous to my children, but, please remember, digital photography for the masses has been with us for less than 10 years.

I vividly recall during my time at *Dazed & Confused* how Rankin and his assistants were tentatively experimenting with their first digital camera. They were a forward-thinking professional photographic studio, not everyday people at home, and that was as late as 2001/02. When I was at art college in 1990, the idea that I could have simply taken a large volume of photos, viewed them instantly on a screen, made a quick edit, cropped the frame and enhanced the colours and exposure at the click of a button, and then sent them wirelessly to a desktop printer would have felt like a storyline in a Ridley Scott or Spielberg movie.

By injecting certain technologies into the creative mix, you immediately unlock an array of fantastic developments provided to an artistic community hungry to constantly push boundaries, and to collaborate with partners from different but complementary creative disciplines. Until you see The Creators Project (thecreatorsproject.com), you might perfectly and reasonably deny the possibility of a successful marriage between irreverent youth brand Vice and the blue-chip tech giant Intel, but this growing global network dedicated to the celebration of creativity, culture and technology is an amazing thing. At a time in the history of the arts when digital technology has revolutionized distribution, democratized access and reimagined the scope and scale with which an artist can create a vision and reach an audience, The Creators Project is a shining example of our new technologically advantaged creative world.

For a month in 2011, IBM created the breathtaking 'Think Exhibit' at the Lincoln Center in New York City. Featuring a sparkling 120- by 12-foot LCD screen that drew people from the front of the building and through a tunnel into the bowels of the iconic arts venue, this was an exhibition of a different kind. At the meeting point between art, technology and interaction, the exhibition was in celebration of IBM's 100th anniversary and illustrated, via multimedia, the possibilities that science and information technology offer to 'make the world work better'. I thought it was genius.

What excites me more than most other things about these developments in science and technology and the empowerment of everyday 'you and me' is that it breeds, possibly more strongly than at any other time in the entire history of humanity, a 'nothing to lose' or 'get up and have a go' culture, where little experimentation is prohibited by cost, and in the truest sense there is no stigma attached to failure – more likely a kudos for trying, and appreciation of the knock-on benefits for those who pick up where you left off. I am not suggesting for a minute that it's easy, but technology has levelled the field. The tools for development are no longer afforded simply by the few. This is a new world where small garage businesses and lone teenagers can compete on a world stage against the behemoths, get noticed, and quickly, and win.

For a recent summer half-term break I went with my wife and children to the far side of the wilderness that is the Isle of Skye, some eight solid hours' drive north of Glasgow, and for most people in the wrong direction. If you get good weather it is heaven on earth, but it's a stretch too far even for a reliable cellular signal. That week away from computers, technology, e-mail and virtually also television and voicemail was a tonic for us all and something that I would wholeheartedly recommend to everyone, to briefly wallow in a digital-free state – but would I want to return to the technological winter of the 1990s? Absolutely never.

SOCIAL (MEDIA) ELITISM

Until recently, in my last in-house role, I had ultimate responsibility for the social media team within one of the larger UK media agencies. Whilst a crowd-sourced, 'social' approach to brand marketing makes perfect sense to me, it was a role I held with some irony. My idea of a good time has never been Facebook; nor was Twitter really created with me in mind. With further irony, however, it wasn't until I finished that job, which coincided with the mass adoption in Britain of the second wave of social tools, tools that focus on the image (read: Tumblr, Pinterest, Instagram, etc), that the 'social' digital penny absolutely dropped for me.

Writing this chapter alone has taken considerably longer than it should have on account of the remarkable number of hours I've devoted this summer to my 'generationcreat' Pinterest account (for a daily dose of creative inspiration feel free to check out my boards: pinterest.com/generationcreat). Having caught the bug on my terms, I can now appreciate someone's addiction to Facebook, and can clearly see the parallels between my hours of enjoyment searching and posting my own unique image and design references, and the 'need to tweet'.

The way users curate and contrive on Pinterest fascinates me. The arrangement of inspirational images in a selection of 'boards' allows one to follow, edit and segregate, against very personal criteria or a very personal agenda, to my mind much more successfully than on any other social platform.

I will confess I suffer from a virulent case of 'art and design snobbery', and further suffer mild irritation at the fail-proof success of pictures of cute puppies, being squeezed close to equally pretty owners. It's just that I feel compelled to execute any craft (painting, photography, printmaking, design, illustration, etc) at the highest possible level and harbour incredibly high expectations of the creators that *I* admire. Clever bloggers gain staggering numbers of followers by humouring the middle-American or middle-English desire for 'naff content', and at the same time impress the cognoscenti with their prowess as exceptional arbiters of taste, across a rich variety of subjects, without diluting or undermining one or the other. Try as I might, I just cannot bring myself to post innocuous content purely to attempt to appeal to a larger crowd.

It's similar in many ways to the phenomenal act of contradiction created by the original iPod, in which millions upon millions of people across the planet sat in lines, in Maoist harmony, on buses and trains, sporting identical white headphones, but all with the very real belief that they were ultimately totally original. I fear that there's a global cultural homogenization happening in front of our very eyes. Whilst everyone believes that they can follow whoever they want, at whatever time and on whichever platform they choose, and like and respond to an intensely personal selection of whatever they feel is nice or important to them, the sad truth is that like lemmings we actually follow a tiny amount of unique thinkers, funny people and pranksters, and constantly therefore recycle an increasingly diminutive selection of the same ideas.

I have nothing against Stephen Fry (on the contrary, his combination of intellect, wit and overall Wilde-esque charms make him an exceptional human being); it's just that, along with perhaps Ricky Gervais, he now seems to me omnipresent, and a founder of the pathetically small cabal of people that 'we Brits' want to watch, follow, listen to and read about.

I wonder whether our 'collective tastes' are becoming frighteningly clichéd, in defaulting to the same reliable few. What of the new generation of talent out there? Where are today's best B-sides? Who will find the lesser-known stars of tomorrow and dare to give them exposure? In making content exceptionally easy to access and share, and by hanging too wholeheartedly on the word of the people with the largest amount of followers, aren't we in danger of losing *our* identities altogether? As if it's not bad enough that the whole world now favours the same brand of fizzy pop, eats the same brand of cereal at breakfast, drives the same six makes of car to work, and wears the same branded jeans on the weekends, whilst overusing the same smartphone, do we also all have to now listen to just the one band, enjoy or deride precisely the same film, read only the one book at a time, and like the same video? To my utter astonishment, 470 million people have watched a baby boy bite his brother's finger on YouTube in the now infamous 'Charlie bit my finger'.

Sadly this is aided or accentuated by the financiers and commissioners of our new, sometimes one-size-fits-all, 'content' world. New-and-original is a risk. Tried-and-tested is a safe bet. Better to put old content on new platforms and rinse a profitable content product to near extinction than take an uncalculated gamble on something new. No one ever got the sack for investing in Potter (Harry or Beatrix), and both are great examples of franchises that can do no wrong and are more likely to be repackaged, stretched and endlessly morphed into new incarnations of the same tales than passed over in favour of a brand-new, perhaps creatively astounding, but yet-to-be proven content product.

In 2012, YouTube finally admitted that their eye-wateringly large worldwide audiences now deserved to be served a higher quality of content than its mainstay of 50-second, hand-held curiosities. To that end they have been busy receiving proposals from content creators and producers for a series of eagerly anticipated YouTube channels – but, surprise surprise, their guidelines to prospects suggest that strong proposals are likely to involve proven stars or digital super-users. The current rumour is that YouTube plan awarding the first of their channels in the United States to Ryan Seacrest (US radio DJ, *American Idol* host and, although entirely different as a person, the United States' answer to Stephen Fry). If rumour becomes fact, then sadly my concerns are playing out.

INFORMATION OVERLOAD

Occasionally I wonder whether I suffer from mild dyslexia. My natural ability to very easily digest, organize, judge and edit a large amount of images against a variety of criteria (genre, aesthetic, craft skill, famous artistic style and its influence or historic significance, etc) makes me feel that my processing speed for reading and consuming arrangements of words, by comparison, is somehow sub-sufficient. This marked difference in my own personal abilities does make it clear to me that the potential for information overload is a very real issue for many. Now check your phone for messages.

Consider for a second the autistic mind's brilliant ability to perform outstanding feats of calculus or memory. As I write this, the London 2012 Olympics are in full swing, and the other-worldly physical abilities that we are witnessing are no more than a few hundred in 7 billion human beings. If some of us are tall and others pretty, some scientific and others musical, some gregarious and others agoraphobic, then of course it stands to reason that our brains are not at all identical in their capacity to consume and process the gargantuan volume of data that is being pumped into the ether, moment to moment, by the media, businesses, creators, governments and social beavers alike. Now check your phone for messages.

In the thread of a conversation that I was following (slowly) recently, these statements were made:

> *Many people do feel in over their heads when scrolling social media streams... Many of us feel positioned directly in the path of a growing avalanche of information, scared of missing out and afraid of losing our ability to slow down, concentrate, connect and daydream... While it seemed fun and harmless at first, have we found ourselves drowning in the information streams that we welcomed into our lives?*

This doesn't sound exactly like a success story to me.

Our society is endlessly driven to conceive better, smaller, more intuitive machines that feed larger, more robust networks, which make it easier and faster to interact with greater volumes of people and achieve the impossible through the exponential growth of the Digital State – but where in all of this is the self-protectionism?

There is a stigma attached to drinking a bottle of whisky a day, or smoking 40 cigarettes. We indirectly accept that recreational drugs are in the main a folly of youth. Now check your phone for messages. To a lesser degree, we monitor the amount of fat in our diets, or the size of our carbon footprint; but for some reason we haven't yet found it appropriate to meter our own digital addiction. Is this because doctors haven't yet linked a significant number of total mental breakdowns specifically to information overload, or recognized it as a credible and present phenomenon?

Nick Harkaway, in his brilliant book *The Blind Giant: Being Human in a Digital World*,[1] makes some hugely valid points around information overload. He states that such is the immensity of the amount of information and theory now available in the public domain, on any subject, that 'Universities are complaining that they cannot bridge in three or four years the gap between the end of the school syllabus and the place where new work is being done either in industry or Academe', and that the very same quagmire creates an added complication that 'even the simplest of questions or decisions have now acquired nuance, controversy and multiple interpretations' as a result of the volume and variety of extreme opinions pushed gratuitously into our lives (no longer merely the preserve of grave issues such as humanitarianism or nuclear power but now too on the benefits of almond milk over cow's, or even which coloured Smartie is best). Now check your phone for messages.

Harkaway goes on to say 'that every action in our lives now carries a tacit burden of complexity', because 'digital technology possesses the ability to bring it to the forefront; to report it live, to bring to our notice obscure but poignant crises, to connect us to matters far away and make the problems of people we do not know seem close'.

The more we know, the more we feel we need to know, and have to keep up to date with any given situation – and technology feeds this hunger. Sooner rather than later, I wonder, will we be checking ourselves into the Priory for 'social media addiction', or joining semi-circles of contemporaries in church halls for Technology Anonymous?

Now check your phone for messages. Some of you will have hopefully played along with my game in the previous few paragraphs, others will have no doubt ignored it as a cheap gimmick, but I bet even more still will have ignored my instruction, yet at the same time inadvertently checked their phone or BlackBerry, or glanced over at their computer (regularly and unnaturally breaking their mind's train of thought as they read), just for the tiny confidence boost that the big bad world hasn't forgotten them.

I was publisher of *Wallpaper* magazine when I got my first BlackBerry, and had teams in eight different markets worldwide. I fooled myself that my new-found self-importance meant I should jump out of bed at two in the morning in response to its beeps, and reply to e-mails from LA or Australia in a rather sad 'always on' fashion. I am pleased to say that this was short-lived.

Technology will only ever get faster, and the volume of things that we track and record will certainly never diminish, so we are powerless to slow down the exponential procreation of information around us. What we as human beings must learn to do is appreciate when our brains have reached their full capacity, on any given day, or across a week or month or year, and meter our excessive digital activity. We must learn to switch off more regularly and allow our minds to meditate (by which I don't mean expensive wellness clinics, but simple nothingness, a walk in the park, some gentle conversation with friends, a peaceful stare out of the window or a daydream) in a digital anti-state. I could certainly recommend the Isle of Skye.

INTELLECTUAL 'PROPRIETY AND SURROGACY'

I remember hearing just over 10 years ago that Bill Gates had apparently bought the licence to show digital reproductions of the entire collection of the British National Gallery... on large screens around his US home. Whether the rumours were true or not, it is easy to imagine how such personal wealth and technological access could have made this possible, but in most cases these days intellectual property is so much more complicated than a simple transaction between a global philanthropist and an exhaustive rights owner, and as a publisher and editor I've certainly more regularly looked on IP as a minefield.

An 'original thing' these days so often comes with a history of collaborators. There are the rights of the organization that funded the project, the variety of different creative brains, experts and craftspeople (all in some way involved in the production), the permissions of any participants (models, actors, performers), considerations for different sizes of audiences and platforms, and often too a complex international web of reproduction rights and further licences. This makes identifying the 'owner' of the work, and therefore the beneficiary of profit, a very opaque business – particularly when there arises debate over what an 'original idea' truly is, as so much of today's clever or fresh thinking is based, often indirectly and unconsciously, as a reaction to a predecessor's efforts and ideas.

Having had the fortune over my early career to work for some amazing magazines, I had always had in the back of my mind the resolute desire to create a magazine of my own. It was equally resolute that it had to be original and, in a sense, have its own specific raison d'être. Around 2005/06, I had my Isaac Newton 'apple' moment. Sitting by that time comfortably in the nursery slopes of the new digital frontier, and already much exposed to debates around information overload and the endless possibilities afforded by technology, I'd become interested in the idea of content 'curation' – as being as necessary and important in our futures as content creation itself. It may seem strange that this digital inspiration spawned an idea for a simple magazine, printed using ink on paper, and sent in bulk as hard copies around the world, but it did.

The magazine was called *Distill*, and as the name suggested it was a curation of the finest editorial content from fashion and style magazines, from around the world. The international style press at that time was enormous in number, ranging from Condé Nast power glossies through to back-bedroom cult titles residing in the obscure cities of far-off lands, but most of these titles, in spite of an extremely loyal following, were quite small in terms of circulation and overall exposure. It was time, I thought, that someone trawled the globe for all of these wonderful magazines and gave them suitable exposure for their amazing talent. *Distill* didn't claim ownership of any of this content, and credited all of the originators (including the magazine itself, photographers, illustrators, stylists, etc). It showcased the work as displayed on the page in its original context, with the addition of an explanation behind the idea and technical approach to the shoot. We acted as trusted editors to what I and my editorial board (an amazing selection of fashion and design heroes, from Colin McDowell, Matthew Williamson, Stefano Pilati and Donatella Versace, to Tom Dixon and Deyan Sudjic) considered the best content of the day.

The collapse of AIG, and the domino effect that had on the world's trading floors, meant that *Distill* was ultimately the right kind of thing at undoubtedly the wrong time. And timing is everything. The wind robbed from our sails to make a real go of it, we were forced to close after not nearly enough issues. I still consider *Distill* to be a hard-copy precursor to things that followed, a pragmatic, pre-digital and pre-social version of ffffound.com, Pinterest, Tumblr and so on.

Whilst *Distill* was not more than five years ago, in contrast with today what I find particularly telling is this: we had to get permissions and obtain original artwork files from the creators in question. We couldn't simply rip from the internet, or copy and paste, or guesstimate the best (or least offensive) credit, and share it with our audience and expect it would be all right. In order to include any editorial from any magazine I first needed a signed clearance agreement from the magazine publisher, the photographer and in some cases the model's agent too. By today's standards, our then hugely diplomatic and painstaking approach to IP attribution seems positively archaic.

I wonder if we're fast approaching a new era of 'intellectual surrogacy'. In this place that is so far beyond the traditional notions of IP and ownership, if I have carefully and intelligently built through common social channels a positive reputation and a significant following, and *I* spread the word to my disciples about *your* work, and I credit you accurately and associate your work with a larger selection of the finest craft and talent – even without your permission – am I in fact not doing your marketing for you, and as the term suggests playing a significant role in the birth of your project and success? It is after all why leading talent once had publicists and those publicists would secure coverage in 'the press'. A solid feature article in the right magazine could equal a huge spike in a product's sales. But, if I'm not a magazine, newspaper or TV show and instead an individual, how is that relationship going to play out?

THE TREE OF KNOWLEDGE

Dr Sherry Turkle, Professor of the Social Studies of Science and Technology at Massachusetts Institute of Technology and author of *Alone Together: Why We Expect More from Technology and Less from Each Other*,[2] describes how in the extent of our addiction and love affair with our companion machines we have 'sold our souls to technologies that were designed to save us time to do more real-life things' and, as people, 'have reached a state of emotional readiness in which we are willing to seriously consider robots – not only as pets but as potential friends, confidants or even romantic partners'.

Perhaps I am already in love with technology. After all, I regularly spend time away from my wife and children (my loved ones) but wouldn't dream of leaving home without my iPhone and absolutely couldn't go overnight anywhere without my Lumix GF1 or MacBook.

I feel quite strongly that there are some issues to be resolved around the net and public IP and that the need to switch the Digital State 'off' occasionally, in order to free our minds, will soon become an anxiety *du jour*. We probably *are* going to have to work harder than our parents before us to save our teenage children from losing 'real' social skills through an over-reliance on texting and artificial 'social media' friendships, and will almost inevitably need to begin somehow to meter our own technological addiction and live by the mantra that just because technology means we can doesn't mean we should.

But the Digital Revolution is upon us and to all intents and purposes it promises to be *ace*.

An entire century before my personal technological journey, Britain was coming out of the Industrial Revolution and experiencing a remarkably similar set of reactions to advancements in manufacturing and the ability to make everything and anything, and concerns about the responsibilities that went with that. With the benefit of hindsight we now appreciate that it was perhaps, until now, one of the finest moments in the history of humanity.

Technology has blurred the boundaries between work and pleasure. *Technology is fun.*

Technology has facilitated previously unimaginable possibilities for family entertainment. *Technology makes me and my family happy.*

Technology has reinvented the world for the creatively minded. *Technology is my saviour.*

Technology has made almost everything easier and quite considerably better. To my mind, therefore, technology is *good*.

CL
London

NOTES

1 Nick Harkaway, *The Blind Giant: Being human in a digital world* (John Murray, London, 2012).

2 Dr Sherry Turkle, *Alone Together: Why we expect more from technology and less from each other* (Basic Books, New York, 2013).

9 'I'VE BEEN EXPECTING YOU'

Law for a digital state

Tamara Quinn

> “In the early days of the brave new digital world, a few pioneers, some of them influential (or at least vocal), envisaged a democratic, stateless, anything-goes online universe, unsullied by such real-world considerations as the law. I don’t know how many of these people really believed that this was desirable. No significant society exists without some kind of law...
>
> Why on earth would anyone think that the internet can function without law? And why would we want it to? There’s a reason why the word ‘lawless’ is pejorative – and in fact, there is a lot of law relevant to the internet. My own specialism, intellectual property (IP) law, is right there at the heart of it.”

I'd like you to meet... Tamara Quinn

Most Bond girls fall into one of two camps. You have your meadow-fresh, open-faced blondes, who specialize in being comely and either racy or rather ditsy, and then, by way of counterpoint, you get your mysterious and much more complex brunettes. Maybe brunettes are just smarter at dodging stereotypes, sporting the kind of colour-coding that's able to keep guys guessing?

Tamara Quinn would make a smart casting choice for a dark and mysterious Bond girl – but it's truly not why I invited her to this particular party. It was because she's a dear friend and because I needed a really good lawyer.

Of course, it's always nice being able to introduce a little glamour into any proceedings. And it's nicer still when that glamour is accompanied by some icy smarts. That, you see, is the double-up with Tamara Quinn. She's the kind of class act that, Bond girl looks aside, might just carry her own double-O licence, only (of course) you'd never know about it, and if you did it would be short-lived.

Tamara heads up the non-contentious intellectual property practice inside law firm Berwin Leighton Paisner (BLP), 'advising on the protection, enforcement and ownership of all types of IP rights'. I can't even begin to imagine how complicated that must be. What I do know is that there can be no limits to the amount of special operative resourcefulness and ingenuity required to navigate through our Digital State, because 'open source' can't suddenly be open season, and with so much creativity and commentary going on you need to meet it in equal measure with some common-sense controls. Copyright, defamation, privacy laws: these things are all here to help.

*

All lands, whether physical or digital, need the rule of law. The internet is no different to anywhere else, nor should it be and nor can we afford it to be.

We can briefly, albeit naively, smile with charming sugar-plum notions of social structures that build bottom up, self-regulate, and protect through some all-embracing sense of kindness, nurture and humanity. But, let's face it, these fairy tales would turn dark pretty damn quick. Ultimate laissez-faire can quickly descend into *Lord of the Flies*. It's a fine line between commune and cult, and civilized society stays civil only because there are clear boundaries and enforced rules, because the majority need protection from the malevolent few and because the greater good is upheld by good governance, and good governance is born of laws and good order.

So, Bondian parallels aside, Tamara Quinn is also something of a lawman, a much prettier and more petite Gary Cooper, someone essential to 'The Cause', who ensures that the internet, like the Wild West, is a place that can be won.

Surely enough, 'the law' acts and reacts and plays catch-up with the Digital State, because the Digital State moves with the speed of technology and mavericks and impulse. But 'catch up' the law does. Not even cyberspace is, or should be, beyond its reach. It can be anticipated, and countered.

Over to Tamara. (She's been expecting you.)

My first encounter with the thing-that-would-become-the-internet was in the mid-1980s. Snug in the wood-panelled library of an Oxford college, we gathered, curious, around the tiny screen, as the glowing words appeared. 'What is it?' I asked the super-bright mathematician who plugged at the keyboard. 'I'm talking to a researcher at Cambridge.' I sipped my mug of hot Vimto, and we looked on in wonder.

My next encounter was less awe-inspiring. At the dawn of the 1990s, I was funding my legal training by developing software for a big consultancy company. (My coding was at best indifferent, but I won acclaim for the lucid prose of my comment boxes.) We had for weeks been attending meetings in which the organizer complained that no one had received his agenda memos. Largely unconcerned (they were dull meetings), we vaguely blamed the post room. In fact, it turned out that the memos had been sent direct to our PCs via some new-fangled internal electronic memo system. We were bemused. Why would anyone send messages via a system that you had to separately log into every time you wanted to check it and that there was no point in checking anyway, because no one else used it? And that was at a company that specialized in IT.

More staid professions progressed more slowly still. Twenty-odd years back, officials at the Law Society, responding to a book that predicted that one day lawyers would routinely use e-mail, denounced the idea as 'bringing the profession into disrepute'. A barrister friend tells how, until about five years ago, his e-mails were delivered to a communal inbox in the clerks' room, printed out and borne to his office on a velveteen cushion. OK, I made up the cushion bit, but you get the picture. We lawyers were not exactly at the cutting edge of internet usage. No early adopters here. Now, however, we have pretty much embraced it.

In the early days of the brave new digital world, a few pioneers, some of them influential (or at least vocal), envisaged a democratic, stateless, anything-goes online universe. Their cyber-frontierland would not be sullied by such real-world considerations as the law. I don't know how many of these people really believed that this was desirable, let alone possible. Give or take a few academic quibbles, it's pretty clear that no significant society exists without some kind of law. There are some traditional societies that don't have much in the way of law – no statute books, no courts, no lawyers – but closer observation reveals that they do have rules, and that departure from these rules results in sanctions, even if these sanctions may be collectively decided on and enforced.

So, if the most simple, non-hierarchical communities have law, why on earth would anyone think that the internet can function without law? And why would we want it to? After all, there's a reason why the word 'lawless' is pejorative – and in fact there is a lot of law relevant to the internet. My own specialism, intellectual property (IP) law, is right there at the heart of it.

I fully appreciate that many of my fellow contributors to this book would rather saw off their own leg with a spork (google it) than work as a lawyer, but I consider myself fortunate. IP law is challenging, fun and fascinating. More practically, with an eye to the mundane business of earning a living, it's an area of law that has grown rapidly in recent years. It will keep on growing, because IP law is one of the most fundamental supports underpinning the explosion of modern technology.

Because there is so much relevant law out there, it can be difficult to know where to stop. Rather than attempt any sort of comprehensive overview, I have focused on three related areas that I believe are key: copyright, defamation and privacy. By happy chance, they are also some of the most interesting areas. They illustrate how law and the online world interact, the law lagging some way behind but always adapting its existing rules to make them relevant to the digital environment, and the environment changing in response to the law.

IP 101

There are many common misconceptions around IP, so it's worth a few words of explanation. IP laws vary between countries, sometimes dramatically. An example: each time you copy a song from a CD to your iTunes account in the UK, you break the law, but not if you do the same thing in the United States. In this chapter, I am usually talking only about the law in England and Wales (Scotland has its own system). It is often broadly similar in many Western countries, but can differ greatly, especially in the United States.

More than one type of IP right can cover the same product. The IP rights that are most relevant here are copyright, patents, trade marks, confidential information, privacy and defamation. (Strictly speaking, the last is a different area from IP law, but I'm ignoring this for now.) Take your mobile phone. There is copyright in the maker's logo, the layout of icons on the home screen, the software, the words of your texts and the photo of your kid you've set as your wallpaper. There are patents covering the battery, the wi-fi and the 'slide to unlock' screen access. The maker's name and logo are trade-marked. There is confidential information in the algorithms that handle the compression of data, and in the content of texts and e-mails. And there may be defamatory gossip simmering in your social media app.

Of all the IP rights, copyright is of surpassing importance in the digital world, because it is the main form of legal protection not only for the content that you see (photographs, text, video), but also for the underlying software, apps and databases that make it all work.

Copyright does what it says on the tin: it is a right to stop copying. It won't stop someone copying a mere idea or concept. Rather, it protects the form in which an idea or concept is expressed, but only if that form is original (ie you had not copied it in the first place) and if that other person has actually copied it from you (rather than, say, coming up with it independently). So, if you write an opinion piece for your blog and someone copies it without your consent, you can sue the person for copyright infringement, but you can't stop people from doing their own opinion piece using the same arguments and structure, provided they do it in their own words.

There are two other features of copyright worth knowing. Firstly, copyright protection arises automatically, without registration, payment or other formalities, as soon as the piece of work is created. Secondly, protection terms vary, but it generally lasts for a very long time. In the European Union, in most cases (eg writing, software, photos) it lasts for the life of the author, plus 70 years.

Because of these last two there is, in my view, simply too much copyright. Copyright was originally intended as a way of incentivizing people to be creative, but it has mutated into something quite different, something much grander than can possibly be justified as a reasonable reward for the creator's efforts. In short, too many things are protected by copyright, and for too long. It is not difficult to see how this can stifle what should be legitimate innovation and development. But there we have it, and there is no sign that this will change any time soon.

The realities of our digital world drive developments in the law, but this is a two-way process, as the law creates pressures that change technology and change the way we use technology. The law and its subject matter co-evolve.

COPYRIGHT

Remember Napster, the peer-to-peer music file-sharing site? Napster software on your PC uploaded music files that you'd recorded from CDs, etc and made them available to all other subscribers. For a couple of years at the turn of the century Napster allowed millions to download their music free of charge. Record companies, caught off-guard, were horrified and rang their lawyers.

Napster claimed that it was not itself infringing, merely facilitating copying by users and it was up to the users to make sure they did not upload copyright content. But the law caught up, with a US court ordering the company to block access to infringing tracks. Unable to comply, Napster shut down its operations. By then, the public had developed an appetite for online music downloads, a demand that the music industry was unable, or unwilling, to meet as it grimly clung to its existing, CD-based business model. This now appears to have been a colossal mistake, not merely because of lost profit from the legitimate sales that would have replaced many illegal downloads, but also because the popularity of Napster and similar services reinforced the attitude that internet content should be available free of charge. This mindset still permeates the online world.

How often have I had to explain patiently (usually to marketing people) that just because a photograph they'd used is available on the web it doesn't mean that it is 'in the public domain' and can be freely used and copied? The existence of the web means that content such as the photo is easily found and copied, but it also means that unauthorized copies can often be traced, their users identified and lawyers' letters dispatched. This readiness of copyright owners to sue (or threaten to sue) is surely an important factor in changing user behaviour, which will lead to increasing numbers commissioning the work they need, seeking out images that are licensed free of charge, or paying licence fees.

The examples above are straightforward, from a legal point of view – the owner of the IP in question would have a pretty much open-and-shut case, and always has, from the dawn of the internet age. However, there are also greyer areas of law in play. What's been interesting here has been admiring the law's flexibility as it has been shaped and stretched to fill in the legal gaps created by the digital world.

Take cyber-squatting (the practice of buying up domain names that are, or include, someone else's trade mark). As the world started to get to grips with domain names, entrepreneurish types realized that there was money to be made by registering these domains and then offering to sell them to the trade mark owner at an inflated price, with the threat of a sale to a third party if the price wasn't met.

It was not immediately clear what laws, if any, this would break, but the lawyers worked on it, arguing by analogy from earlier cases where people had been prohibited from incorporating companies with the name of a soon-to-be-created merged conglomerate. Once the law was firmly established on the side of the trade mark owners (and swift, cheap online dispute procedures were set up by internet organizations such as ICANN), behaviour began to change. Nowadays, cyber-squatters typically demand far less money to hand over the disputed domain name. I still see clients with serious problems, but they tend to be different: many are battling outright fake websites set up by fraudsters intent on taking as much as possible from gullible users before being shut down (often not by IP owners, but by the credit card companies whose facilities are vital for relieving the punters of their money).

As the internet matures, the basic legal positions have been established, and our focus is shifting to more sophisticated problems. Take something as apparently straightforward as clicking on a link to an article on a newspaper's website. Assuming there is no pay-wall, the article appears on your screen and you peruse it at your leisure. In the unlikely event that you gave any thought to the legalities of this, you would of course assume all was well. After all, newspapers have websites precisely because they want you to read their articles. Don't they? Well, yes, but it is, as lawyers are fond of saying, a little more complicated than that. In a case that was being considered by the UK Supreme Court at the time of writing, it is suggested that, if the link was sent to you by a paid-for commercial media monitoring company, you infringe the newspaper's copyright if you click on the link, because the permission to read does not apply where the link came via a commercial service (ie where the media monitoring company charges for providing you with the link).

Some internet users have taken a radical approach to the IP laws they are unhappy with. There are many who believe that the spirit of the internet requires that software and content should be freely available, and that this will speed progress, as other users will be able to change and develop that content or software. This ethos has found expression in the concepts of open-source software and creative commons content and allied movements.

The idea here is that a person creates a piece of work (eg software, a photograph or information) and makes it available without charge, but subject to a specified form of licence. The terms of the licence vary depending on the scheme in question, but in essence anyone is allowed to use the software, photograph, etc (though perhaps with restrictions, eg banning commercial use) provided that they in turn make their version of it freely available on the same basis. These restricted licences are amusingly dubbed 'some rights reserved' rather than the traditional 'all rights reserved'. The success of organizations such as the Open Source Foundation and Creative Commons has been astonishing. Content made available on this basis ranges from the hundreds of millions of photos uploaded to Flickr, through the research databases of international R&D companies, to the website of the US president.

It's remarkable to see these developments unfold, and on such a vast scale. Rather than just wishing that copyright law was what they thought it ought to be, these people used (subverted?) the existing law to make it so.

DEFAMATION

Another hot spot for legal developments is defamation and privacy, fuelled by the growth of blogging and news and gossip sites, and the rise of social media. Everyone has an opinion about everyone else, and they want everyone to hear it. The law of defamation allows you to take action if someone has made derogatory and damaging comments about you, either in print (libel) or orally (slander), which cannot be defended, eg by proving they are true or fair comment.

Until quite recently, few people had the resources to make their words widely known. If you were a publisher, you would be aware of the laws of libel, and could take care to check facts and craft published words with care. As for slander, unless you were a well-known orator, your spoken words reached few ears, and you would have known the owners of each pair. If you exercised common sense in choosing your audience, your comments would probably not make it to the ears of the slandered person, and even if they did your identity might not.

Legal sanctions are tailored to reflect the severity of the defamation. The damages ordered for slander are usually significantly less than for libel, reflecting the fact that the words will have reached far fewer people, and those listeners may well have given them less weight than if they had seen them in writing.

With today's widespread use of social media, there is a problem of perception. Twitter, for example, is written (and so the law of libel applies), but many users see it as closer to chatting (and so might expect the law to treat it like slander). The difference is important: chat is intimate and ephemeral, whereas a tweet can be instantly retweeted, potentially spreading virally if picked up by someone with many followers. The lack of face-to-face interaction, coupled with the character number constraint, means that there is little scope for subtle nuance. A tweet intended as ironic or humorous can easily come across as rude or aggressive.

A 2012 high-profile case may turn out to have a big impact in this arena. Lord McAlpine, a high-profile former senior member of the Conservative Party, was falsely accused of being a paedophile. *Newsnight*, the BBC's flagship news programme, had discussed the allegation. Whilst *Newsnight* stopped short of naming the alleged offender (though it still paid a substantial sum in settlement), many Twitter users were not so restrained. Lord McAlpine was vindicated when the victim said that there had been a mistake in identification, and his lawyers lost no time in making it clear that they would be demanding financial compensation from everyone who had tweeted or retweeted the allegations.

It seems inconceivable that such a well-publicized case will not, at the very least, give pause to the more high-profile user planning to tweet or blog some juicy little titbit. And a pause, followed by reflection on the possible consequences, may be all that is needed for people to modify their words before putting them out there.

PRIVACY

Closely related to these situations are those where the allegation being made is true, but it is private and the person concerned doesn't want it to be made public. The law of confidential information steps in here, entwined with human rights law (in particular the balancing of a person's right to the privacy of his or her private and family life against the media's right to freedom of expression).

Over the past few years, judges have been changing the way they apply these laws in the face of the realities of how gossip spreads online. In recent cases, various public figures have applied for, and have sometimes been granted, injunctions preventing publication of private information, often about alleged extra-marital affairs (eg footballers Ryan Giggs and John Terry) or other sexual exploits (eg Formula 1 racing president Max Mosley). In some cases, the courts have refused to grant injunctions on the grounds that there would be no point, because the gossip was already all over the internet and social media. But, in some of the more recent cases, we see the courts saying that they will grant the injunctions anyway, as it is worthwhile to the celebrity in question to at least keep the stories out of the more authoritative mainstream media.

There are many other examples of the way that the landscape of the internet and social media has been shaped by legal considerations. Websites of multinationals are now tailored by country, not just to cater for linguistic and cultural distinctions, but to reflect differences in local laws. Google changed its Street View service to deal with privacy and data protection issues (blurring faces, stopping its vehicles from scanning data from private wi-fi). The use of cookies has been made more transparent to comply with data protection rules. Online shopping sites have had to stop using a 'one-click' purchasing option in order to avoid infringing Amazon's patent for this method.

But digital technology has not only changed the way the law works; it has also changed the way that lawyers work. One dramatic example is 'disclosure'. This is the step in a legal dispute where the two sides exchange copies of relevant documents. In recent years, the number of these documents has surged, because they now include e-mail and instant messages, which preserve words that would previously have existed only in phone calls and meetings. The legal rules have had to adapt, and now disclosure is limited, as the parties agree to disclose only electronic documents, and only key categories of them, identified by use of agreed search terms.

THE FUTURE

There are plenty of intriguing possibilities for the future. There could be expansion of the use of online dispute resolution services by ordinary citizens, not just for disputes relating to a specific website, but for dealing with more general disputes without resorting to lawyers or courts. We can hope for law guides aimed at the layperson, covering common areas of legal misunderstanding, from a reliable trusted provider (such as the relevant government website). There are good moral and practical reasons for making the law, to which we are all subject, more comprehensible and accessible to non-lawyers. There could be approved standard documents (wills, employment agreements, tenancy agreements, house purchase documents) available free to the public via government websites, in association with the simplified law guides mentioned above.

I hope I've managed to impart a sense of how the law and the digital world are entwined and co-develop, and also given a flavour of the nature and the complexity of the sorts of issues involved. To round things off, I'll leave you with some thoughts on the broader landscape.

WIDER ISSUES

There are bigger-picture legal questions that also deserve to be considered. The likes of Google, Facebook, Twitter, eBay, Amazon and *Wikipedia*, along with a host of smaller companies, naturally insist that you, the user, are subject to their respective terms of use and operational policies. For example, Amazon's and Apple's rules mean that, unlike books, DVDs or CDs, you can't pass on to anyone else the iTunes tracks or Kindle downloads you've paid good money for. This causes problems on divorce and death and, more mundanely, if you've simply finished with the item in question and want to give it to a friend. YouTube's policy is to remove offensive footage reported to it, but it is YouTube's employees who decide what's allowed. Are we happy having them as our censors? And eBay might take down offers to sell fake luxury goods, but the owner of the IP has to jump through several hoops, of eBay's choosing, to persuade them to act.

Even if someone (like me) bothers to read the small print, and is able to understand fully its implications, there is little I can do beyond putting up with them, as a refusal to click the 'I have read and agree to' button results in me being denied any access at all. The sheer scale and ubiquity of use of these services mean that, in a very real sense, their policies have become the law for hundreds of millions of users worldwide. This is interesting. It will strike many people as disturbing. It will even strike some people as an insidious undermining of how law is supposed to be created and enforced: with due process, consideration and respect for democratic principles.

As a lawyer, my legal auto-pilot naturally nudges me towards this last point of view, but this instinctive reaction would be too narrow-minded. Yes, companies' terms and policies are often heavily biased in their favour, can change with inadequate notice, and may show scant regard for users' privacy, but remember that it is early days: even the largest online behemoths are not long out of their infancy, are still feeling their way. As they grow, the pressure on them to do the right thing mounts, not least because of the intense scrutiny of the geeks, and the resulting instantaneous and widely disseminated critical feedback that meets any policy changes.

Instead, I think we should applaud many aspects of online companies' policies and the way they are implemented in practice. The best are practical, pragmatic, responsive, and straightforward for the user to understand and access, which is more (much more) than can be said for the majority of traditional laws that my clients and I spend so much time and expense trying to understand and apply.

TQ
London

10 DIGITAL DARES US TO DREAM

Simon Pont

"These digital days, I think the line between 'reality' and the imagined is a whole lot finer and fuzzier than any absolutist would have us believe. That goes too for the line dividing who we are and who we might dare to me. And I think on all fronts a fine and fuzzy line is a rather wonderful thing.

Being told that our dreams aren't or can't be real, and never will be, is the peevish twaddle of the cynics and naysayers, the closed-minded and the blinkered. Those guys are seriously downbeat company, the kind who drop nicely when thrown from a bridge and make a satisfying splash.

I believe the Digital State is bringing us closer to our dreams. It's opening our eyes, daring us to make our dreams real, and questioning with meadow-fresh vigour just what is real."

I couldn't resist it. I couldn't resist approaching the question from a different direction, cutting it up a different way. There's never only one way to climb a mountain, or ski down it. Maybe I had always planned to have another run at this particular slope.

In Chapter 2 ('Utopia, dystopia. Discuss'), I wanted to look at society as a kind of whole, a bit like an organism, and wonder as to its health, the kind of diagnosis and prognosis as afforded by this onset of 'digital'.

This time round, I want to take a more personal, more intrinsic view, a view of inner worlds, the rise of *invitation*.

This time round, mostly, I want to talk about dreams.

So, if you'd care to join me, let's take once more to the mountain.

> “RYAN BINGHAM: *You know why kids love athletes?*
>
> BOB: *Because they screw lingerie models.*
>
> RYAN BINGHAM: *No, that's why we love athletes. Kids love them because they follow their dreams.*
>
> *UP IN THE AIR* (2009)

What we dream to do, who we dream to be: these are powerful ideas, ideas we hold dear, close to our tender hearts, but they too often remain part of our internal(-only) dialogue. Our dreams can be elusive, like lingerie models. They sit less well in our everyday lives, are harder to follow, where practicalities, obstacles, difficult people and awkward circumstances serve up these fiddly limitations, and endeavour to remind us that wanting to be an athlete, poet, songwriter or rocket man is a pipe-dream and thing of folly.

Of course, I'm in no way sold on the aforementioned way of things. Obstacles are *just* obstacles. They might impede, but they are seldom insurmountable, and are almost never a case of stepping up to the edge of the Earth.

Then there's that other kind of dream, the places and spaces and vast frontier of our imagination, which can be so thrilling, but which we are once again typically told to appreciate as 'unreal'. If you can't 'touch it', if it can't be objectively shared, if it lives *only* in our mindscape, then it is divorced from 'reality'. Once again, I'm in no way sold.

These digital days, I think the line between 'reality' and 'the imagined' is a whole lot finer and fuzzier than any absolutist would have us believe.

That goes too for the line dividing who we are and who we might dare to be. And I think on all fronts a fine and fuzzy line is a rather wonderful thing.

Being told that our dreams aren't or can't be real, and never will be, is the peevish twaddle of the cynics and naysayers, the closed-minded and the blinkered. Those guys are seriously downbeat company, the kind who drop nicely when thrown from a bridge and make a satisfying splash.

I believe the *Digital State* is bringing us closer to our dreams. It's opening our eyes, daring us to make our dreams real, and question with meadow-fresh vigour: just what is 'real'?

A NEW REALITY, A NEW NEVERLAND

> *He'd operated on an almost permanent adrenalin high, a by-product of youth and proficiency, jacked into a custom cyberspace deck that projected his disembodied consciousness into the consensual hallucination that was the matrix.*
>
> WILLIAM GIBSON, *NEUROMANCER* (1984)

William Gibson opens his debut novel *Neuromancer* with the plight of Case, a 24-year-old hacker who once lived for 'the bodiless exultation of cyberspace'. Now denied this exultation, Case downward-spirals, a barfly and black-marketeer playing it fast and loose and grinning at the knowing curve he's riding to suicidal self-destruct.

The separation of body and mind, the thrills of life lived online, an addiction to the imagined, Gibson's then-prescient themes point quite a finger into the chest of our digital today.

With the explosion of social media, for how many is their cyber-self a more accurate image of their true self? At the very least, it's surely a closer reflection of the people we *want* to be and the abridged, 'cool highlights only' life we want to lead. And all this stirs curious thoughts around dual realities and self-curated delusions, or at least self-narrated illusions. But then, without getting too heavy or judging about any of this, what is anyone's *reality*?

On the level that I'm asking, I think the answer is actually pretty straightforward. You can naturally define your reality as the place, the circumstances, serendipitous or otherwise, where destiny air-drops you: above the breadline, below the breadline, into a family that runs a bakery, into privilege, into oppression, the cards dealt at birth making the hand you get. The top-spin on this is then how you *view* that hand, whether you're a glass-half-full or -empty kind of character, your reality being the intersection of your inner and outer views.

Because surely anyone's 'reality' is that which they *experience*? That which they create for themselves and that which is created for them, all making for that thing called 'real', a sum total of any and all experiences. And I use the words 'create' and 'created' deliberately, because I believe so much of our realities are born of imagination and the imagined.

The 'real world' isn't only the hard surfaces and concrete forms. That's the *physical* world. If reality was only our physical space, we'd all interact and react off these solid edges in much the same way. And we don't. You get both happy and sad occupying the favelas of Brazil. You get both happy and sad living in the McMansions of Beverly Hills. What really determines 'reality' is 'state of mind', that theatre of the mind where the real show happens.

I think that mental realities are as powerfully governing as physical realities. Both are perceptual doors we pass through, to arrive in that life-space called 'existence'.

When we sleep, the physical reality is that we're inert, our state one of stasis, of shutdown. But then we dream. What about the mindscapes we encounter? What of the recurring dreams we have, or the dreams where we return to the same place? Those 'dream venues', *those* places are, I think, very real, and maybe no less alive to me than when I walk through my local park or into a nearby bank.

The characters in books, the scenes in films: they are very real memories, of very real characters. *Make*-believe. From the imagination, *made*.

> *Of all delectable islands Neverland is the snuggest. It's not large and sprawly, you know, with boring distances between one adventure and the next, it's nicely crammed. When you play at it by day with the table and chairs, it's not a bit frightening, but in the two minutes before you go to sleep it is real.*
>
> JM BARRIE, *PETER PAN/PETER AND WENDY* (1911)

It's my view that the physical and online worlds are becoming wrapped in a kind of digital membrane, where Barrie's two minutes before sleep are becoming many people's 24-hour cycle.

'Digital' is creating new realities for people. It's transforming how we interact with the physically concrete world. We don't jog the way we used to, listen to music the way we used to, party like we used to. Just consider the following three exhibits:

Exhibit 1: Nike+

Going for a run, 'jogging' as it was once called, used to be an obviously solitary affair. Today, with Nike+, your running performance can be a thing of automatic Facebook updates, with your friends' typed encouragement and congratulations fed to your earpiece in a soothing electronic voice. Now even going for a run is a social media moment to be shared. For those who don't want to 'escape', they never have to.

Exhibit 2: Shazam

Still on the subject of ears, services like Shazam have come into being by bending technology to meet longstanding human need, even if the need isn't exactly the kind of thing Maslow was ever talking about. A combination of database and smartphone is all it takes to satisfy that once niggling, borderline chronic frustration of not recognizing a song. Within earshot, you hear music, and you're either not early adopter enough or your internal aural encyclopedia is failing you. With a Shazam app, you just have to hold your phone up to a song, record a 10-second fragment, and the 'acoustic fingerprint' is then cross-referenced with an 11-million-song database. Once the song is successfully matched, Shazam then texts you top-line information like title and artist, as well as links to the likes of iTunes and Spotify.

Once upon a time, something so simple would have sounded so impossible, a kind of magic, which today is just a simple case of pairing a mobile phone's microphone with a very large pile of digital spectrograms.

Exhibit 3: Spring Break

> *Spring Break Gets Tamer as World Watches Online*
>
> *Key West, Fla. – Ah, Spring Break, with its copious debauchery, spontaneous bouts of breast-baring, Jager bombing and après-binge vomit... But today's spring breakers say they have been tamed, not by parents or colleges but by the hand-held gizmos they hold dearest and the fear of being betrayed by an unsavory, unsanctioned photo or video popping up on Facebook or YouTube.*
>
> *NEW YORK TIMES* (16 MARCH 2012)

If booze-fuelled, party-hearty spring breakers are now keeping covered, reckless impulse suddenly stemmed, then there's no more vivid yet denied illustration of how 'digital' is creating new behaviours. When bright young things hold back on flashing their bright young assets for fear of becoming 'Facebooked', we can all conclude that it's a new world order.

The Digital State is a very *real* place, a place where our inner and outer worlds overlap. It's the confluence of imagined fiction, documented act and physical fact, a brave new Neverland for spring breakers to fear and latter-day Barries to excitedly explore.

WHEN FICTION BLEEDS

For the Ridley Scott *Alien* prequel *Prometheus* (2012), I just loved how 20th Century Fox's viral promotion fed the imagination. There were three virals prior to the film's theatrical June 2012 release:

- First was Peter Weyland (as played by Guy Pearce) at TED2023: 'I will change the world'.
- Then came 'David 8', a kind of 2-minute-30 'corporate' ad for Weyland Industries' new eighth-generation android.
- And third up was Noomi Rapace, in character as Dr Elizabeth Shaw, making a video appeal to Peter Weyland, to fund her space mission to 'find God'.

The three digitally seeded virals were back-stories (to the back-story), oblique glances at the Prometheus story universe. It was 'Transmedia' theory (if you want the parlance), put into the most compelling practice. The second instalment, 'David 8', was short-form film-making of the finest kind: mesmerizing, creepy in a cool way, curious as hell.

Robert McKee, Fulbright scholar and champion of story craft (*Story*, 1998)[1], argues that back-story is a waste of time. If the back-story is so good, then set the story in it, tell *that* story instead. While McKee makes a very solid point, storytellers like JJ Abrams and Damon Lindelof have pretty much lined McKee's argument up against a wall and shot it. Parallel and non-linear timelines, 'multi-verses', grand narratives with crazy-rich character arcs, the TV show *Lost* turned 'back-story' into *more* story, added byzantine layers of meaning and depth. You don't create a world by stripping away, but by *layering*. Lindelof, who co-wrote TV show *Lost* and

Prometheus, seems to approach 'story' as if throwing a stone at an uneven surface, taking joy in the unsuspected angles, delighting in the ricochet. He creates story worlds you can disappear into and get hit by.

For me, the ultimate highlight of *Prometheus*' viral campaign was its first TED viral. It showed Lindelof ignoring the limits of where you can take 'story', overlapping fiction and reality, bleeding 'story' into our 'real world'. It marked the first time TED had involved themselves in a promotion, in a marketing tie-up, but then there was no reason to get precious and say no. The brand fit couldn't have been snugger. It was the most conspicuously obvious kind of mutual win; *Prometheus* lands some higher-brow associational kudos, and TED gets some Hollywood glam and is introduced to a broader audience.

When Lindelof discussed the canvas of *Prometheus* at Comic-Con in July 2011, he said, 'We're exploring the future... Space exploration in the future is going to evolve into this idea that it's not just about going out there and finding planets to build colonies. It also has this inherent idea that, the further we go out, the more we learn about ourselves.'

Imagination, like space, has no boundaries. In the Digital State, storytellers like Lindelof are exploring just what that can now mean, blurring the borders, playing story-games in the new frontiers of our digital universe. And, of course, story-games in the Digital State aren't just the preserve of Hollywood.

SECRETS AND LIES

Eric Schmidt and Jared Cohen state:

> *There will be a constant struggle between those striving to promote what US Secretary of State Hillary Clinton has called 'the freedom to connect' and those who view that freedom as inimical to their political survival.*[2]

WikiLeaks is a high-def illustration of fiction colliding with fact, a whistle-blower hunted, a digital bogeyman manufactured, crimped, pimped and popularized by the propaganda-peddlers.

> *On 28 November 2010,* WikiLeaks *began releasing some of the 251,000 American diplomatic cables in their possession, of which*

over 53 per cent are listed as unclassified, 40 per cent are 'Confidential' and just over 6 per cent are classified 'Secret'.

WIKIPEDIA

Overnight, and from almost out of nowhere (for the mass-media-consuming majority at least), *WikiLeaks* editor and founder Julian Assange became a very public figure. The suddenly everywhere photos of the sharp-eyed, prematurely grey 30-something Australian looked like a caricature of Bond villainy. Circulated images of the *WikiLeaks* HQ looked subterranean, high-tech, the perfect lair for a megalomaniacal master of misinformation and general ill-doing.

Assange's early life read off the page like a spy novel. At the age of 16, he had been a hacker operating under the moniker Mendax ('nobly untruthful'). Twenty-three years later, in outing the confidential musings and missives of US diplomats, Assange was now posturing noble truth, contending no regime should have transparency purely on its own terms. The US government and its allies felt otherwise. Both US vice-president Joe Biden and Senate minority leader Mitch McConnell labelled Assange 'a high-tech terrorist'. House speaker Newt Gingrich suggested Assange be treated as 'an enemy combatant', and vice-presidential candidate Sarah Palin trumped them all, proposing Townsville, Queensland's (all-of-a-sudden) most infamous son be 'hunted down like Bin Laden'.

No photos emerged of Assange attending a Bin Laden family BBQ, or stroking Blofeld's white cat, but an angle was worked by Western puppet-masters. The highly charged hullabaloo of *WikiLeaks* took further turns as rape allegations and arrest warrants surfaced, Western governments appearing hell-bent on nabbing Assange, even if it was just to contain him briefly, somewhere, anywhere, so they could work out which laws he'd broken and whether anyone could justify water-boarding him. The 'somewhere' became 10 days in Wandsworth prison, with food, water (and of course no boards) before making bail and being offered a roof in the form of Ellingham Hall in Norfolk.

On 6 December 2010, Fox News political commentator Bob Beckel stated, 'A dead man can't leak stuff. This guy's [Assange] a traitor, he's treasonous, and he has broken every law of the United States... And I'm not for the death penalty, so... there's only one way to do it: illegally shoot the son of a bitch.' Other guests on the program agreed.

WIKIPEDIA

In poignant contrast with Fox's familiar über-right-wing stance, Assange was nominated in 2011 for a Nobel Peace Prize (by Norwegian parliamentarian Snorre Valen), and remains a hugely divisive figure within our Digital State, where one man's whistle-blower remains another woman's Bin Laden.

Right-wing cries for assassination aside, Assange's spiralling legal bills alone suggest it's seldom wise to make an enemy of the in-residence superpower. However, judgements also aside, he remains living testament to the shock waves that can be caused by one man exercising his 'freedom to connect'.

DIGITAL ENSURES THAT 'DOING' IS 'BEING'

I've never been driven by an inner calling to expose the secrets of others, but before I knew what I wanted to do when I grew up I did know that what I *really* wanted to be was a writer. Writing was how I wanted to express and freely connect. Up until that point, of course, writing had been one of the things I'd done the most: writing essays, writing answers, writing letters, writing stories, in school, then university, a pre-adult life spent writing, and reading, and really liking words and how they go together and have something to say. Of course, I also appreciated that writing and 'being paid' are twain that far from necessarily twine.

Journalism was an option, but death knocks and hacking around on provincial titles carrying the high-likelihood moniker of *Bugle* or *Echo* or *Evening* wasn't the kind of big-city-glam ticket I was looking for. I didn't much fancy suffering for my art, 'the penniless writer', living in a bedsit (or perhaps 'garret'), drinking impossibly cheap red wine, an electric fire and scrappy wall of second-hand books for company. I don't much acknowledge there being nobility in adversity. I only acknowledge the existence of adversity.

Fortunately, even in my 20s, I also realized that writing, like anything expressive that could broadly be termed a 'passion with no guarantee of paying its way', wasn't an either–or deal. Dream of being an actor? Then act. Go join a group or workshop. It doesn't cover those pesky utility bills? Go wait tables, and while you're waiting them just make sure the lights and heating are turned off in your garret. Dream of becoming a painter? Then paint. Can't find the time? Make the time. 'No time' is no damned excuse. You can't want it badly enough or love it enough.

In *On Writing*, Stephen King slams it home with cut-through-everything smarts: 'Writers write.'[3] In just the same way, actors act, painters paint and, yes, hackers hack. No need to agonize about authenticity and self-definition. If you write, act, paint or hack, you are one (just ask Sarah Palin). And if you don't, you're something else. It's that seriously simple (like Sarah Palin). Whatever it is you do, your *doing* defines who you are. And a lot of what you don't do adds further depth and definition. What we chose to do, what we chose not to do: this is who we are.

My point in all this... is this. The Digital State's 'freedom to connect' is providing wonderful new tools for self-exploration and self-expression. If you have something to say, something to put down and put out there, the barriers to doing so have pretty much vanished. Blog, micro-blog, share, like, the act is within arm's reach and fingertip. There's an audience there, if only you can draw it in, and if you've got it, what it takes, whatever that thing happens to be, then the odds of rising up and breaking through are odds worth playing.

One development, loud and clear, in this digitally enabled world, is the proliferation of opportunity, where 'talent' can freely audition itself, in the open space, open-eared and -minded, of the internet marketplace. Our dreams are moving to within grasping distance, the Digital State giving everyone their shot. It's giving everyone everything to play for, the binary-oiled dynamics of absolute competition daring everyone to slalom and jump the virtual contours of each and every zero and one.

Now, to my mind, it's never just about getting down the mountain, but how you ski it, and I'll finish with two illustrations of two very different types of skier. From Hollywood storytellers and Australian whistle-blowers, let's talk of female soft porn and crowd-sourced T-shirt designers.

FROM JK TO EL

> *On 1 August 2012, amazon.co.uk announced that they had sold more copies of* Fifty Shades of Grey *than they had the entire Harry Potter series combined, making EL James their best-selling author ever, overtaking JK Rowling.*
>
> *WIKIPEDIA*

Well-written, well-paced tales of a schoolboy wizard, I think few would claim much real surprise to the ultimate appeal of Master Potter and his chums (even if it was the 13th publisher, Bloomsbury, that ultimately said yes to JK and her Philosopher's Stone). But female erotica, formerly print-on-purchase 'fan fiction' (based on Stephenie Meyer's *Twilight* characters), who figured on the from-underground-to-epic rise of 'mommy porn'?

In 2012, *Fifty Shades of Grey* was *the* publishing phenomenon that had everyone talking. Indeed, its success had everything to do with being such a word-of-mouth cultural juggernaut. A heavy-loader that maybe no one saw coming, *50 Shades* caught on, captured the imagination and became absolutely huge.

In hindsight, the success formula was wonderfully obvious. EL James wrote something that titillated, deemed 'naughty but nice' by the middle classes, who suddenly had something new to whisper about. It was satisfyingly risqué, while falling just the right side of risqué to have mainstream potential. And the real thrill in reading it was being able to read it without embarrassment, inconspicuously, but in public, on a Kindle.

By the time enough Kindle readers had excitedly eulogized and giggled with friends about how clit-lit was really hitting their spot, *Fifty Shades* had reached a critical enough mass to be mass-market, permissible, and OK to buy in Waitrose without danger of blushing at the checkout, while for those too easily prone to embarrassment Amazon represented the purchase without stuttering excuse or comeback.

In an analogue world, EL James would never have become a multimillionaire, would very likely have remained a wannabee Black Lace novelist. As it is, *Fifty Shades of Grey* might just be the first great digital novel.

THREADLESS

One of my absolute favourite examples of an e-business built on crowdsourcing self-expression is Threadless (threadless.com). Threadless sells T-shirts, via a website, but what Threadless is *really* all about is building a global community of artists and designers, letting crazy-good print design flourish, and encouraging everyone to wear cooler T-shirts. Y'know, there are *less* noble causes in the world than championing a bit of T-shirt cool. Of Threadless, I'm a fan.

> *Threadless is an online community of artists and an e-commerce website based in Chicago, Illinois. In 2000, co-founders Jake Nickell and Jacob DeHart started the company with $1,000 of their own money.*

> *Threadless designs are created by and chosen by an online community. Each week, about 1,000 designs are submitted online and are put to a public vote. After seven days the staff reviews the top-scoring designs. Based on the average score and community feedback, about 10 designs are selected each week, printed on clothing and other products, and sold worldwide through the online store.*
>
> WIKIPEDIA

For me, Threadless is all about the Digital State's proliferation of opportunity, an open invitation to talent, a sourcing of audience, and the removal of former bottlenecking intermediaries. I wanted to ask the guy who founded Threadless, Jake Nickell, whether he felt similar.

> *Threadless started as a hobby while I was in art school. I just wanted to make cool things together with my friends. Today it's still the same, just a lot bigger! Artists around the world submit designs, they get voted on by our community and then we print and sell the best ones. Our mission is to give the creative minds of the world more opportunities to make and sell great art. In the beginning we mostly made T-shirts and sold them on Threadless.com. Today we're expanding on our mission by creating a lot more than just tees and selling them in a lot more places than just Threadless.com.*
>
> JAKE NICKELL, FOUNDER AND CHIEF CREATIVE OFFICER, THREADLESS

If you haven't visited Threadless online, and don't own at least one Threadless T-shirt, then that is your personal tragedy, but it remains something you can remedy. And, rest assured, Jake Nickell's going to make it easier all the time.

THE GHOST IN THE MACHINE... REBOOTED

Philosophically speaking, it was Descartes (aka the Father of Modern Philosophy) who teed up the idea of dualism (the doctrine of duality), that to be human is to be two parts, a physical *and* a 'non-physical'. Descartes demarcated that we are a mind (you could also call it a 'soul') and we are matter, a physical vessel, of 'corporeal substance'. The degree to which mind and body are divorced from or connected to each other is a philosophical rabbit hole, which probably runs right to the Earth's core. Then chasing that tunnel, a little like the ones in *The Great Escape* (just not running so deep), you've got tunnels two and three, 'monism' and 'pluralism'.

Whether 'existence' and 'What makes our reality?' are points of unified perspective, multiple truths, or someplace in between, this is one dig for (philosophical) victory that isn't going to hit light any time soon. Hip-deep in mud, you just end up in a mind-whirl and some pretty stodgy texts of discourse – and I don't want to go there or add in even the smallest way to that particular canon. But where I do want to go is here, down what I think is a curious and not-so-blind alley...

The Digital State throws a torchlight into at least two of the three philosophical tunnels, contributes examples to the idea of our existing in 'more than one way'. In just the same way that binary is singular *and* combining 0s and 1s, the Digital State it creates allows for each of us to be these singular *and* combined on- and offline versions of ourselves.

In his damning of Descartes's mind–body poser, British philosopher Gilbert Ryle introduced the quite brilliant phrase 'the ghost in the machine'. Now, we can leave the philosophers to argue whether mind and body are connected (or not, or something), but the Digital State *is* a connected one, and by its invitation and opportunity *we* are each projecting and ghosting ourselves into a pixelated, binary universe. We are placing ourselves inside the machine, beyond our corporeal form, in this liberation *of* self – not *from*, but *of*.

And, on a somewhat cautionary note, thinking about all this made me think not of Case in *Neuromancer*, but of Wolfgang von Kempelen, a Hungarian inventor. His most famous invention: The Turk (also known as The Strange Turk). The Turk, built in the 18th century, was a chess-playing automaton. You could play against The Turk, where pieces would move around the board in response to any human challenger, and very often The Turk would win. The Turk was *that* good at chess.

The Turk was not, of course, the first days of artificial intelligence. It was a hoax, powered not by Intel, but a very human chess master secret-squirrelled inside. The alleged storyline I particularly like is where von Kempelen gave The Strange Turk as a gift to Empress Maria Theresa, last ruler of the House of Habsburg. Von Kempelen had hidden a midget inside The Turk for a performance of the knight's tour. Soon after the first knight set out, Empress Maria Theresa freaked and ordered the machine shot – on the spot. The chess pieces were unscathed. The midget didn't make it.

Empress Maria Theresa was clearly a technophobe, and these days her numbers are dwindling. While dwindling technophobes would be considered a good thing by many, we don't want to end up like the fated midget – a bullet in the form of delusion and detachment, the two watch-outs in this new Digital State of ours.

But, in counter-argument, why should we be fearful of our imaginations? There's little reason our imaginations should estrange or alienate us, should *disconnect* us in the convergent age.

For me curious, the political theorist and Cornell professor Benedict Anderson (b. 1936) describes nations as 'imagined communities', 'imagined' because it's not literally possible to know every nation member, but it *is* possible to feel emotionally wedded to the idea of a national collective. I think our ever-expanding Digital State is becoming no less real than the nation state. Facebook now has a 1 billion population, 'making it the 3rd largest country in the world' (*Social Media*, 2013). Just as in the nation state, in the Digital State there is unity through commonalities, groups forged by shared social mores and cultural practices. There is no 'one language' or singly agreed flag, but there is self-regulation, consent for many languages and no flag, but shared banners, that say things like 'Facebook' and 'Tuenti' and 'Renren'.

Where we physically and emotionally live within a nation, we mentally and emotionally now live too within a Digital State. Both states are immediate to us; both help define us, by nationality and where we've come from, and by the dreams we choose to pursue and the places our imagination will take us.

To cite the subtitle of this book, I believe almost everything is changing and, for novelists and hackers, designers and politicians, spring breakers and ultimately dreamers, the final shape of the Digital State is our shared and brilliant burden. It is ours to imagine, and ours to make real.

SP
London

NOTES

1 Robert McKee, *Story* (Methuen, London, 1999).

2 Eric Schmidt and Jared Cohen, 'The digital disruption: connectivity and the diffusion of power', *Foreign Affairs*, November/December 2010.

3 Stephen King, *On Writing* (Hodder & Stoughton, London, 2000).

11 A NEWER NORMAL AND DEEPER BLUE

Nicholas Pont

Those of us who are the stewards of capital within markets must do all we can. With the widespread loss of trust in the financial system, we run the risk of becoming estranged from a generation of entrepreneurs and investment, right at the very time when markets need them most, to help spur growth, foster innovation and deliver economic prosperity.

The ubiquity of the internet has transformed the ways in which we conduct all business, and new ways lead to new vulnerabilities. I cannot help but sense that we tilt towards appreciating the benefits more than we respect the risks. Connectivity allows for amplification, and an isolated event in the physical world can have a ripple effect in the virtual world of tsunami size. Risk does not respect borders.

I'd like you to meet... Nicholas Pont

This next guy I know pretty well. I've known him all his life, and most of mine. The surname is probably the give-away. His name is Nick, or Nicholas, and he's my little brother, younger by a little over six years.

Nick being my brother might naturally trigger a few whispers of nepotism, something I too thought about for whatever might be the smallest measurement of a second you can break into a fraction, a measurement so small as to be insignificant, because 'shoe-in' just doesn't come into it, and what does is my fine fortune in knowing someone who was a perfect collaborator for *Digital State*, where that someone just so happened (rather handily) to be my kid brother.

Nick walks tall, because he literally is tall, a very straight 6 foot 4 frame carrying a 240-pound body weight that you wouldn't want to get on the wrong side of. Take a Roman gladiator, apply a latter-day high-protein diet, gym discipline and well-cut suit, and you have a fairly accurate first impression. I've always found Nick to be very useful providing ample shade even from a high sun.

And, while I might incline to liken my little brother to a parasol, I might also describe Nick as an overachiever, only that would then come with some kind of judgement call, as though it's possible to *over* achieve, as if maybe it's poor form to achieve too much, or indeed want to achieve too much – a very small-minded, rather English and probably very middle-class kind of twaddle. Nick J Pont is a high achiever, flipped his economics degree into a position at the largest fixed-income trading operation on the planet, and made SVP soon after hitting 30. And a career in finance was the conscious decision, over an alternative life-path in professional sport.

*

'Man and machine in perfect harmony' was a cheesy-but-catchy strap-line from a British car ad, sometime around the late 1980s. I could google the details, and in a few keystrokes have a machine tell me the year of that TV ad, and the car it was for, but I simply don't want to feel tech-dependent right now. It won't bring me a sense of harmony. And anyway the details aren't important. What is important is the sentiment behind that strapline, and the debatable truth of it. Man, machine, the possibility of perfect harmony: is it an equation that stacks up? The answer, of course, can never be categorical. Machines are good, great even, right up to the point when... they're suddenly not. In reality, not all machines are equal, and the spikier issue is the degree to which we rely and over-rely on them. Too smart for our own good, held hostage to our own creations, outsmarted by technology we can't turn off, or turned blind the moment someone accidently presses the off-switch, these are the classical 'man versus machine' paranoias.

In 'A Newer Normal and Deeper Blue', Nick talks of supercomputers and high-frequency trading programs. It all sounds pretty cool *and* rather terrifying. And it is both. It raises some damnably but appropriately loud alarm bells. What happens when we build machines to replace ourselves? While the ideal is that it frees us all up to go lounge on a beach and drink coconut milk, the reality is more that practices like financial trading are built on the basis of humans trading with humans. And the minute you introduce machines to do a person's job they don't do it the same way. They do it one helluva lot faster, so fast in fact that the system can't take it and everything could (flash) crash all at once. And while it's OK for your laptop to crash once in a while, or for you to crash a bumper car, no one's coconut milk is going to taste particularly sweet if the crash in question is the entire global financial system. A simple reboot just won't quite sort that. I'll leave my brother to tell (and terrify) you more.

Over to Nick.

When invited to contribute towards *Digital State* I was delighted. It allowed me to do the most un-digital of things, to take a 'step back' from the financial markets, to avoid the daily barrage of data that my Bloomberg screens so efficiently deliver, and to gather my thoughts on what is not just a cyclical or secular phenomenon, but one that is super-secular in nature and (of course) affects us all.

My interest in financial markets, I am sure, was driven in part by a sporting background. My game was cricket, in which you can measure progress in mass, time, distance, shots and runs. Finance, like few other industries (but like sport), allows you to numerically record and judge progress, to chart winners and losers on a real-time basis. Furthermore, financial markets sit at the very intersection of geopolitics and technological evolution, where any significant advancement is most acutely felt – all with the added benefit of measurability via price declines and falls, percentage gains and losses. My 'step back' and view upon the Digital State is from this intersection.

The theory of economics, the practices of financial markets and indeed the technologies of the internet are most interesting, not in isolation but in their collusion and consequence. Financial markets sit at the epicentre of the global system, the potential shock waves they can cause felt (more or less) everywhere and, by consequence, the fated path we navigate through our fast-changing world starts at this epicentre.

We have no historical precedent to serve as our guide. Straight lines of prediction (or navigation) cannot be applied. Esoteric macro and market risks now dominate; we live through a difficult time of monetary experimentation, political polarization, ever-increasing regulation, rising social tension and enhanced technological interconnectivity. The system is one of many moving parts, permanently moving. It is critical that we address these many parts and their risks today, in the hope that we may negate major problems tomorrow.

THE NEW NORMAL

I confess, **www.hangthebankers.com** is not my all-time favourite or frequently go-to website, but its very existence is sharp illustration of the current 'trust deficit' and broader sense of acute uncertainty. Never before have investors, policy makers and the general public been beset by so many conflicting messages about the economy and the markets. The concerns of major systemic financial failure, unforeseen negative consequences of regulation, and the subsequent volatility in asset prices are not shallow ones. Nor are they merely market 'noise'. They reflect deep, structural changes and realignments that are redefining the investment landscape.

Financial instability is often deemed a short-term risk, and (historically) this has regularly been the case. Witness: the dot-com bubble, the Asian financial crisis, Black Monday and 9/11. But such is the magnitude of change and its outcome that we must focus more on the longer-term challenges, consider the possible benefits and make predictions that feel grounded and wholly sensible. We must not be put off course by the short-term spikes in volatility that hallmark today's global financial markets.

This context, our environment, is perhaps best described as 'the New Normal'. We first discussed this term at PIMCO during our 2009 secular economic forum, an annual gathering of some 600 investment professionals from around the world, where we formulate our three- to five-year outlook for the global economy and its implications for our client portfolios. Many of those external to PIMCO questioned our then profound pessimism at the prospect of markets entering a multi-year process of deleveraging, de-globalization and re-regulation characterized by low growth, high unemployment and lower investment returns. Granted, the picture was not overly cheerful. Fast-forward four years and even the most cynical would find it hard to dispute that pessimism had become a present-tense picture of fact. Indeed, so mainstream is the New Normal that simply Googling the term will deliver 1.3 trillion results: it is the name of a TV series that airs on NBC, and the title of a social networking site. The next stop is most likely an official entry in the *Oxford English Dictionary*, even if only the online version. It would appear that a catchy turn of phrase has become a pop-cultural motif, 'uncertainty' the accepted reality of everyone's everyday.

THE FINANCIAL DEMOCRACY

The Digital State has its own defining technologies: the internet, miniaturization, digitalization, satellite communication, fibre optics and, of course, computerization. By extension, these technologies have defined the behaviours and practices of our Digital Age, at both an individual and a corporate level, and how they interplay.

The Digital Age has involved the inescapable integration of markets, states, technologies and individuals, allowing us all to reach around the world faster, deeper and cheaper. The internet has enabled business and social relations to acquire 'distanceless' and borderless qualities. Much of what we do and how we do it may now be conducted in this one singular 'state'.

The internet, an invention by scientists for scientists, spread across industrialized countries via e-mail in the 1980s, and then higher-speed access in the 1990s, with the most rapid acceleration occurring in the past decade via mobile access. Ever-increasing global interconnectedness has created co-movements in economies and financial markets – a point reinforced by Harvard Business School professor Rosabeth Moss Kanter: 'The world is becoming a global shopping mall in which ideas and products are available everywhere at the same time.'

The defining document of the Cold War was 'the treaty'. The defining document of the Digital State is undoubtedly 'the deal'. The Cold War was a world of friends and enemies. The Digital State, by contrast, has turned all friends and enemies into competitors.

The costs inherent in finding information, communicating and transacting have all dramatically reduced. Often, pre-internet, the cost of getting things done was so high they simply did not get done. This efficient mix of improved access to information, increased knowledge power of consumers and reduced transaction costs has mobilized a once inert buyer base, creating the potential to have a meaningful impact on global financial markets.

One cannot underline enough the significant importance of the trend of information availability to all, at all locations, at low cost. That said, information availability no longer provides you with the edge that it once did. It's the ability to *decipher* information that is rewarded. The constraint now is not how much information we can find, but more the question: how much information can we process?

THE HERD

The Digital State is not a place constrained by many of the barriers to entry that once limited the sphere of influence of the individual, and because we have wired the world into networks it gives more power to individuals to influence both markets and nation states – on an unprecedented level. We now have a shifting world order in the form of super-empowered individuals, who have both access to information and the ability to transact. The impact of this once dispersed and disparate group has the potential even to affect nation states. James Surowiecki of *Slate Magazine* argues that this impact has the potential to trigger the downfall of governments: 'The US can destroy you by dropping bombs, the [financial] supermarkets can destroy you by downgrading your bonds.' Irrespective of individual motivation, good or bad, the fact remains that we, as 'super-empowered individuals', are able to act directly on the world markets, *without* the traditional mediation of governments, corporations or any other public or private institutions.

Until only recently, individual investors had little collective impact. But as they have grown in size and sophistication, accessing real-time information through a variety of digital media, their influence has become much more pronounced. Investor aggression and sophistication are running well ahead of historical norms and, whereas the Old World order was one where markets traded on fundamentals, the New World order is one that often trades on noise over signals, and image over performance. Integration of many new entrants into the global system has the potential to destabilize the system.

Realism once posited that no single individual or minority voice could make a significant impact. Explain then how in the early 1990s, without the knowledge of the US government, a hedge fund (Long Term Capital Management/LTCM) in Greenwich, Connecticut (established by two Nobel laureates) amassed more financial bets around the globe than all the foreign reserves in China.

Of course, individual impact is not exclusive to financial markets. From the Nobel Prize in Economics to the Nobel Peace Prize, consider Jody Williams, the US political activist known around the world for the banning of anti-personnel landmines, and her important work in the defence of human rights (especially those of women). When asked what her secret weapon was in helping achieve the ban in 1997, when she mobilized 1,000 different human rights and arms control groups on six continents, in the face of opposition from the five major powers, her answer was simple: 'E-mail.'

Unlike the fragmented analogue state, the Digital State can mobilize en masse. In previous eras this political, economic and cultural homogenization occurred only at a regional scale: the Hellenization of the Near East and the Mediterranean under the Greeks, the Turkification of Central Asia, North Africa, Europe and the Middle East by the Ottomans, or the Russification of Eastern and Central Europe and parts of Eurasia under the Soviets. Perhaps 'regionalism' has become a thing of the past.

'TURN THOSE MACHINES BACK ON!' MACHINES NEED AN OFF-SWITCH TOO

> *Get those brokers back in here! Turn those machines back on! Turn those machines back on!*
>
> MORTIMER DUKE OF DUKE & DUKE, *TRADING PLACES* (1983)

At the time considered by many as a cheap marketing trick to boost IBM's stock price, the appearance of supercomputer Deep Blue was in fact rather significant. In May 1997 the chess match between Gary Kasparov and IBM's supercomputer Deep Blue was dubbed 'the brain's last stand'. Deep Blue was capable of evaluating 200 million chess positions per second, compared to a human's meagre three positions per second. After the inevitable loss, Kasparov said that he sometimes saw 'superior intelligence' and even creativity in the machine's moves. Kasparov simply concluded, 'Deep Blue sees so deeply, it plays like God.'

Imagine therefore if we could apply that power of analysis to financial markets. Well, we did. Deep Blue was a precursor. Welcome to high-frequency trading (HFT).

THE CRASH OF 2.45 PM

HFT is a trading system whereby all portfolio-allocation decisions are made by computerized quantitative models. The success of HFT strategies rests in their ability to simultaneously process volumes of information, something ordinary human traders cannot do. It is highly quantitative, employing computerized algorithms to analyse streams of incoming market data, and then implementing proprietary trading strategies. So efficient and prolific has HFT become that, in the United States, HFT firms represent 2 per cent of the approximately 20,000 firms operating today, but importantly account for 73 per cent of all equity orders.

On Thursday 6 May 2010, the Dow Jones Industrial Average plunged 9 per cent, only then to recover those losses within minutes. Temporarily, $1 trillion in market value disappeared in an instant, in what has been termed 'the Flash Crash'. In a five-month investigation led by the US Securities and Exchange Commission it was concluded that the market was so fragmented and fragile that a single large trade could send global stock markets into sudden spiral. In this instance, it was brought on by one significant market trader selling an unusually large number of contracts, which was in turn further exacerbated by HFTs starting to sell aggressively. As a response, HFTs traded nearly 30,000 contracts – in the space of 14 seconds.

What *then* followed was without precedent. The stocks of eight blue-chip companies for a short time fell to 1 cent per share, including Accenture and Exelon, whilst other stocks, including the digital (Apple and Hewlett-Packard) and the traditional (Sotheby's), increased in value to over $100,000 per share.

By 3 pm, 15 minutes after it had all started, it was all over. The market reverted to trading at prices that reflected true market consensus and value.

Former cocoa trader Nick Gentile put it as well as anyone: 'The electronic platform is too fast; it doesn't slow things down like humans would.' Certainly, HFTs may see deeply, but trade like God they do not. Mortimer Duke was more right than he knew when he appealed to 'Get those brokers back in here!' The human touch will always provide a deeper (or at least more agreeable) hue of blue.

Whilst 'the Flash Crash' was a substantial blip, the high-speed trading arms race being waged in markets had yet to claim its first victim. Of course, it was only a matter of time.

Enter Knight Capital. On 1 August 2012, the US brokerage firm Knight Capital lost $440 million in less than an hour, when the company's high-powered proprietary trading algorithm was accidentally set on autopilot, to buy high and sell low (which is not the right way round), losing money on each trade at a rate of 40 trades a second. Previous concerns held by Wall Street, Main Street and policy makers around the globe about structural flaws in the US financial system, and the over-reliance on computer-driven trading, were done no favours when Knight's chief executive said on television that the error was down to 'a bug, a large bug'.

Knight Capital had been the largest trader in US equities, with a market share of 17.3 per cent on the New York Stock Exchange, and a heyday trading volume of 3.97 billion shares per day. The 'large bug' did not however lead to Chapter 11 bankruptcy. Getco (another HFT firm) stepped in and acquired Knight Capital in a multimillion-dollar deal, creating one of the largest US electronic trading and market-making companies on Wall Street. Seldom has a cautionary tale had such a 'happily ever after'.

WHERE NEXT?

Trust is the most precious commodity in the financial system. We have already borne witness to its demise when, in 2008, trust in the financial system vanished overnight and liquidity evaporated. Contagion spread at previously unseen speeds, with financial markets nearly collapsing through that September and a wave of institutional stalwarts toppling. An infamous list included Bear Stearns, Fannie Mae, Freddie Mac, Merrill Lynch, Lehman Brothers, AIG, HBOS, WaMu, Fortis and Hypo Real Estate. When everything started going south, every hour brought significant news of change, as more dominoes fell.

Those of us who are the stewards of capital within markets must do all we can. With the widespread loss of trust in the financial system, we run the risk of becoming estranged from a generation of entrepreneurs and investment, right at the very time when markets need them most, to help spur growth, foster innovation and deliver economic prosperity.

The ubiquity of the internet has transformed the ways in which we conduct all business, and new ways lead to new vulnerabilities. I cannot help but sense that we tilt towards appreciating the benefits more than we respect the risks. Connectivity allows for amplification, and an isolated event in the physical world can have a ripple effect in the virtual world of tsunami size. Risk does not respect borders.

The more complex the system, the greater and deeper and potentially more fundamental the risks. Our daily lives increasingly depend on hyper-connected online systems. Operating systems and platforms, by their nature, are continuously revised and upgraded, and technological changes can lead a sentiment of uncertainty, in just the same way that any upgraded operating system can come complete with the odd gremlin or glitch or Knight Capital-sized 'bug'. We must build more resilience into our businesses, and into the financial industry as a whole, and we must adapt to a new set of unusual and complex variables, and do so in ways that are long-lasting and profound. All a lot easier said than done, but intent and pro-action start that journey. Firms with the ability to adapt and absorb change can and will succeed in a world plagued by heightened volatility, and we will all look back at this time as one of fundamental change, and one that further separated the strong from the weak.

It is hard to justify a stubborn faith in inferior, old-fashioned ways when technology has served as a beneficial accelerator to so many. Over the course of the last several decades, world trade has continued to expand and the subsequent efficiency in productivity has created millions of jobs, with trade and investment rising to such a degree that living standards have risen at a rate once thought impossible.

We have some decisions to make. Technology can be either a force for increased productivity or a trigger for accelerated social unrest that exacerbates volatility and is the catalyst for contagion.

Genuine responsibility rests upon this current generation of investment professionals. The challenge is one of delicate and considerable balance, of return generation and risk mitigation. It is therefore critical to rethink any approach to investing in a world of unprecedented uncertainties. Think: risk-factor-based portfolio constructions; increasing international diversification of investments; maximizing yields, income and position for reflation.

Investors have always had to live in a world where any decision is one of trade-offs and, whilst the principle remains true today, never before has the scale of possible loss been so great. We can only afford to get it right. We have to accept, perhaps even embrace, 'the New Normal', but we cannot afford to be beaten down by it. We have to navigate our way through it and determine its positive outcome. It is a matter not of hope but of conviction. This is the Newer Normal.

NJP
London

12 RESISTANCE IS POINTLESS

Vicki Connerty

> “Massive corporations and true giants of industry now have meetings about specific individuals who regularly post complaints on their Facebook page. There are numerous papers and articles penned daily about how best to manage social communities – and quite rightly so. Social media wields the power to seriously damage and even destroy a brand's reputation. Regardless of whether those customer complaints are spurious in the extreme, brands have little choice but to react, apologize and attempt to compensate. The customers, once bullied, ignored and dumped in a bottom drawer by the corporate giants, have risen up. The tormented have become the tormentors.”

I'd like you to meet... Vicki Connerty

I hadn't seen Vicki Connerty in nearly 10 years. In that time, she'd moved to Sydney, built a whole new life, nicely progressed her career, racked up a lifetime of holiday 'flash-packing' memories, and managed to look not only 'just the same', but arguably a bit younger. The Southern Hemisphere clearly agrees with her.

Vicki heads up the content division of media agency ZenithOptimedia, 'content' being one of those industry-darling nouns that has turned into an entire brand discipline.

I guess being a Brit living in Australia and working for an international organization puts you on opposing sides of the planet quite often, and so there we were, Vicki and I, drinking Italian coffee in a London side street, catching up and flipping back into the same rapport, the last decade immaterial.

Vicki is always high-energy, animated even when seated, with this rather brilliant balance of optimism and realism. Her glass is always half-full, but she's never up for drinking anyone's Kool-Aid. I've always thought she'd be great at stand-up comedy.

Into our second round of skinny, but whipped, double-shot lattes, Vicki was lightly frothing on the treatment of the English language, as adopted not by Australians per se but by her younger, cooler, hipster friends. A world of acronyms and abbreviations (think: wuz for what's, abt for about, obvs for obviously) was jarring with Vicki's grammatically correct analogue upbringing. 'It was when a friend of mine replied by text "Mabes Paddo?" that I felt compelled to answer, "Babes, mabes has the same number of letters as maybe."'

'Vicki,' I said, 'let me tell you about this anthology I'm working on.'

*

Candid and impassioned, Vicki's chapter is part confessional, part soap-box eulogy, part toast, part head-shake on the current 'digital dilemma'. You see, Vicki was a digital non-believer who's subsequently gone native. She hasn't been able to help herself, because 'social media' has proffered its utility, made its benefits clear. If you move to the other side of the world, then any tools that can help shrink space and time can be rather useful. And, while digital adoption was never a point of resistance for Vicki, there's a chord of clear bemusement running through her commentary, a bemusement that extends to how 'digital' has changed not only her personal 'everyday', but her professional one too. In the everyday world of marketing, 'digital' has risen up the agenda, has often become the point of the meeting, irrespective of which hemisphere those meetings are taking place in.

Firm opinions and common sense very quickly elbow past Vicki's opening tone of self-deprecation and, once she's at the front of the stage, it's clear that her view is a global one, endemic of our 'Now', with stand-up exhibits in the form of P&G, McDonald's and Woolworths, and also a rather fine near-final word from her mum.

The chapter considers the almost-out-of-nowhere explosion of social media dependency and (because they're naturally connected) the proliferation of 'social media agencies'. Whatever our Digital State is, know this: 'Resistance is pointless.'

Over to Vicki.

> *The Internet is a shallow and unreliable electronic repository of dirty pictures, inaccurate rumors, bad spelling and worse grammar, inhabited largely by people with no demonstrable social skills.*
>
> *CHRONICLE OF HIGHER EDUCATION* (4 NOVEMBER 1997)

I'm on a plane from London to Australia. I have 24 hours of total liberation from the internet to enjoy some device-free solitude and make some sense of the question: how is the internet changing everything? My hand has hovered anxiously over the keyboard for about six hours already, waiting for inspiration or indeed the semblance of a thought to strike, epiphany-style. In actual fact, I've spent about four of those hours grumbling to myself that there's no wi-fi on this plane, thus making it impossible for me to google 'internet' and 'Digital State'. The internet (or lack of it) is currently responsible for ruining a perfectly pleasant plane journey.

I am, in my humble opinion, not the ideal person to be either commenting on 'the Digital State' or attempting to articulate how the internet is changing everything. I don't feel remotely equipped to explain how the gods of technology went about literally making these changes, and I have accepted, after far too many years spent ringing IT helpdesks in a fit of frustrated rage, that my brain will simply never be wired that way. I continue to marvel at all the things the Digital Age has brought us, both good and bad, and I'm frequently awestruck by the e-mails detailing new web-related inventions that land in my inbox daily. The reality is that I'm no digital guru, and this chapter will only uncover trends unwittingly and statistics will be kept to the barest of minimums. In fact, by the time I've finished this sentence, there will probably be another game-changing innovation that I've missed.

That said, I do know that in or around 1991 (the exact dates are up for debate, from what I gather), with the arrival of the first-ever web page, our world changed irrevocably. At the time I, like many of my fellow fresh-faced undergraduates, was utterly oblivious to this remarkable and life-changing event and indeed I was busy telling anyone who would listen that I'd never end up in a job that required me to use a computer anyway – O, the blind naivety and arrogance of youth!

I genuinely thought I'd sold my soul to the devil when I gave up my leaky biros after three years and in 1994 bought a shiny new Canon Starwriter word processor to type up my dissertation. If only my surly student self could see me now, tapping away on my shiny laptop, with a tablet device to my left and a smartphone to my right. In truth, I felt distinctly underwhelmed and unaffected by the arrival of the web and the ensuing Digital Revolution. Nowadays the opposite is true.

When I actually stop to think about where we are now versus where we were then, I feel largely overwhelmed by the furious advances in technology and communication and secretly yearn for the halcyon days of handwritten diaries and clumsily scrawled thank-you letters to my nans at Christmas. Sometimes I miss the blind optimism of handing in a roll of film to the chemist and waiting a week for all 24 photos to be revealed as the work of a sausage-fingered, focus-averse idiot. I even miss the days of driving in the wrong direction for an hour because of a basic inability to read a road atlas. I certainly miss the reassuring weight of encyclopedias. I miss the simplicity of the pre-digital era. Just don't tell anyone.

I work in an industry that embraces the Digital Age, gazes adoringly at new technology and worships at the altar of all things clickable. I work with, and indeed actually enjoy, the company of those who often confound me with their seemingly bottomless pits of digital knowledge. I frequently ponder, how do they find the time to read about all this stuff? I can't ask them, of course, because they're far too busy Instagramming themselves or checking their Klout scores or creating a new Spotify playlist or mocking me for not understanding the true benefits of Apple TV. And, in fairness, I'm too busy googling 'Why is my Apple TV not working?' to care.

The coming of the Digital Age means that my professional world, the world of media, marketing and communications, has developed a wild-eyed unquenchable thirst for digital knowledge and technological advances. Our daily lives revolve around the best or next or newest way in which to persuade a wary and largely weary audience to buy our shiny products, and we have become almost obsessed with what might be the quickest and most effective way in which to reach them, connect with them, amuse them, engage them and make them actually care about us. The horrifying realization some years ago that TV advertising may not be all things to all people has set us off on a frantic and never-ending quest to find the Holy Grail of Communication. And the advance of technology and this digital world has opened our eyes to a whole new treasure trove of opportunity.

The opportunities are truly endless – apparently. The sands of change are constantly shifting, and the well-worn premise of 'Out with the old and in with the new' has never felt more relevant. As soon as something is in, it's out. As soon as something is new, it's old. I can barely keep up. And that's the problem. Five years ago, I distinctly remember a conversation with a good friend about something called Facebook. She was attempting to explain to me what it was and why I should be 'on Facebook', which in itself sounded like a ridiculous notion. 'It's this website where you add photos, add friends you're already friends with and befriend people you haven't seen for years, and then poke each other. It's fun', she explained. Unconvinced, I raised an eyebrow, told her she needed to get out more and said it wasn't for me. Fast-forward five years, and I'm living in Australia, I have 628 Facebook friends (most of whom I haven't seen for years), I have uploaded 142 photo albums and I have been tagged in 1,433 photos where my facial expression generally says 'Please don't judge me. This is *fun*!!' Ironically, the same friend who introduced me to Facebook got married last year. The invitation included the line 'Please don't upload any photos to any social networking sites.' How quickly we forget, I thought.

The global phenomena that are Facebook and indeed Twitter are truly fascinating. The way in which they seem to have fundamentally affected and changed human behaviour in a relatively short space of time both impresses and terrifies me. No longer restricted by time zone or extortionate phone charges, Facebook has become for me personally the most frequent way in which I communicate with the majority of people I know across the globe. I'm using the word 'communicate' loosely – I realize that simply liking a picture of someone's cat wearing a hat is not the highest form of communication. It's also become a cyber-storage unit where I can store memories and pictures of events and places and people that are important to me. It allows me to keep in touch with all the friends and family I left half a world away. Uploading one photo lets my family know I'm still alive when they haven't heard from me for three weeks. At least that's how I justify being on it so frequently to those non-Facebookers who raise an eyebrow when, like an evangelical social networking desperado, I tell them they too should get involved.

But while I've fully and (almost) unashamedly embraced the Facebook era, I still struggle with Twitter, despite legions of colleagues and tweet-happy friends encouraging me to get involved. I suspect this may be largely driven by the 140 characters limit that I firmly believe is at least partly responsible for the bastardization of our beautiful language. I'm thus refusing to get fully involved, out of both an old-school love for proper punctuation and grammar, and an ongoing disdain for vacuous celebrity tweets.

For brands, however, it's a different story. When I worked for a media agency back in London as little as five years ago, social media at the time wasn't even a commonly used phrase, let alone a dedicated communications channel for brands. Yet now, just a few years later, there are thriving businesses dedicated to it. Advertising spend on social networks is expected to reach US$9.2 billion by 2016, according to new research from BIA/Kelsey. There are experts and specialists in social media within every major media-buying agency in town, in what feels like every town. Some of the brands I work with in Australia even have a dedicated social agency as well as a digital agency on their roster, and I know this similarly applies across EMEA and North America, with so many now clamouring for a piece of the social pie.

Just like us mortals, brands have been forced to adapt to the Digital Revolution or face the harsh realities of being left behind. By adapting, brands have been forced, albeit reluctantly, to relinquish a large portion of control to consumers. In doing so, they have unwittingly handed over the power to make or break a brand. Power to the people indeed. Not so long ago, if we had a complaint about a product or a service, we might have called customer services and sat on hold for a few hours; we might have got into an angry and ultimately futile exchange with an adolescent store manager; we might even have fired off a 'Disappointed of Dulwich' (or 'Seriously Pissed of Palm Beach') letter to head office. But that complaint would have remained pretty much between the individual consumer and the offending company. Now, courtesy of the internet, all that has changed for brands.

According to Nielsen's 2012 Social Media report, 50 per cent of social media users are now complaining about brands and services at least once a month. It has never been easier or quicker to voice our discontent. We, the customers, can pop on to a product website, can bombard HQ with e-mails, can angrily tweet to our numerous followers, can write daily posts of rage on their Facebook page (that are shared with other customers as well as our own friends), can write a stinging review and share it all, instantly. In short, one's 'grievance' rarely stays within the confines of a linear 'brand-to-customer' relationship. Brands can't bury it in an overflowing in-tray to gather dust. It gathers shared momentum within seconds and can send PR machines into a frenzy of white-faced panic. No matter how many traffic light systems or response matrixes are put in place, there's another example every day of a brand or a service being beaten by the stick of social media, and no one is immune.

The mighty McDonald's launched their #McDstories social media campaign in early 2012, wanting diners to recall their great meals at McDonald's, only to find their hashtag predictably ambushed by a wave of less-than-positive feedback, such as 'Ate a McFish and vomited 1 hour later... #McDstories'. 'I'm Lovin' It' became 'I Wish I'd Never Asked Actually'. The campaign was pulled two hours later.

Closer to home in Australia, massive retail giant Woolworths handed their Facebook 'fans' a golden opportunity to berate them by posting on their page 'Happy weekend, everyone! Finish this sentence, I can't wait to _____'. Five hundred and eight comments later, many along the lines of '... go shopping at Aldi' and '... finish working at Woolworths', and it's probably fair to say that Woolworths' social media manager was no longer enjoying the weekend quite so much.

Massive corporations and true giants of industry now have meetings about specific individuals who regularly post complaints on their Facebook page. There are numerous papers and articles penned daily about how best to manage social communities – and quite rightly so. Social media wields the power to seriously damage and even destroy a brand's reputation. Regardless of whether those customer complaints are spurious in the extreme, brands have little choice but to react, apologize and attempt to compensate. The customers, once bullied, ignored and dumped in a bottom drawer by the corporate giants, have risen up. The tormented have become the tormentors.

According to Jack Daniel, a former digital manager for Procter & Gamble Australia, the power of social media is a huge threat to brands:

> *Social media offers a phenomenal opportunity to go to market in a new, efficient and modern way and, in industry terms, marketers often think it can demonstrate that you're a smart and progressive company. Most companies go straight to Facebook, as they think*

> *this is the way to show they have consumer-centric brands. But to get success in social media you need to plan very smartly with a long-term vision, risk management and solid pipelines of material and engagement methods, something most brands don't necessarily do. The result is this. Someone writes a negative comment that is within Facebook rules but wildly slams a product. The Community Manager sees the post and alerts the Brand Manager. The Brand Manager is unsure what to do and contacts the PR and digital agency. A 45-minute meeting follows and the decision is made to ignore the post. The amount of time and money big organizations waste discussing one person's wallpost is staggering. Social media is a great way to have a dialogue with your consumers but also it's a huge complaints forum, which can turn the most progressive corporate office into a swirl of confusion and debate. If a brand has a skeleton in its virtual closet, social media will find it and ensure more people see it, and see it on a page with your logo right next to it.*

Whilst I would never suggest that social media is the overarching symbol of our Digital State, and indeed one could argue that Facebook is the modern-day equivalent of a telegram (just a bit quicker and slightly less private), it does go some way to representing how far we've travelled and how the digital world has changed us in such a short space of time.

When I moved to Sydney in 2008, I sent an e-mail to pretty much everyone I knew or liked so that they'd have my e-mail address and we could stay in touch. I've just dug out that e-mail and there are 87 names on it. There were fewer than 100 people whom I liked enough to want to share my e-mail address with, upon leaving UK shores. And yet now, just five years later, I'm happily sharing my holiday photos, locations of my lunch dates and various whimsical musings with 628 people. So either I've excelled myself in the popularity stakes over the last five years (unlikely) or I've become far less rigorous in my definition of friendship (equally unlikely). The truth is that I'm no longer restricted to just one or two ways of connecting with people, such as via e-mail or phone, and consequently this leads to quicker, easier and more frequent connections. Now I have e-mail addresses, phone numbers, a Facebook, Twitter, Skype, LinkedIn, WhatsApp and even an Instagram account (for those who prefer pictures to words). And if all else fails you can google me. Frankly, there's no excuse for not being able to contact anyone any more. No wonder stalking is on the up.

The Digital Revolution has made it impossible to hide. It has effectively killed the once-reliable 'I did try but I couldn't get hold of you' excuse.

And yet there's a sense that things are already moving on. Facebook, once the cool new kid in town, has started wearing a blazer and a prefect badge and is wafting through the corridors of the Digital State school with an air of smug superiority. It is becoming a bit, dare I say it, passé. My much cooler (and, in fairness, considerably younger and probably smarter) colleagues and friends in Sydney, when they're not creating lavish Pinterest boards, updating their blogs or furiously tweeting their innermost thoughts to total strangers, are starting to sneer at my perceived loyalty to Facebook. And really, I'm no more loyal to Facebook than I am to a brand of toothpaste. Lethargy has simply been mistaken for loyalty. Not that I'm casting myself in this particular role, but, akin to the footballer's wife loyally standing by her errant playboy husband, I simply don't have the energy, motivation or frankly time to get involved with something new again.

For a while, I laboured under the illusion that the technological advances of the modern and Digital Age would liberate me from the shackles of time pressure and fling me headlong into a utopian life of hedonism, where I would be able to enjoy everything the world had to offer, whilst gaily checking the odd e-mail. I think it was in 2004 when my friends demanded that I hand over my BlackBerry battery in Heathrow's departure lounge (before we all went on holiday) that I realized I had a problem. Actually, that's not true. I thought they were just being melodramatic. I realized I had a problem when I waited for them to leave the hotel room before rooting through their bags and drawers, wild-eyed and desperate, only to discover them standing in the doorway, holding the battery and shaking their heads like disappointed parents.

With the benefit of hindsight, having instant access to my e-mails on the move brought a whole new world of pain. I thought it would free me up and allow me to get away from my desk without fear or guilt. I thought I would spend the time travelling back and forth to client meetings cunningly answering the e-mails that awaited me upon my return. I'm sure I threw the words 'better work–life balance' around with gay abandon. I genuinely thought I would save time and thus waste less, which would in turn make me enormously productive. Looking back, it feels as though I was half-right. Certainly, digital access on the move freed me from the fear of an overflowing inbox upon my return to the office, and for a while it felt as though I was indeed living a working life made easier, but cracks started to appear quite quickly. E-mails would be read but not answered, problems posed but not solved, the lines of responsibility became blurred, and the age-old practice of buck-passing came back into fashion as 'forward e-mail' became the new black and 'reply to e-mail' sat forlorn and forgotten in the corner.

Professionally, I was that person with 57 half-written e-mails in her draft box, who would of course *need* to finish them over dinner with friends. Socially, I became much like an over-anxious parent, constantly checking my BlackBerry for a flashing red light and rewarding only a glowing screen with full eye contact as opposed to my friends' lovely faces. My previous sparkling repartee and witty banter became limited to 'Has anyone got a charger on them?'

Frankly, not much has changed. Fast-forward a few years and smarter smartphones are everywhere, abbreviations are slowly murdering the English language, and opinions are great, but if we could keep them to 140 characters or fewer, please, that would be tremendous. *Time* is at an all-time premium. As a race, we are claiming to be busier than ever, and yet technology has theoretically made life simpler, quicker and easier. So why do we feel as if we have less time than ever before? The Digital State has stroked our faces and offered us time with one velvet glove and then whisked it away again with the other iron fist. We have so much to think about, so many new toys to play with, so much to absorb and learn and then re-learn about this Digital State of ours that it's no great surprise that we all feel as though we're moving at 200 miles per hour.

Logically, though, I know that the Digital Age has probably made life 'easier'. On a recent trip home and with this subject in mind, I asked my mother how the internet had changed things for her, and she replied without hesitation, 'Sat nav. You wouldn't have caught me driving round central London before sat nav came along. It's changed my life.' She makes a fair point, even if it wasn't exactly the answer I was expecting. Getting from A to B is certainly easier when you don't risk slamming into the back of a truck every time you check your road atlas. Thank God for the Digital Age indeed.

For my mum, the technological advancement of our world means she can get from Peckham to Pall Mall without any major drama and, even better, she can tell you to the minute when she'll arrive. Magic. To others, the internet is responsible for them meeting their fabulous new wife or husband, thanks to the wonders of online dating (one in five straight couples, and three in five gay couples, now meet online). To some, it means that via Skype they can see and talk to their family living on the other side of the world in full Technicolor glory. To someone else, it means he can upload a video to YouTube of himself singing, get spotted by an agent, signed up to a record deal, and go on to make millions of dollars and become a world-famous pint-size pop star called Justin Bieber. Thirty-one million Twitter followers can't be wrong, can they?

The internet, the web, the online revolution, whatever we're calling it has changed everything for everyone, but no two answers as to how will ever be the same. We simply pick and choose the parts that work for us as individuals and ignore those that don't. The Digital State is upon us; the opportunities are endless and the innovations relentless. The world has changed and resistance is pointless.

VC
Sydney

13 DIGITAL THROUGH A HUMAN LENS

And why we need to look at it that way

Malcolm Hunter

> "Technology transforms life, but not always as intended. Gutenberg imagined the printing press would enable more people to read the Catholic Bible, but it actually led to the Reformation. Benz saw the car as a replacement to the horse, but it created the modern sprawling city. The internet was developed to enable the military to communicate in the event of a nuclear attack, and look how we use it now. It is the law of unintended consequences. People use the technology in a way that its creators could not have foreseen. So it is in the world of brands.
>
> The Digital Revolution has driven us to look at brand communication through the lens of technology... and the technology-led view is based on false assumptions and flawed thinking."

I'd like you to meet... Malcolm Hunter

Sometimes, when you think of people, it's hard not to place them in context, to give them a 'scene', even if it's a purely fictitious one. When I think of Malcolm Hunter, I always feel tempted to place him at a pavement café, Les Deux Magots if I wanted to give it real detail, chain-sipping espressos, a packet of Gauloises close at hand, looking out on the world with knowing irony and cool surmise. I don't put Malcolm in a beret, that would be a cliché, and for the record Malcolm doesn't actually smoke, but he does tend to dress in black, and he wears black, a turtleneck perhaps, as I imagine him sitting, watching, thinking, a kind of latter-day public intellectual in the Camus or Sartre mould.

And just in case you were wondering, Malcolm's not French either, though he is fluent in the language, has worked a good portion of his career in France, and has a family home there. For me, it's enough back-story to feed my imagination, but it's really the bigger facts that build my street-scene, in regard to Malcolm's smarts and how he sees the world.

Malcolm Hunter is an impressive thinker, wastes zero time cutting through nonsense, and tends to be economical in his commentary, because there's little reason repeating yourself when you get it right the first time. He's recently launched his own consultancy, The Human Strategist, where he's applying his trade-mark insight and concision to the only-getting-harder task of modern-day brand building. I was hugely curious to read about how he'd tackle our Digital State.

*

Malcolm's written a manifesto – not a young angry man tirade against a world that doesn't understand, not an older angry man venting at a world that's lost sight of what's truly important. Malcolm's perspective and appeal are much more human and heartfelt than either of the aforementioned. It's a humanist's view underlining how real people behave, as *real people*, and how 'digital', how technology, can help in all of that.

When we start with how people are, rather than what a technology can do, then the implications for how brands should behave and how marketing should be approached change rather radically. No longer does it become a case of everyone meeting up and announcing with burning need, 'Let's build an app! Our brand *needs* an app!' (or a new, better, faster app, to replace the old one). The 'app meeting' is instantly replaced with 'What's our consumer up to, and why, and how can our brand help in that?'

Technology is a facilitator for meeting human needs, and that's the role of brands too. Assume the wrong start-point, worship at either altar, of brand or technology, and, no matter how loud and earnest your devotion, it's highly likely no one will hear you.

Over to Malcolm.

Technology transforms life, but not always as intended. Gutenberg imagined the printing press would enable more people to read the Catholic Bible, but it actually led to the Reformation. Benz saw the car as a replacement to the horse, but it created the modern sprawling city. The internet was developed to enable the military to communicate in the event of a nuclear attack, and look how we use it now. It is the law of unintended consequences. People use the technology in a way that its creators could not have foreseen. So it is in the world of brands.

The Digital Revolution has driven us to look at brand communication through the lens of the technology. Every day, questions are asked in marketing departments such as: what does 4G mean for us? What does the new cookie legislation mean for search? What are we doing about Pinterest?

However, there are unintended consequences at play. People are not using the technology (in the world of media, brands and advertising) as intended or predicted. The technology-led view is based on false assumptions and flawed thinking about how brands need to communicate in the new digital era of media. If we flip the lens and look at the impact of digital through a human lens (rather than the lens of technology), it leads to a very different conclusion.

The more technology transforms marketing, the more we need to put humanity at the heart of everything we do. The most human brands will be the most successful brands. It is especially true for the mass-market consumer brands that still dominate global ad investment. Here's why.

DIGITAL TECHNOLOGY HAS TRANSFORMED LIFE

Digital changes everything. As Mary Meeker points out in her 2012 'State of the Web' report, digital has transformed the way we connect with each other, seek knowledge, learn, read, photograph, navigate, find out news, take notes, file, organize content, shop, pay, sign for things, take holidays, fund businesses, hire people, design products, take care of our health and heat our homes, to name just a few. And it's only heading in one direction, namely more change at an ever deeper and ever faster pace.

DIGITAL TECHNOLOGY HAS TRANSFORMED MEDIA

Digital technology frees us from time, place and form. If we want, we can watch a movie on a laptop in an airport, read the news on a tablet, watch an ad on YouTube, search and Facebook on a phone. We are in control of what we consume.

There is more media content than ever before. It's difficult to estimate. Some people say compared with 2000 there's 10 times more, some say 20, some 100, some thousands. But, whichever way you look, there's a lot more media in a lot more forms, and 'advertising' now represents a much smaller part of this much bigger media world. In 1990 advertising-related communication was estimated to account for 5 per cent of total media in most markets. Today this is estimated to be 0.5 per cent or less.

People love the media. They spend more time consuming media (up to 8–10 hours per day in many markets) than they do anything else, apart from sleeping. Because there are now so many different types of media to interest us, brands and their advertising have a smaller cultural impact than they used to. The latest video game, who did what on Facebook, cats attacking printers on YouTube: all have stronger 'social currency' than advertising. The social impact of 'advertising' in this new world is less important than it was say in the 1970s, 1980s, 1990s, when it was a significant part of popular culture. People simply don't talk about Levi's ads, Heineken ads, Smash ads, in the way they used to.

By contrast it is the media we love that has the highest social impact and deepest consumer engagement. For every hour that *Glee* is on air, hours of online media activity are created by people chatting, posting, sharing.

Media's transformation has meant that people have become more powerful. Not only can they choose and control what they consume, but they can also use digital media to magnify their influence. Fashion bloggers have become so high-profile they have even started to feature in ads. Powerful interest groups appear out of curious places. Mumsnet, for example, played a very significant role in the 2010 British general election, dubbed the 'Mumsnet election'.

In this new world there is more media, and consumers are more engaged in it, have more control over it and more influence. Brands and their advertising are a much smaller part of this much bigger world.

DIGITAL TECHNOLOGY HAS TRANSFORMED MARKETING THINKING

Marketing and communications professionals looked at this new world of media and concluded that people would be rejecting mass media, and that the big opportunity was deeper consumer engagement and influence. There was an all-out attack on the traditional mass-marketing model. Mass marketing is by nature broad, shallow and occasional: big, imprecise audiences, one-way, TV-driven push advertising and occasional bursts of activity, punctuated by long periods of silence. It is interruptive. It relies on the consumer being trapped and passive. The language is targeting, strike, hit, reach, frequency, eyeballs – the language of warfare. It is a brand-centric model, based on forcing largely unwanted selling messages into people's lives. Invented for another era, it is challenged in a world where the consumer is active and empowered.

Surely, they said, the consumer will avoid all this stuff? The Digital Revolution meant a new model and way of thinking was needed. It's human nature to throw up a counterpoint, counter-argument, opposing view. In contrast to the old TV-led world, the new model is technology-led, and often described as 'digital at the heart', 'digital by design', the 'participation model' or the 'engagement model'.

The underlying principle of the new model is this: let the technology lead the way. In contrast to the mass-marketing approach, digital-led is focused, deep and continuous. By embracing the new technologies, brands can focus on valuable consumers and influencers, get them to participate in the brand and interact with it, be there for them all the time, and let positive word of mouth do the rest.

The language is about invitation, participation, permission, conversations, involvement, user-generated, liking, sharing, recommending. The extreme version of this model is a small number of impassioned consumers deeply engaged in the brand and spreading the word to a much broader group. It's a marketing nirvana where consumers spread the word about the brand free of charge. In this new world, it was presupposed that people would be engaging en masse with new technologies, and applying them to the world of brands and advertising just as they do in their lives.

The old 'lean-back' world where consumers sat passively on the sofa (supposedly) absorbing whatever was thrown at them was declared dead. While people were laying into the old model, nobody really questioned the new one. Many took it on faith. Anyone who questioned it was an 'old-school' reactionary. But there is a danger in this Orwellian new-think, a flaw. It is where the law of unintended consequences comes in.

TECHNOLOGY-LED THINKING FORGETS PEOPLE (AND HOW THEY REALLY ARE)

Technology-led thinking in media assumes that people will rapidly replace the old with the new. They don't. Yes, some people do wholeheartedly and rapidly embrace the new technology and reject the old, but many don't. They combine the old and the new to suit themselves.

Technology-led thinking in marketing assumes that, because people are embracing the new technology in their lives, they will use it in the same way for brands and advertising. They don't. There is a belief that brands and their advertising are important and interesting in people's lives. Unfortunately (with one or two exceptions) they are not. A few of us may want to have deep relationships and conversations with brands, but most don't.

Yes, loyal, passionate consumers are vital and need to be loved and made to feel important. But, in many categories, the technology-led approach ignores the fact that the vast majority of purchases come from the lightly engaged, the less loyal and the new.

The participation model is questionable because it ignores how the majority of people feel, think and behave in the context of their lives, technology and brands. It ends up focusing on the few to the exclusion of the many, and it focuses on what people may do in the future as opposed to what people are doing now. Both are dangerous for the commercial prospects of brands, which need broad appeal to succeed, and sales today, not tomorrow.

FIVE (UNCOMFORTABLE) HUMAN TRUTHS

The truth is uncomfortable. The consumer is often a figment of the marketing department's imagination. The importance of brands in people's lives and how we use technology to engage with them is exaggerated. The reality of life (and where brands and their communications fit) may not be what many marketing and communications practitioners want to hear, but it will actually help us build better and stronger brands in the digital age:

1 *Life is more important than brands.* People apply technology to what matters to them in their lives (life, death, the weather, sport, weddings, stars behaving badly, according to Facebook's 2012 study), and use it to avoid the things that don't matter to them. Unfortunately most brands and their advertising fall into the second half of this equation, not the first. In Google's Zeitgeist for 2012, only two brands appear in the most searched topics of the year – Apple and Red Bull. In the grand scheme of things, most brands aren't that important to people.

2 *Media is more interesting than advertising.* The media we love is media that enhances our lives in some way, stuff that entertains us, moves us, informs us and is useful. This is what we remember, talk about and pass on. Unfortunately most brand communication does not seem to fall into this category. According to Yankelovich, 59 per cent of people in the United States say advertising is of little or no use to them. In general, whether it is traditional or digital, we don't really care about or like advertising, especially the stuff that we feel is just selling to us.

3 *We're not looking. We're not talking.* We gather around the things we love (physically and virtually). Family, friends, romance, holidays, sport, music, movies, hobbies and interests: these are the things we look for, spend time with, share, and talk about. 'Digital' has meant we can access whatever we like, whenever, wherever. We are not out there looking for content from brands; we have plenty of other things to interest us. Just build it and they will come is the logic of many content creators, but they *won't* come, because they're doing something else. According to Deloitte, 80 per cent of brand apps have fewer than 1,000 downloads. Nor are people looking for continuous conversations with brands. Most of us would rather have conversations with other people. According to Nielsen, fewer than 1 per cent of fans have any active engagement with 'their brand' (and that's the fans).

4 *We are passive and lazy (and enjoy it).* We like to veg out in front of the TV, simply read the news, a book, flick though a mag (online or offline). We are not excluding all that (old-fashioned) passive entertainment from our lives. We are watching more TV than we have ever watched before (including the young). Only 5 per cent of TV viewing is time-shifted, and 98 per cent of all video consumption is on TV. For every minute of 'active engagement', there are hours of 'passive absorption'. In fact, active participation is rather low

(especially in the context of brands). Of all interactive ads, 99.9 per cent do not get clicked on. There is a 0.00001 per cent chance of a video being clicked on in YouTube.

5 *We are superficial and forgetful.* We don't know a great deal about brands, and most of us don't want to or need to know a great deal. People rarely remember more than two or three things about brands, if that. Many decisions are based on feelings, beliefs and a little bit of knowledge. Yes, of course, buying a car merits research, but the thought that goes into the soap powder, cat food or even banks and insurance companies we choose is often quite superficial. Because brands are not that important in the grand scheme of things, we tend to forget them and what we've been told unless they remind us on a regular basis. After all, if we only remember 10 per cent of what we read (and that's the stuff we want to remember), what chance is there for brands? We are suggestible, and sometimes a nudge is reminder enough, but out of sight is out of mind, and out of mind is not good for sales.

Apologies for bringing up the truth about human nature. What it points to is this: in our relationship with brands, we are mostly shallow and only occasionally deep. Occasionally some people want to go deeper, may want to find out more, hear what other people say, to get closer to the brand, for example if I'm a teen and Adidas let's me get closer to my sporting heroes. But most of us for most of the time have a shallow relationship with brands. The unintended consequence of the Digital Revolution for brands is that there is still a lot of passive, shallow media consumption amongst the many, and deeper engagement is (more often than not) reserved for more important things in life than brands and their advertising.

THE MANY MATTER

In most markets it's the big shallow group who account for a larger volume of sales than the narrow deep group. Mass brands need mass purchasers. In most markets, growth comes from increasing penetration (getting more consumers), rather than frequency of purchase. In most markets more volume comes from light purchasers (the less loyal and the less engaged) than it does from heavy purchasers. Most brands need a lot of people a little, not just a few people lots. In many FMCG categories well over 50 per cent of volume comes from lighter purchasers. Growth comes from engaging the unengaged: the many people who have no real desire to have a deeper, closer relationship with the brand, no matter what the technology enables.

Focusing on the human condition forces us to look at how we really are, not how the world of marketing and digital technology likes to see us. But this is not bad news. By changing the way we see, by looking at the world of digital through a human lens, we have the opportunity to create more powerful, exciting and engaging communication than ever before.

THE HUMAN BRAND MANIFESTO

We need to think about brands and their communications in the context of life, not technology. The brands that win will be the brands that are born out of life, fit into life and enhance life – in short, human brands. In this world technology becomes an enabler to create a more human brand, not an end in itself.

There is an almighty battle for the attention and interest of people in a world where the technology enables them to focus on the things that are important and interesting to them. Human brands think in human terms. Here are five very human principles, the starting point for any brand that wants to grab and hold on to people's attention in today's Digital State:

1 *How can the brand have greater importance in life?* We are emotional creatures. We are driven by our big emotional needs: fun, friendship, belonging, security, control, recognition, power and adventure. The satisfaction of these needs is the most important thing to us: to be a good mother, to go on adventures, to be attractive to the opposite sex. As society changes, the cultural norms surrounding these big emotions shift. Consider how our views on motherhood (and fatherhood) are constantly shifting. Brands can make themselves more important in life by playing a big role in our big emotions and the culture that surrounds them. Some brands have memorably done this in the past. Today, it is more important than ever. It is possible for all brands to achieve this, not just those that are in the more interesting categories. For example, both Axe and Dove made deodorants more important, by focusing one on sex (aimed at teen boys) and the other on attitudes to beauty (aimed at women). People notice and engage with what is important to them. The brands that

tap into the big emotional needs and resonate in culture will be the brands that people notice, spend time with and prefer.

2 *How can the brand make life more interesting?* It's the idea, and how it is told, that still makes the biggest difference to the effectiveness of any communication. Brand communication competes with all other forms of communication. It cannot simply deliver a message. To grab people's attention, and encourage further engagement, the communication has to enhance life. It has to have a value in its own right – to be entertaining, useful or interesting. It could be in numerous forms – an entertaining ad, a stunt, an experience, an education – but it needs to have a utility beyond a selling message. People love 'the John Lewis ad' because it entertains and moves, the Red Bull space-jump because it excites, Canon 'Shoot like a Pro' because it educates. Communication that enhances life will be embraced and exchanged. Communication that does not enhance life will be ignored.

3 *Where does the brand fit into life?* Our moods, feelings and needs change as we go through our daily lives. Media permanently accompanies us in every moment, enabling us to engage with the media that best suits us wherever, whenever. We can use the technology to welcome in brand communication or screen it out. Brands need to identify when, where and how they best fit into people's lives. By mapping out the emotional as well as rational journeys people go through in their lives, brands can identify those moments where people will be most receptive. Nokia launched its mapping service in and around places where people might get lost. HSBC, 'The World's Local Bank', famously dominated airports, the place where different cultures come together. By fitting into people's lives, brands will be welcomed into their lives.

4 *How does the brand make life simpler?* People don't want to and can't take too much in. The more technology complicates our lives, the simpler communication needs to be. One big idea adapted to fewer channels is more effective than lots of little ideas across many channels. People don't have the attention or the curiosity to work out complicated communication programmes. Many ideas, across many channels, simply don't get noticed. IPA studies show three to five channels as the optimum number, with diminishing returns setting in as the number of channels increases. Choices need to be made. Communication needs to be focused. Less is more.

5 *How can the brand be part of what people love?* We gather around the things we love. We are there in huge numbers. It's much easier for brands to be where people are and to be part of what people love than it is to try to force them to come to you. Brands should ask themselves what the people that they want to attract love, and how they can be a part of it, or even better how they can *improve* the experience. O2 promoting their sponsorship of the O2 Arena, and giving preferential access to customers, has been very beneficial to the brand. Gordon's Gin posted its first growth in 15 years by embedding itself in British food culture, through Gordon Ramsay.

JUST BE HUMAN

'Human strategy' recognizes that, in this Digital Age, brand building still needs to cater for the many as well as the few. Focusing on making brands more important in life, making communications enhance life and fit into life, does two things: it creates broad appeal amongst the many for whom engagement is relatively passive; and it invites deeper participation and active engagement amongst the few.

'Human strategy' challenges the digital convention that has emerged: where technology empowers consumers, so killing off the (old) mass-marketing model and replacing it with the new model of 'participation'. The presupposition is that, because technology empowers consumers to engage in brands and their communication, they will. The premise is *false*, because it ignores the human condition.

As the digital revolution continues to drive more profound changes in our lives the question is not: how can we use technology to get consumers to participate in the brand? The question is: How can we make brands important and interesting to people in their lives? Then: what role can digital play in establishing importance and engaging interest?

The more technology changes our lives, the more we need to put humanity at the heart of everything we do. As a model we could call it the human-interest model, or as a way of thinking: just be human.

MH
London

14 ESCAPE THE WALLED GARDEN TO THE PARADISE BEYOND

Greg Grimmer

> “The internet was supposed to encourage freedom, the proliferation of brands and consumer choice. The actuality is that it is dominated by the hegemony of super-brands – Google, Facebook, Apple, Amazon, eBay, Twitter. The web is increasingly offering consumers a paucity of choice – in search, in video, in social, in microblogging, in auctions, in retail, in phones, in operating systems...
>
> Forget Chris Anderson’s long tail. Consumer herd mentality has meant that the internet is like a docked Weimaraner – nothing wagging here except the tongues in Mountain View.”

I'd like you to meet... Greg Grimmer

I met Greg before I landed my first job in advertising. More specifically, meeting Greg was the path to that job. He interviewed me. It's a rare thing to keep in touch with someone who once interviewed you, made less rare of course if you go on to accept the job, work together and then continue to move within the same industry circles.

I remember my first encounter with Greg very well – and I know *why* I remember that interview. Because I enjoyed it. I genuinely enjoyed the conversation, thought, here's a smart guy, heaps of confidence, high-energy, properly interesting to talk to. The questions Greg asked were fun, you could have fun with the replies, and he showed a genuine interest in those replies, in me.

While I won't give away any of his interview questions here, I can confirm that all those first impressions I had of Greg still stand. And those qualities help account for much of what Greg has gone on to do in his career, from a crazy-young board director, to a commercially astute managing director, to a founding partner of an agency where his name sits above the door. None of those achievements surprise me, because you can learn a lot about people by how they conduct an interview – and if you're lucky, once in a while, you get to meet someone like Greg Grimmer.

*

> *Our computers, our tools, our machines are not enough. We have to rely on our intuition, our true being.*
>
> JOSEPH CAMPBELL

At the heart of this matter, this Digital State, is not 'a machine'. I believe the heart is a beating one, a very human one. And that's as it should be, new technology, new tools, allowing us to show our true nature and our potential.

Where Icarus was cocky, his wings his downfall, Icarus' father Daedalus kept his head, showed his character and flew safely to land. Daedalus was the inventor, had invented the wings in the first place, but we hear less of him, because Daedalus doesn't serve as a cautionary tale.

Greg Grimmer doesn't want us to fly too close to the Sun or, by consequence, crash into the sea. Greg doesn't want us to be a cautionary tale, and his message is clear – the big digital brands should have their place, and know their place, and we as consumers should be the ones to put them in that place. Greg's appeal is for a healthier perspective, where we retain, even claw back, our humanity, our 'true being', rather than becoming slaves to our own digital creation.

You see, the reason Daedalus had built two pairs of wings was so he and his son might escape the Cretan labyrinth, the irony being the labyrinth was something he'd created. Greg's been making wings, believes we can 'escape the walled garden', and his flight plan's a smart one.

Over to Greg.

The Digital Age was supposed to set us free. The Digital Age was supposed to be an enlightened age. The Digital State was supposed to be a global, boundary-free utopia where all our dreams were realized, our work compressed and our leisure time enhanced. But now we find ourselves prisoners to our own digital devices. *This* is the Digital State we are in.

This chapter will take you on a journey. It starts with the wonder and awe of our early exploration into the newfangled digital world, a cornucopia of choice that was first presented to us as the 'world wide web'. From happy beginnings, we then entered into 'the channel of tyranny', where our every waking hour is dominated by the plethora of digital screens in our domain. Perhaps finally we are ready to cross these badlands, begin a path to enlightenment, where we can wrest control again of our lives, and control rather than be controlled by the Digital State.

WONDER AND AWE

Those of us who will never be able to claim the moniker of 'Digital Natives' will always have one over on those for whom the internet is now just another part of the learning process: trigonometry – check; conjugating Latin verbs – check; remembering numerous online passwords – check; managing multiple relationships via various social networking sites – check.

For anyone over the age of 21 in 1994, the learning process of e-mail, the information superhighway, mobile phones and the rest of the technology charge that greeted the end of the last millennium provided a test not experienced by any previous adult generation. However, to be fair to us 'Digital Immigrants', we have acted more with the hope of the arrivals at Ellis Island at the turn of the 20th century, than refuseniks being transported to a hostile new land.

The awe and wonder provided by the new digital devices quickly saw uptake from virtually every audience. Gladwell's much lauded 'tipping point' is arriving faster and at lower penetration levels with every next generation of digital device. Mobile penetration hit 20 per cent, then 80 per cent, in a small matter of 24 months, broadband speeds became the prevalent internet modus operandi in an even shorter space of time, and the growth of tablets, smartphones and netbooks will outpace even that phenomenon.

We seem (especially in the UK) to embrace every aspect of the new Digital State. The UK's Napoleonic status as a nation of shopkeepers has been replaced by a new-found global leadership as a nation of e-shoppers. Every possible form of commerce (business-to-consumer and business-to-business) is not only utilized, but also greeted with incredulous outrage if a transaction cannot be completed in a completely virtual state. 'Clicks and mortar?' No thanks. 'Click and oughta be with me in a max of 24 hours' – this has become the UK consumer's maxim to prospective online retailers.

I personally took great pleasure in buying everything I possibly could as early as possible in the new world of awe and wonder. I wanted to experience the braggadocio of being the first in my network to have bought a book, CD (ironic, isn't it, how two of the most successful sectors that entered the e-commerce arena became two of the first real victims of a virtual world), holiday, car and house. I have set up companies, paid my tax bill, done share dealing and banking now for over a decade, and it gets easier and easier every year. Oh the bliss, oh the joy.

Just about the only thing I haven't got over the web in the last 10 years is a wife or a child, although the constant barrage of online dating and relationship site advertising I currently see obviously makes the former very possible, and a quick Google search for the latter suggests it's scarily straightforward.

It is too easy to forget these days about some of the very mundane tasks that were either incredibly time-consuming and laborious to complete in an offline world or impossibly tied up in professional service or government red tape.

I still remember the dumbstruck reactions of friends and family when I first called them from a mobile, showed them a web page, or set them up with an e-mail account. The Digital State truly can evoke awe and wonder, a place where we can be free of the drudgery of the mundane; the allure of 'something new' is now available to all of us, frequently. Yesterday's choice is wrong, but tomorrow can belong to me.

THE PROMISE OF FREEDOM FOLLOWED BY PAUCITY THROUGH HEGEMONY

The internet was supposed to encourage freedom, the proliferation of brands and consumer choice. The actuality is that it is dominated by the hegemony of super-brands – Google, Facebook, Apple, Amazon, eBay, Twitter. The web is increasingly offering consumers a parsimonious choice of suppliers. We have a paucity of choice – in search, in video, in social, in microblogging, in auctions, in retail, in phones, in operating systems. There seems to be an unbreakable trend in the virtual world that only one brand can survive in any one sector and, perhaps even more interestingly, it is then incredibly difficult for that brand to transfer its dominance to another sector. Perhaps the best example of this was eBay's investment into Skype (albeit that they did make a profit on their investment). Add to that the failure of Google Video, under that brand name, before its purchase of and subsequent investment in YouTube.

Even in tertiary services such as genealogy (ancestry.com), car sales (AutoTrader.com), dating (Match.com) and ticketing (Seatwave.com), there seems to be a clear market leader dominating. Interestingly, this also appears to be the case across platforms, with the same brands dominating again and again across PC, mobile and tablet.

Google should, of course, be applauded for managing to transfer their search technology to all devices, but it surely is the consumer's prior experience with the brand and not the bespoke product that has driven this?

I recently read yet another piece of hardworking research[1] looking into the 'unexplained' success of Facebook. There appeared to be some surprise that there is a key youth market that actively interacts with the website as well as the smartphone app! 'Have we really had enough of social networking?' the headline asked. What!? The biggest global phenomenon since Google and the world is already telling us it is all over? To be fair, the piece concluded that the time when we have had enough of social networking will only arrive when 'the next big thing' comes along, a point that coincides with some work I did previously, many thousands of moons ago in the digital world (about 2006). I used to have a theory about social networking sites. This theory was that they had a half-life, a bit like a piece of radioactive waste. The theory stood up quite well for a season of conference speeches, as Friends Reunited, Bebo, Second Life (I like to think my 'Get yourself a first life' comment helped this particular site's demise) and even the mighty MySpace lost favour with their previously fanatical users.

Then along came Facebook, and I needed another theory (or a longer time span to judge it by). However, as *The Social Network* (2010) was going big and hitting Hollywood, the latest piece of mass-owned technology (geo-tagging on smart phones) was spawning a number of threats to even Facebook. Gowalla, Rummble, Foursquare (and numerous other location-based services) had been gaining traction by getting users to 'check in' their location via their smartphones in order to let their friends, fans or mere digital acquaintances know their whereabouts.

Briefly, Foursquare became the digerati's new favourite social app. I was staggered to hear that over 4,500 people had earned an 'Epic Swarm' badge by checking in simultaneously at an American football game... until I realized that it was a 49ers' game in San Francisco, down the road from Silicon Valley, where smartphone penetration was probably about 200 per cent – therefore the market usage figure for Foursquare was disappointingly low!

Then Facebook Places was launched and pretty much killed Foursquare overnight. Well, not quite, and it is still around today, albeit the growth rates (and therefore VC valuation) are nothing like they were before the Facebook Places launch. So why is this?

Before starting my advertising agency HMDG, I ran a digital media company full of bright young things who had already binned Facebook as it was too mass, and not cool (or geeky) enough for their liking. No doubt this lot will be part of the 5 million current users of Foursquare and will, for the time being, carry on gathering mayorships and earning badges.

The problem for Foursquare (and don't feel too sorry for the founders, who took out $4.6 million in the last round of funding) is that the launch of Facebook Places will not only stymie their consumer growth plans, as Facebook Places is automatically added to Facebook profiles, but the companion service Facebook Deals also drives a sledgehammer through Foursquare's commercial aspirations. Facebook has spent the last seven years getting brands to set up pages and fan bases. These communities can now be carefully harvested, and the investment payback started, through offering Facebook Deals to those checking in.

So is this the future for new brands on the web? To launch, wait for one of the big players to copy your best bits and deliver it seamlessly to their larger audience base, and then quietly drift into the ethersphere and become a distant memory? It wasn't supposed to be this way.

Maybe the Instagram model is the better one, land-grab as many users as you can, as quickly as you can, and then sell out to one of the big players for a quick billion before they launch their own version of your easily replicable product or service?

But back to the premise that the internet was supposed to encourage freedom, proliferation of brands and consumer choice. This hegemony of super-brands – Google, Facebook, Apple, Amazon, Twitter *et al* – seems to have set the pattern for the whole state of digital. Forget Chris Anderson's long tail. Consumer herd mentality has meant that the internet is like a docked Weimaraner – nothing wagging here except the tongues in Mountain View.

Talking of Google, its corporate motto of 'Do no evil' is all well and good until you realize that it means it will attempt to operate in any sector, and if that means the wholesale dismantling of the current status quo within that sector then so be it. No evil has been done only so long as the consumer chooses to use the new model ahead of the old.

If Google's latest attempt at a social network, Google+, was a shot across Facebook's bow, then the e-mail service for all 1 billion Facebook account holders is a broadside against the Big G. There is no love lost between these two digital superpowers, and both their populations and their reach outweigh anything in the 'real' world. It is not so much a rerun of the Cold War, as a digital arms race in which stalemate is the most obvious lesson from history.

Those who have seen recent user stats from the United States[2] will have seen Facebook overtake Google in terms of time spent with each brand – the addition of Places, Deals and Instagram will have ramifications in even the most powerful boardrooms of the West Coast, and potentially the legislatures of Washington, Brussels and London.

THE TYRANNY OF DATA

If Google and Facebook are the superpowers of the Digital State, then the plutonium of this dystopia is Big Data. The collection of data has become a crusade by the powerhouses of the Digital State, and they appear to be playing the long game, despite the unremitting presence of the privacy lobby. This small but vocal group – who maybe because they choose as their weapon of choice the place known only as the 'bottom half of the internet' – seem to be making little to no headway in stopping all that Big Data heading off to ServerVille in the Valley. This lobby group, despite their good intentions, are not getting their message across in a controlled and articulate manner. I'm sure that I, like many, are reminded of the Ralph

Waldo Emerson quote: 'You speak so loudly I cannot hear what you say.' Only time will tell if the Facebook mantra of 'share everything' (drunken graduation photos, mobile phone numbers, previous girlfriends/boyfriends, etc) comes back to haunt the first Digital Natives.

Without torturing this analogy too badly the League of Nations – in the fight for data control between the superpowers of the Digital State – appear to be the archaic medieval legislatures of the real world, powerless to stop truly global operations collecting, using and moving data, revenues, taxes and technologies around their amorphous organizations, virtually (pun intended) free of any meaningful legislation.

Despite this, the inhabitants of the bottom half of the internet have yet to really prove that the evil, all-powerful Digital State cabal have used their monopolistic power to *harm* the consumer. They seem to ignore the fact that the likes of Google[3] and Facebook are key participants in the freemium economy, and have never hidden the fact that advertising revenues are their key source of revenue, in order to ensure their services remain free.

The best example I can find of 'digital hegemony' is the as-yet-unproven claim that Amazon are using 'price-setting software', based upon the browser being used (Mac users being seen as more likely to pay a higher price), or the cookie information showing previous keenness to purchase. For me, as a free market capitalist (albeit one with liberal leanings), I can see no difference between this and the King's Road branch of H&M having a different pricing policy to the Kingston upon Hull branch. Or, to draw further parallels, just try to buy a box of Nurofen at the airport for less than a fiver, when the same product is available for pennies on the high street. The Digital State here is not acting any differently to a savvy market trader in ancient Greece.

Moreover, the real Big Data issue is *not* primarily a privacy problem. OK, you need to be on constant vigil and ideally a Stanford computer science graduate to stay on top of your Facebook privacy settings, but this isn't really a) a problem; b) something in your control.

Well before Orwell's masterpiece *1984* (as an aside, as I write this, I am filled with some sense of horror that we are now nearly as far *past 1984* as good George was as far away from the eponymous year he was prophesying), there had been fears of too much information collection. While I am talking of data collection mainly by governments, or government-controlled organizations, and not by corporate behemoths, this compiling has always gone on and has always been feared, from the Domesday Book to the first census collection.

So, if not privacy infringement, what do I see as the issue? Well, for me it is not one that concerns individuals, but more so the corporate world. It is the explosion of data and the 'paralysis by analysis' that this constant quest for Big Data brings. This is perhaps most obvious in the world of web design, where the prevalence of A/B testing and multivariate analysis produces googols of data every day.

As a long-time fan of the data-driven (inside and outside a pharma lab) sport of road cycling, I have enjoyed British cycling's rise to the top of the tree, as led by Team GB's supremo Sir David Brailsford's mantra of 'marginal gains'. This is the same philosophy as used by Obama's digital election team, the Facebook start page development squad, and any countless host of 'web neeks' looking to improve yesterday's 'performance' today. However, what I see more often than not is a corporate state of bewilderment, a paralysis driven by new data falsely labelled as 'insight'.

How can we possibly learn when all we do is live in a sea of flux? If this is true of the enterprise world, it is increasingly true of our personal lives as well.

THE PATH TO ENLIGHTENMENT

The 'always on' culture, as afforded by our possession of multiple digital devices, has encouraged most of us to be jacks of all digital trades and masters of none. The do-it-yourself culture has been a bad thing. The type-it-yourself, design-it-yourself, check-it-yourself, send-it-yourself culture has led to a falling of standards across the board. The very speed at which we can send messages, documents, bons mots and love letters to multiple recipients, *simultaneously*, has made us all worse citizens in the Digital State, as compared to the former, slower-moving, more judicious and considered inhabitants of the analogue state.

Nevertheless I do see a way out of this vortex of digital horror. As humans we are physically limited by our senses and limb count and must curtail both the amount and the type of digital activity we consume. (Audiovisual content and the written word are still the mainstay of the Digital State.) Whilst *The Man Who Fell to Earth* multi-screen environments may be commonplace in every Western household, it is our future capability to make both personal and social decisions that will influence how we start to live better in the Digital State.

The omnipresence of cloud computing will mean that we will all have constant access to our own personal preferences for music, art, literature, drama and learning. We must start using the Big Data world for our own time-saving purposes. As individuals we must realize that sending e-mails is not the same as a face-to-face meeting or even a phone call. A FaceTime call will *not* replace the sensual meeting of two bodies, and the tangible look and feel of the printed page will always convey more than type on a screen.

Big and live events in sport, entertainment and pageantry are already more popular than ever before, brought together and then shared by devices of the Digital State. To say 'I was there!' will become even more prevalent as these experiences can become more shared. 'Making the unmissable, unmissable' can be more than an ad slogan for a VOD device – it can be the mantra for each and every one of us, whether that be a child's sports day, friend's birthday or key business meeting.

I shall end this chapter with my favourite quote for the Digital Age, one that we should all seek to remember in times of digital or data paralysis, one that perhaps should become the motto on the coat of arms of the Digital State. It is one that was written over a hundred years before the onset of the internet age, with the unrivalled perspicacity of one Oscar Wilde: 'It is a very sad thing that nowadays there is so little useless information.'

GG
London

NOTES

1. http://mediatel.co.uk/newsline/2010/12/02/have-we-had-enough-of-social-networking-yet/
2. http://mashable.com/2010/09/10/facebook-overtakes-google/
3. Although this is true now, I am always buoyed with a slight sense of *schadenfreude* that the twin geniuses of Page and Brin did *not* foresee this in their original business plan for Google!

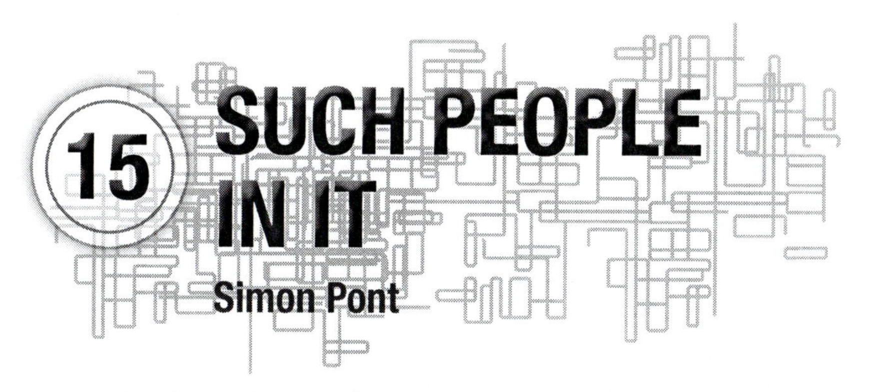

15 SUCH PEOPLE IN IT

Simon Pont

> When Team Romney announced Project Orca, a week before election day, it was hailed as an 'enormous advantage': a highly sophisticated poll monitoring system, built on a smartphone platform, taking the form of an app that would put real-time voting data in the hands of Romney volunteers, so they could then focus on low-turnout areas. It was a (high-)tech-enabled idea that sounded great – only the Orca app didn't work. It wasn't properly tested and it kept crashing. Volunteers complained, labelling it an 'unmitigated disaster'. One aide confided to the Washington Examiner, 'Orca is lying on the beach with a harpoon in it'.
>
> While you can't blame a whale-named app for losing an election fight, there's no question – digital and democracy are a long way from forming a perfect union.

Earlier, did I say there would be two chapters from me? Yes, I think I did – but, when it came to it, three just felt more rounded. It's funny how odd numbers can feel less odd. There's visual balance to three. Interior decorators, I've noted, just love putting three vases together to make a set. I've always liked paintings and photos done as triptychs. No vase arrangement served as inspiration for this third chapter. Simply, I liked the idea of a trilogy, and personally I wanted to take the theme of our 'Digital State' in a couple of other directions.

'Such people in it' came out of having lunch in London with one of the chapter contributors (Hans Andersson, Chapter 7), and watching the US presidential election results at the LA home of another (Bettina Sherick, Chapter 4). I love the way that disparate events and thoughts can connect, and in fact the two events connect because they haven't borne similar thoughts, but opposing ones.

It was over gourmet game pie and thick foreign lager that Hans and I talked of 'funnels' and how opinions and written words can break through and hit the mainstream. In amongst this image of a funnel is a very thrilling idea around digital giving everyone voice, and where talent outs. I've always thought that most people end up doing the thing they're meant to be doing. It's not a coincidence that some people become astronauts, others teachers, others accountants. People often talk of 'falling' into what they do, but if they do 'fall in' *and* end up staying there then isn't that more their doing than anyone else's? Outcome is hardly a matter of coincidence, if 'falling in' becomes 'sticking with'. And, while all I'm saying is that things maybe happen with a degree of design, 'digital' is an opportunity maker for many people. It potentially provides more options for folk, as it did for one former employee of Hans's agency, who was hugely passionate about interior design (and would have known a thing or three about arranging vases), and who started blogging about it, ultimately drawing a huge following and the opportunity to become a full-time and handsomely paid interior designer.

'Digital' has already happened for some people, has helped them to find their way in the world, to become who and what they want to become – and that's amazing. The second, opposing point, however, is that, while 'digital' can help individuals advance at pace and in their preferred direction, it's a tool with yet-to-be-identified utility as far as most large organizations and institutions are concerned. Of course, I'm not talking about digital-derived businesses, but those that pre-date, that started out in an analogue world, whose practices might still be very analogue. The democratic process, the very process of 'voting', couldn't be more archaic. The 2012 US presidential election underlined how far 'digital' has to go. 'Digital' is still borderline 'nowhere' in the voting process, and I think it's a suitably levelling example, just before anyone starts getting too giddy and ahead of themselves and wanting to join hands and skip gaily into a digital sunset.

'Such people in it' completes my own little trilogy on the Digital State, because trilogies can work rather well, I think, and have the right kind of balance. It didn't work for the *Godfather* franchise, and many would say the *Rocky* movies only went downhill, but George Lucas pulled it off with Episodes 4 to 6, and *Toy Story 3* provided a real 'completeness', even if it did leave me too close to tears. But it's OK. For you, what follows shouldn't involve tears, unless, that is, you happen to be a Republican.

The thinking goes that modern humans, the very same *Homo sapien* tag we go by today, started thinking in abstractions and concepts and showing some serious smarts around 50,000 years ago. Some anthropologists believe our epochal evolutionary leap, the so-called Great Leap Forward, was the result of some major genetic mutation, our use of symbols and language like a sudden superpower, as if just bitten by a radioactive spider or exposed to a detonating gamma bomb. Abstract Thought: like developing a Spidey-sense or being able to turn big and green when angry.

Irrespective of cause, whether near-instant or subtly incremental, the *effect* is that human 'intelligence' and 'thought' have been around for a good while. Take a generation to be roughly 25 years and we're clocking 2,000 generations of human endeavour. That's 81 generations in the AD, each and every one trying to work it all out, pursuing those damned-elusives called 'experience' and 'wisdom' and 'understanding'.

With each revolution, we take a giant leap. 'Evolution' is where the small incremental baby-steps happen, but a revolution is (by definition) a big shake-up. And now we have our big digital shake-up, a full-on judder, and I, like a lot of people, find it all really rather exciting. Certainly, there are pitfalls, with spikes at the bottom, but with care we might just be one step closer to those 'damned-elusives'.

Where we've been sentient beings for quite some time now, our latest leap presents new possibilities, where we can be and feel more connected, more widely conscious, potentially achieve a wider understanding of one another's needs, and even share and support in the *achievement* of those needs. Now, I'm not going to start penning some kind of *Star Trek* episode, infer the emergence of a sentient society, founded only on collective responsibility and pay-it-forward reciprocity. Simply, we are in the arc of a giant leap, where we're still trying to find our feet and work out where we might all land. The internet is a lot more than just realizing how much we love home videos of cats and find them funny.

Fundamentally, 'funny cats' aside, the internet *is* changing everything, or starting to. From the democratic path to the White House, to the way everyday folk work and don't work together. The internet is undermining how we function within many conventional organizations, as large and formal groups, and it's encouraging personal initiative and the formation of looser, more enlightened collectives. But then it's flat-serving a 150-mile-an-hour missile in the form of: how does wealth creation derive from people exchanging ideas and collaborating on fun projects? Because, even in an internet-triggered 'social economy', folk still have to pay their rent.

First up in all of this: democracy in the United States and killer whales.

DIGITAL AND DEMOCRACY

I had the fine fortune of being State-side on the day of the 2012 US presidential election. I had even greater fortune in being invited to an election night house party, getting to watch it all live, as everyone talked and drank and ate chilli and ribs (different plates) with crossed fingers. Would a disappointed nation oversold on hope and too little follow-through put a right-wing Republican in the Oval Office? The crossed-fingers present hoped not, prayed that liberal America would shout sufficiently loud and in sufficient number to give Obama another four-year run at making a difference.

Incidental of political persuasion or outcome, for me the 2012 US election showed how far digital has come and, more so, how far it has to go in driving the democratic process. There is of course no purer expression of 'the invitation to like' than the exercising of our free will within a democracy. The act of voting is surely the ultimate thumbs-up. This I mulled between mouthfuls of fiery house-party chilli and a friendly Malbec. When CNN called it (8.25 pm PST), declared Obama was back and that the Florida count was incidental math(s), the room went nuts, shed tears, hugged, and the party-people started to party, and tweet, and drink, all with fresh hope.

Folk only took brief pause when re-elected Barack Obama took to the stage, once more a US president, once more *their* president, and within the first three minutes of his victory speech he praised them, pointedly thanked each and 'every American who participated in this election, whether you voted for the very first time, or waited in line for a very long time'. Almost *sotto voce*, Obama then added, with what one sensed was planned ad lib, 'By the way, we have to fix that.' 'That', a long line, because we're not in a place yet where the Apple Store is offering any quick fix, say a free downloadable voter app. The only way to flex your right to 'the ultimate like' is the analogue way, a slow process involving a wait in line, a voting booth, a slip of paper and a pen. At some US polling stations, voters had queued for an hour, some sidewinding like hell in the key swing states of Florida, Virginia and Ohio. Parochial, archaic, yes; it feels as though both labels too easily apply.

As the polls officially closed, Obama had even tweeted:

> *Reminder: If you're waiting to vote in Florida, #StayInLine! As long as you were in line when polls closed, you can still vote.*

Obama could only be commended for how he was trying to work around the problem, administering a digital tool to a bureaucratic and physical-world dilemma. But then, hadn't Obama and his crew always been digitally savvy? Didn't such savvy explain why (as of November 2012), Barack Obama had 33.5 million likes and 2.3 million talk-abouts on Facebook, and Mitt Romney had only 11.9 million and 250,000 respectively? Certainly the use of social media has been oft cited as an 'in-touch' positive of Obama's 2008 campaign bid for the White House, when 'Yes We Can' seemed to say all the right things, 'feel' in all the right ways, and marshal all of the right kinds of people. And yet...

While social media has moved on a whole heap in the four years since 'Yes We Can', becoming more graphical, considerably more concise and ever more social, thus implying even greater potential to 'mobilize and influence', analysts were quick to analyse how the vast majority of presidential campaigning dollars went 'above the line', on mass-media and push-marketing techniques. The figure spent on the 2012 US presidential election ran to $6 billion, an all-time high in any presidential race, and negating the need for anyone to ask: 'What is the cost of *free* speech?' Of that $6 billion, the

New York Times reported that Obama had overcome 'an unprecedented torrent of advertising'.

With donations gratefully received from the likes of Goldman Sachs, Bank of America and Morgan Stanley, Romney had gone all in, buying mass media at top-dollar rates, reportedly throwing money at the problem of how to outshout and overpower Obama.

> *The disparity, with Republicans spending $41.7 million and Democrats spending $23.5 million, illustrates a strategic gamble on behalf of the GOP presidential nominee [Romney] to bury President Barack Obama and burn past him during the closing weeks of the campaign.*
>
> WWW.HUFFINGTONPOST.COM, 15 OCTOBER 2012

In the final analysis, it was clear that the digital young guns lost out to the media old guard, who'd been busy burning campaign dollars. Where Zac Moffatt, Romney's campaign digital director, had declared pointedly and plainly in the *New York Times* (October 2012), 'The more people you talk to, the more likely you are to win', Romney's 'strategic gamble' was not to talk *to* the American people, but to shout *at* them, with a 'torrent' of TV ads and faith-shaking vitriol.

In point of (balanced) fact, TV airtime buying was the mainstay of *both* Romney *and* Obama's media schedule. Where Romney spent $492 million on airtime in 2012, Obama spent $404 million. It wasn't a case of which side deployed *digital* communication best, more a case of which side tanked less. And it played out that Romney's side mostly talked a far better digital game than they played.

When Team Romney announced Project Orca, a week before election day, it was hailed as an 'enormous advantage': a highly sophisticated poll monitoring system, built on a smartphone platform, taking the form of an app that would put real-time voting data in the hands of Romney volunteers, so they could then focus on low-turnout areas. It was a (high-)tech-enabled idea that sounded great – only the Orca app didn't work. It wasn't properly tested and it kept crashing. Volunteers complained, labelling it an 'unmitigated disaster'. One aide confided to the *Washington Examiner*, 'Orca is lying on the beach with a harpoon in it.' It was later reported that the Orca debacle cost Romney thousands of votes.

Of course, you can't blame a whale-named app for losing an election fight. I was still clear on this thought, even after finishing my second bowl of chilli and finding repeat glasses of Malbec far too easy to swallow. It's only ever good to get the tech right, but getting the tech wrong is unlikely to determine political destiny.

Powerful, persuasive communications, born of strong, simple, single-minded ideas, consistently told: I'd argue that's the winning formula. Now a keen tweeter, Alastair Campbell (director of communications and strategy to Tony Blair) formerly had an anti-tech stance that was a telling one, given his Svengali skill in positioning New Labour with the media and electorate alike:

> *For the entire period I worked for Tony Blair, almost a decade, I did not use a computer. This was not any old decade of course, but the one in which computer technology advanced further and faster than during any period in our history.*

Digital and democracy are a long way from forming a perfect union, where the former has yet to provide the latter with a well-oiled path to electoral voters. In time, it will happen, though, like a murmuration of caffeine-crazed starlings, the 'social economy' is a shape yet to take coherent form.

While digital infancy, tech teething trouble, and old-fashioned mass-media practices all played their part in Election 2012, I think there is a fourth dimension to consider. While having a highly political, heavily bureaucratic skew, government is little different to any other large institutional body, and I believe institutions per se are struggling.

BIG COMPANIES NO LONGER WORK SO WELL

So this is where it gets a little punchy.

Once upon a time, 'decision by committee' was a tenable (even productive) process. Now it is not. Committees don't decide quickly enough, and seldom do they think, feel and act as one. There are almost always a few conflicting agendas and personal motives, making for delay and non-commitment.

By exception, large but autocratic organizations as formed in the maverick image and attitude of their founder still stand a chance, because strong and inspiring leadership can railroad through damned-minded purpose. Think: Apple's Steve Jobs, Virgin's Richard Branson, GE's Jack Welch, all hugely known, revered even, because they have (or had) the ability to define, align and drive a large institutional collective. It tends to be that either the institution stifles entrepreneurialism or it is led by an entrepreneur. And, of course, you only want to work in and for the latter – or be one, an entrepreneur, yourself.

There are many large and *less* autocratic companies, in many sectors, that I believe are feeling pretty damned sour about the whole digital deal. Because in the face of CHANGE, individually and institutionally, there are really only two ways to go: you either cheer or you panic. You either feel buzzed by the excitement and thrill of it all, or you entrench, anticipating a cold winter and a tough fight. Embracing or going foetal, optioning front foot or back, either action is first a decision, an *emotional* decision.

Of course, let's be clear, not all change is good. Far from it.

Certain changes are true-blue and out-of-the-same stinkers. And you'd rightly counter, in the face of any change, what about a little pause and consideration? What first of a little shrewd judgement and formulated thought? It's yes to both, of course. Think; *then* act. I'm all for that. I'm not proposing introducing bulls to china shops, but my underlining (overarching if you prefer) point is this: change, by its nature, is a shift in circumstances, with unknowable consequences. The bottom line is: we can either feel good or we can feel bad about the loud door-knock of 'unknowables'.

What we're living through is technologically assisted, turbo-charged change. Social–economic–political... *change*, with a ruddy great big Boeing jet engine strapped on its back. And it's the *emotional* response to this kind of acceleration that I believe is key. We can either put our hands in the air or our hands over our eyes.

At an organizational level, I get to see both responses first-hand and at pretty close quarters. I get to sit in meeting rooms with clients, the custodians of global brands and businesses that stretch across the planet, and it seems to me that businesses the world over are in only one of two states of seeing (and feeling): they are either open-minded hives keen to experiment and learn and adapt, or they are closed shops, gated, guarded, guarding, even resenting the shifting sands beyond their walls.

The music, publishing and movie (retail) industries are three sectors that are (arguably) at the sharp end of a world gone digital. Their business models pre-date digital. They were born in an analogue world, operating to the tramline practices of physically making, physically distributing, and then promoting through controlled mass media. Then 'digital' came along, robbed their margin, undermined their control and made their 'product' potentially non-tangible, because it stripped away the need for box sets and disc cases, turning proud physical collections into dust-gathering clutter. Of course, the irony is that, while they may sometimes feel as if their heads are on the chopping block, the music, publishing and movie industries are potentially future-proof, because their true product is entertainment and escapism, a 'product' that people will always crave and pay for.

But, without hesitation or pause (I have no doubt), the music industry would gladly turn back the clock if they could. Hell, they'd bite your whole arm off just to get within fingertip of a reset button. Record a track, bulk-buy and burn a truckload of CDs, send them out on to the shelves of the high-street stores, and then buy poster space and TV airtime to drum up weekend shopper purchase. Ah, the good old days, when life was simple and sepia, with few parts, all controllable, and a healthy margin baked in!

The last time I visited HMV, I was near overcome with bone-aching depression. Adapt or die? Five minutes inside an HMV was like witnessing 'old retail's' final convulsions. Not long now, I thought,[1] with a spring returning to my step only once I had inhaled the thick London air back on the pavement outside. I had left empty-handed, not tempted to buy impulse jelly babies, baseball caps, T-shirts, discounted DVDs or 'bargain' paperbacks.

I've heard global television broadcasting companies very openly acknowledge that they remain baffled by our convergent world. They openly invite industry debate and professional discourse, but they freely admit that they are 'not going to rush into anything'. They add, 'We don't want to commit just yet. We'll go slow in this space. There are risks.' For 'space', they're talking about social media, about how people like to talk and interact. To such 'statements of reservation', as I hear them it's as if I can see cobwebs gathering, the walls fossilizing, the business historians ready to ink a new addition to the column of cautionary tales. 'There are risks.' The biggest risk is in resenting the changes around you. 'We'll go slow in this space.' Then get left behind.

You don't have to be the very first in line, but you do have to get up off the couch. There's advantage in being the first-mover; there's advantage in being the second. The ultimate reason is that both are *moving*. In the history of humanity, this is the least sympathetic age for indulging procrastination, with the only past exception being our dealings with fast-moving, sharp-toothed combatants across a frisky food chain. 'Man or meal?' was no moment or 'space' to go slow in either.

I perfectly acknowledge that loss of control over the message you 'put out there', and how it may be echoed, rehashed or derided, is hard to stomach for most organizations and big brands, and particularly for any that have formerly enjoyed high levels of control. How can you keep a brand, a campaign, a company's PR 'on message' the moment it enters the ether of unpoliced cyber-chatter? It's almost impossible; you of course can't. You have to roll with it and hope for the best.

I've seen 'Heads of Business' shake their heads, throw their arms aloft and proclaim with wide eyes: 'We tried! We tried Facebook. We tried Twitter. We wanted to control the conversation and, you know what, we couldn't control it!' 'Stop wanting to control the conversation' is the only answer. Learn to loosen that grip. Be part of the conversation; get in the mix; be happy if you manage to *start* a conversation. Look out over the lake and lob in a ruddy big rock, ripple the zeitgeist, and then watch (even try to enjoy) what happens next. In the want to be liked and the hope to influence, chasing after a Twitter feed is pretty reactionary and short-sighted. The answer to influence does not lie in chasing technology's tail. I believe it's this not wanting to get stuck in and have a go, of holding back rather than taking to the dance floor and dancing as if you just don't care, that will be the downfall of many companies. Reluctance to try, and to adapt as necessary, can only end in tears for organizations.[2]

In the Digital Age, companies (and individuals) need to be less fixed on who and what they are. Terrifying as it might be, they need to be more naive, more childlike, more open to constant redefinition. Michael Lewis said:

> *When capitalism encourages ever more rapid change, children enjoy one big advantage over adults: they haven't decided who they are. They haven't sunk a lot of psychological capital into a particular self.*[3]

INDIVIDUALS CAN WORK VERY WELL

For me, the Digital State is all about revisiting and (in a good many cases) ripping up former definitions. It's a cheerful kind of iconoclasm, a bloodless kind of revolution. Consider the medium by which you're reading this, and the long-held definition of a book:

> *BOOK – noun*
>
> *Portable written or printed treatise filling a number of sheets, fastened together, sewn, or pasted hinge wise.*
>
> OXFORD ENGLISH DICTIONARY

Printed? Numbers of sheets? By past definition, today a book is no longer just a book. Certainly, a 'book' prevails as a collection of articulated ideas and themes – but it's no longer bound to its physical spine. We now have iPads, Kobos and Kindles, where the very discreet nature of e-books has made the likes of EL James very wealthy indeed. And it's not a contentious and emotive case of pixel versus page, screen versus paper. It's not a publishing format death-match that has to be terminal for one party. It's much more interesting and expansive than that – and one small example that gives broader sense to the kind of revolution 'digital' is.

Gandhi stressed that a 'non-violent revolution is not a programme of seizure of power. It is a programme of transformation of relationships, ending in a peaceful transfer of power'.[4] In this 'Digital Revolution' of ours, the true opportunity sits with 'the Individual', the opportunity being one of potential transformation, to explore and express passions and interests, to pursue convictions, where the destination is unknown. Yes, it is a potential two fingers to 'the Man' and the status quo, and it is potentially non-conformist in spirit, but it is happily bloodless, the two fingers never becoming a pitchfork.

But the opportunity for 'the Individual' is one that comes with small print, print that has everything to do with Michael Lewis's comment on 'psychological capital' and self-definition. The mandatories stipulate some bravery and the taking of risk. Whatever 'psychological capital' was formerly invested in the 'self', there now has to be a willingness to walk away and start afresh. Break down, rebuild and make new, that's the idea of it.

You're an insurance underwriter who wants to become a landscape photographer? A primary school teacher who wants to design glass vases? A copywriter who wants to be an interior designer? No reinvention is without risk. 'Self-defining by deed' is insanely exciting, but the act is also potentially undermining of the *former* self, and that's rather daunting, even when it is in the cause of 'making better'. It's easier for children to do it, it's harder for adults, and it's close to impossible for certain kinds of organizations. Organizations typically move slowly and flinch from 'transformation agendas'. Individuals (by contrast) can act fast, and if they incline to chance their arm they don't need sign-off from a boss or boardroom.

In the Digital State, I believe 'the Individual' is rising ascendant over 'the Institution'. There's a 'transfer of power', as Gandhi describes it, brought on by new means and partly out of necessity. There are no more 'jobs for life'. There is a fast-ailing sense within the private sector that 'the Company' will do the right thing. The only thing 'the Company' will do is pledge allegiance to its stakeholders and a commercial imperative. The moment it becomes everyone for him- or herself, employees rightly start looking for the angles and playing the short-game, and who can blame them?

Changing context, as created by the internet, is creating a new generational breed of entrepreneurs and creative independents, who know there's no guaranteed PAYE comfort blanket, but also no pay-grade to keep them in their place, and where the upside is that they could, even at a massive stretch, be the next Mark Zuckerberg.

THE FUNNEL FLIPS

Everyone now connected can respond to the internet's call – to pass comment, critique and create. That kind of open invitation didn't use to be there, but the internet has taken tiger-sized bites out of former paradigms and then spat the gristle far across the room. Put less gruesomely, 'the funnel' has flipped.

Just imagine a funnel for a moment, an average, everyday kind of funnel, a round, wide opening reducing to a narrow neck, a spout. Two holes, two very different apertures, the one end very different to the other. A funnel could easily be applied to the mass-media principles of an analogue age (broadly the 1950s to the 1990s), where the funnel's entry and exit points were very clear. The entry point started narrow.

You had high competition, lots of people clawing and clambering for space in the narrow spout, to create content and share ideas. Entry was not just narrow, but also gated, controlled by a broadcast media elite. You couldn't of course just shoot a 15-minute documentary on your smartphone and upload it to Vimeo. It was with much luck, bundles of tenacity and talent (and ideally some helpful nepotism) that you might get employed or commissioned by a broadcaster and ultimately get to make some kind of 'content', but the percentage likelihood of destiny making you part of that chosen few was, well, as slight as the neck of the funnel. Of course, the mass media that delivered the content was always then going to find its audience, because it was as defined; it was 'mass'. From an audience point of view there was very limited choice: very few TV stations and a modest number of newspaper and magazine titles.

The funnel flips

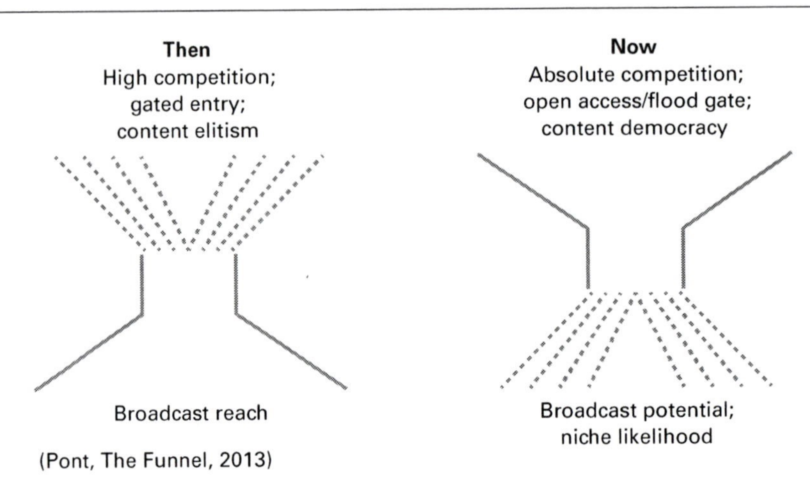

(Pont, The Funnel, 2013)

From analogue came digital, and the funnel went 180. No more starting with a narrow spout. It's open season, wide open, where everyone's invited to the party. The internet has put 'everyone in the room', and there's tons of elbow room. How we respond, who we meet, introduce ourselves to, what we reveal of ourselves, what we curate and produce: this is all up to us.

That's really quite amazing, don't you think, in a 'talent will out' kind of way? And I'm not of course talking just about individual endeavours, but about the forging of new collaborations. Tim Berners-Lee said:

> *I wanted to be able to have it [the internet] as a very collaborative play space, and still the web hasn't fully provided what I wanted then in terms of being a really powerful collaborative medium.*[5]

When I read this quote from Berners-Lee, three words popped, exploded even, right at me. I thought, 'Yes! That's it! A "collaborative play space". The guy who invented it has just nailed defining it.' The Digital State, essentially, is about collaboration, of encountering and sharing new ideas, perhaps leading to partnerships and original outcomes, sparking new directions.

The internet *connects* people. It connects consumption (people buying) to production (people making and creating, where something may potentially be sold). Consider the success of Craig's List, Gumtree, eBay. Consumers and producers: connected by a PayPal or a 'One-Click' purchase. And all the time producers are becoming more closely connected to *other* producers. When you mash Craig's List with LinkedIn, you start to get a sense of what 'the social economy' could really be all about. For 'social economy', think: connectivity leading to a transaction of human skills, of creativity and specialism, the exchange leading to creation and originality, where the produced outcome generates new value. The real thriller in all this is it's so open-ended, so dependent on who meets who. It's the convergence of newly introduced talents that defines what the thing becomes.

COLLABORATION, CASTING AND CHARGING FOR IT

Oscar Wilde once said, 'The world is a stage, but the play is badly cast.' Always pithy, I think the line captures Oscar on a black day, pissy of mood. Maybe he'd been slammed with a parking fine or harangued by a chaser from the tax office? (We've all been there.) On the days when the cosmic forces of bureaucracy and mild persecution don't strike, I tend to feel pretty good about the people in my world. I think the play is well cast, because I hold myself responsible for making the casting decisions.

When my novel launched, I made a short film, three minutes long. I liked the idea of making a movie trailer to promote a book, hoped it might create a bit of buzz. The 'short' was made on a shoestring, brought in on a production budget close to the cost of a nice pair of brogues. What I found most affecting was how so many talented, skilled people bought into the creative idea and simply lent their expertise, time and talent free. They gave of themselves in exchange for no more than a couple of beers and a few slices of pizza. I mentioned this to my director, Babis Tsoutsas, who replied with wonderful simplicity: 'There are a lot of talented people out there.'

I find this truth humbling, and inspiring, and even a little tragic. People with talent are crying out to use their talent. They're looking to do something exciting and rewarding, and doing it free is still a whole lot better than not doing it at all.

'O brave new world, that has such people in it'; it's this line from *The Tempest* that spars with and then, for me, easily bests Wilde's bleak view. Of course, feeling creatively rewarded nourishes only to a point. 'Such people' still need to eat. Caitlin Moran's cutting assessment of the internet layers a further truth, which would probably make Wilde smile:

> *The internet is currently split into two halves. The bit that's making all the money is the bit selling holidays, dishwashers, weekly groceries and fake V1111agra. It's San Francisco during the Gold Rush over there. Then there's the other half that makes*

> *no money at all – where you can download music, films, TV shows, photography and journalism for free. When Lily Allen spoke up against downloading, the internet exploded, castigating her for wanting to get paid for her work. We're at the odd point where it now seems reactionary for artists to want to earn a living. By way of contrast, the comparethemeerkat.com crew are driving around in a golden hovercraft, wiping their arses with fifties.*[6]

Caitlin Moran writes for *The Times*. You have to pay to read *The Times* online. They call it a 'paywall', meaning it's not a freebie. And, quite frankly, why should it be free? It's *The Times*, after all, and if you want that kind of journalism, from quality journalists who themselves need to eat, then there should be a price tag. Those criticizing Lily Allen's gripes about getting screwed on residuals just sound naive, foolish, actually both.

However, if you *want* to be a journalist and don't work at *The Times*, or you're a singer–songwriter without a record deal, then your path to recognition and revenue is most likely going to have to start with a few freebies, and that's where the internet comes into its own. Gain a big enough following based on your uploaded freebies, and you can create your own demand. Then you might just be in the market for your own golden hovercraft (as well as having an alternative use for your fifties).

NO BOUNDARIES

Technology is moving at a lick. It's relentless, causing never-ending change, and change worries people (and it worries institutions even more). It pulls up the rug we're all standing on, to reveal there is no floor. Some feel vertigo, some fall, and some know how to hover. They don't know where they learnt how, whether it was a spell they picked up from reading Rowling, or an invisible jet pack they put on one time and forgot about... but they do not fall. They are open-minded to change, prepared to adapt.

It felt fine when technological change appeared to restrict itself to technology: the falling cost of VHS tapes, then a CD, then a DVD, then a Blu-ray, then a hard drive. When technology operates within a defined space, as relates to gadgets and 'machines', most feel pretty relaxed about getting to feel as if we're beta-testing the output of Q Branch. But then technology went invisible, became 'digital', and it crossed over. It no longer restricted itself to the confines of some kind of physical shell, as operating and sparking within a box of plastic or metal. Software fast evolved out of being programming code, and spreadsheets, and presentation slides, and turned into 'apps', finger-touch software offering help on almost anything, even able to 'augment' our physical world. And the technology crossover has now entered a bigger universe, the ultimate universe, the social universe.

Where the internet was once about computers connecting to computers, it's now about people connecting to people, and about the consequence of all these new connections. As Tim Berners-Lee underlines it: 'The web is a social invention as much as a technical invention.'

At the opening of the London 2012 Paralympics, physicist Stephen Hawking reminded us: 'There should be no boundaries to human endeavour.' This from the guy who wrote *A Brief History of Time*, who was perhaps also reminding us that our time is brief and that we should get on with it, strive, aspire, and shoot for the stars.

I choose to feel excited by 'right now'. The Digital State is borderless, and what that really means is that it can be without boundary and limitation. The Digital State is the outcome of technical invention, accessible in physical form, say, as a device in the palm of your hand. But don't think of it as a piece of hardware. It's really a calling card. An invitation. To connect. To collaborate. To play. To be human. And, most of all, to endeavour.

SP
London

NOTES

1 It turned out to be about eight months of convulsions. HMV Group entered administration on 15 January 2013.

2 'On January 16, 2013, Blockbuster placed their UK subsidiaries in administration, putting over 4,000 jobs at risk' (*Wikipedia*).

3 Michael Lewis, *The Future Just Happened* (Hodder & Stoughton, London, 2001).

4 MK Gandhi, *Non-Violence in Peace and War* (Navajivan, Ahmedabad, 1948).

5 Andrew Edgecliffe-Johnson, Lunch with the FT: Tim Berners-Lee, *Financial Times*, 7 September 2012.

6 Caitlin Moran, *Moranthology* (Ebury Press, London, 2012).

16 HOW 'INTERNETS' INVENTED US

Stefan Terry

> “As the 21st century approached, our newest and bravest internet arrived to shake things up again. The internet of connected computers, with its roots in the 1950s and its heart in the 1960s, is the most radical and revolutionary yet. No internet in history has been more disruptive or more liberating, not even the printed word. Why? Firstly, because it was built that way by idealists, with community and democracy in its DNA. Secondly, because it contains and supersedes all the previous internets – it trumps TV and cinema for mobility and flexibility, it’s richer than radio, it beats books for speed and simplicity, and it even finds ways around language gaps. And thirdly, because it hands out the power to build to absolutely anyone... All you need is a strong enough idea, a heartfelt opinion or an interesting experience to share and you have the bricks and mortar needed to make a mark.”

I'd like you to meet... Stefan Terry

Stef and I first worked together when we were trading on the percentage play that we were smart enough to compensate for how naive we feared we were. Saatchi & Saatchi was an office jungle of big names, bigger egos, account barons, super suits and political power-plays. It was a place where everyone strutted or swaggered, or merged a self-styled version of the two. At the time, everything and everyone at the agency felt a little bit dangerous, in an exciting way. Dangerously smart or dangerously good-looking. Dangerous implications followed dangerous conversations, where you might walk away not only fleeced but one limb down, only you wouldn't know it until retracing your steps and the trail of blood returned you to the water cooler... where you'd find your arm part-gnawed and the vultures bold enough just to grin back at you. It was a great time and a great place.

Stef was too smart to stay long at Saatchi's. I suspect I still remain too naïve. When we parted company, Stef went on to co-found his own company, a brand shop called Heavenly. I always wondered whether the name was a soul-cleansing attempt to counter his Saatchi years. Most recently, Stef has ventured forth again, setting up Leap of Being, which I doubt is much of a leap of faith, given how outrageously smart and genuinely talented the guy is. On Stef's LinkedIn profile, there's a very on-the-money comment from a guy called Mike Fleming: 'Stefan has a massive brain. But quite a small head. I've been trying to figure out this conundrum over the past 3 years that I've worked with him. How can all that insight, inspiration, knowledge, clarity of thought and charm fit into the space normally occupied by human grey cells?' FYI, Stef's head is pretty much normal-sized.

*

The role of editor, I've come to learn, is one of panic and pleasure. It's not exactly ideal for anyone who ideally rather likes to control, but a little self-coaching and a few soothing words can work wonders. I kept reassuring myself that the folk I'd involved in *Digital State* would do themselves and the idea proud. Stefan Terry did himself proud. Stefan's taken on the history of civilization, started not so long after Day 1, wielding an ambition not dissimilar to Kubrick and the way he started *2001: A Space Odyssey* (1968).

On reading, I absolutely delighted in Stef's approach, the angles of understanding, the words and themes so threaded to make up a chapter whole. Stef's constructed his own kind of thematic 'black monolith', like the one in *2001*, only Stef's isn't alien, doesn't randomly squeal with apparent malevolence. Stef's monolith, by contrast, is one we have made, very human, and epochally upgrading. It's a monolith in the form of collective thought – and if that sounds rather obscure and abstract it's because I don't want to give anything away and Stef will do a far finer job of explaining it anyway. You're in for a treat.

Over to Stef.

If you ask it, the internet will tell you its history began with the development of electronic computers in the 1950s. It will tell you its name was coined in 1982, 10 years after the first e-mail was sent and six years after the Queen sent her first e-mail. And it will explain that its name is a shortening of inter-networking, a process of connecting computer networks to create a network of networks.

It's hard to argue with that, but I think there's a bigger story to tell. The electronic computer internet is certainly an amazing, world-changing internet, but it's not our first. If you take a step back, you'll see we've been busy inter-networking for a very long time. In fact, I'd go as far as to say that being inter-networked is the human condition in a nutshell.

With that in mind, I'd like to take you on a journey back in time. I'd like to show you what history looks like through the eyes of our internets, and to tell the story of how internets and humans evolved together. There's quite a lot of ground to cover and I've cut to the chase here and there. I'm also writing from my perspective in London in October 2012, so my skew is to the West. Having said that, I'm confident the principles and patterns hold true beyond the frame of my particular cultural window.

YEAR DOT-COM

When it comes to internets, we humans started early. We were like Mozart and music. It came naturally. Our first internet was language, and the moment it emerged things really kicked off for us. If you think this latest computer-based internet is disruptive, you should have seen the first one. It may even have been the thing that turned our apey ancestors into fully fledged humans, which means it's hard to say for sure whether we came up with it or it came up with us.

Back then, 3 million years or so BC, we were a bunch of missing-link-type hominids doing our thing in Africa. It seems that, back then, as now, our thing was all about coping with climate change. We had to deal with the dangers of living in open savannah rather than cosy forests. We were pretty small, quite slow and very delicious, and we quickly became extremely popular with lions.

Thankfully we had a bigger-than-average brain, a good sense of humour and a lively community spirit, which all helped make life bearable. More importantly, we also managed to take evolution up a notch and, in between our brainy brains and our collaborative approach to life, language happened. It's as if we were clever enough to have ideas and we had the drive to share them, so we came up with a way of passing them around. Language gave us a way to inter-network our brains and that in turn gave us our unbeatable evolutionary advantage.

The moment we started passing ideas around, discussing them, changing them with experience, agreeing things, changing them again and passing them on to more people's brains, something extraordinary happened. In between our interconnected minds a kind of human cyberspace sparked into life. From that moment we humans have lived in an unbelievably rich shared world of ideas, meanings, values and beliefs. I like to call it the Communiverse, and you're in it right now.

Because we're born into it, we tend to take the Communiverse for granted, but we all know deep down it's an amazing place to be. In it, the normal reality of physics, chemistry and biology has extra dimensions. It's a place where ideas live, grow and evolve, where imagination transforms into action, where intangible things have the power to become tangible. It's a place where meaning matters most.

Like cyberspace, the Communiverse started as a place where our ancestors could save information in an easily retrievable form. Classic algorithms like 'how to escape that lion.exe' and 'how to make a net to catch fish.exe' were crowd-sourced, beta-tested and refined. Being able to upload vital life experience like this into lots of different brains meant that the data were less likely to be accidentally deleted by a fatal run-in with an aurochs. It also meant that all the life experience of all the humans connected by language could start to accumulate somewhere. Data could exist beyond the lifetime of one person, the next generation didn't have to start from scratch every time, and the shoulders-of-giants procession kicked in. In evolutionary terms, the internet of language and the human cyberspace of the Communiverse gave us a way of handling and manipulating information much,

much faster than DNA could. In the Communiverse, we could adapt to our environment and evolve as quickly as we could find words to describe our experiences. For old-school nature, adapting still takes generations of hit-and-miss genetic mutation. For us it might just be a matter of seconds. When you look at things in that way, it's not surprising that we're top of the class.

But it wasn't only about pure data. Once someone's experience had been uploaded into the Communiverse, it became a thing in its own right. It took on a life of its own as internet memes do today. This separation meant that we were able to stand back from it, discuss it, understand it and ultimately reimagine it. In this common space, partly held in each person's head and knitted together with language, we started to extrapolate, experiment and tinker. We realized that, by capturing, sharing and discussing the things that had happened to us, we were able to imagine new things that hadn't yet happened. We got creative.

As we grew in confidence, we started creating lots of new things in the Communiverse. Some of them like clothes, tools and shelters were built to be useful in the real world, but other inventions were designed specifically for the Communiverse. My top five favourites would probably include love, law, religion, history and the future. It's worth stressing that, before the Communiverse, there was no past and future, only now. If that sounds ridiculous, ask yourself where the past and the future actually are. They're certainly nowhere in the material world – if you're thinking of calendars or dog-eared family photographs, you're barking up the wrong tree, as these are just representations. You can't get at the past; it's gone. And you can't get at the future either, because as soon as it arrives it's the present. The only place where the past and the future actually mean something is in the Communiverse, where we use them to store experiences in chronological order and as a tool to plan new things.

Of all its magical properties, however, the most important thing about the Communiverse was how it helped us turn theory into practice. While it had infinite scope and dimensions to allow anything imaginable to exist, it was far from ephemeral. It was knitted right into reality, as the mind is knitted into the body, and that gave it and us the power to transform the real world. The process was and remains simple: you build an idea in the Communiverse, you pack it full of powerful meaning, you get lots of people to believe in it and pledge their energy to the cause, and you get stuff done. Our drive to collaborate was as important to our success as our oversized brains and, like cyberspace today, the Communiverse became a place to create communities, forge agreements, spark movements and mobilize.

Spoken and body language worked as one powerful internet to capture the imagination and motivate the community. New layers of protocol developed in the Communiverse: ritual, ceremony, theatre, oration, poetry, dance and music bound its inhabitants together and forged connections between mind and body. People began to understand each other better as their personalities crystallized in the back-and-forth of the Communiverse. They started to build more far-reaching networks of relationships, based on likes and dislikes, and shared friendships, outlooks and values.

Large-scale, long-term teamwork was the powerful result. Activities like hunting were transformed from a desperate life-and-death lottery with wildlife attached into something between a military exercise and performance art. The hunt became a shared experience built and played out in the Communiverse. The tribe would start by visualizing the future together. The hunters' roles would be sketched out and embellished in their shared imaginations. Powerful totems to enhance strength, courage and luck would be downloaded using ceremonies of music and dance. The day of the hunt itself would flow seamlessly from the preparation, with each person bringing his or her own part of the shared visualization as a guide. The animal in the cross-hairs would play its role – it would run, fight, win or lose – and the meaning of it all would be agreed and uploaded in the rituals that followed.

THE COMMUNIVERSE 2.0

As we humans became more and more successful, our numbers grew and we started to spread out across the world. As this happened, the Communiverse split into lots of separate parts that gradually evolved in slightly different ways. There were people early on across these different parts who seemed to have a better grasp of how the Communiverse worked. Maybe they had more ideas; maybe they were better communicators; maybe they were just good-looking. Either way, they realized that they could build *themselves* in this common space. They invented charisma. Through a combination of what they said and did, they built enormous layers of meaning around themselves in the Communiverse. They draped positive values around their shoulders, climbed up on to pedestals built from past glories and donned impenetrable armoured suits of awe and fear. The convincing ones gathered followers around them and, the more people who believed in them, the more powerful and terrifying their Communiverse avatars became. Eventually these early leaders would build avatars for their whole families, creating the first monarchies.

These first kings and queens were helped in their quest for power by the emergence of an assortment of fresh new internets that set the Communiverse buzzing. Writing and visual art started as the same thing, somewhere between the two distinct internets they are today. Suddenly ideas had a new, more permanent way of being stored and distributed.

The written word evolved as an internet capable of carrying much more ornate and complex stuff. Much longer, more sophisticated thoughts could be captured, carried and discussed, and this in turn made the Communiverse into a more urbane place. The quality of our idea environment really started going up in the world.

The internet of art exploded into the Communiverse in a completely different way, bringing a broader, more expressive, emotional intelligence to the proceedings. Cave paintings like the ones at Lascaux, with their dream-time landscapes, give us a vivid insight into what the Communiverse must have looked like to our ancestors in those early days – a fluid, flowing blend of animals from the material world, mixed with the mystical shapes their meanings made in the mind's eye of the community.

In the Communiverse 2.0, much more ambitious things were possible. The oligarchs and tyrants carried on building their ivory towers, employing the majesty and mystery of art and poetry to elevate themselves yet further in the shared consciousness of their subjects. At the same time, new technology was forged in the creative furnaces of the Communiverse: exquisite stonecraft algorithms were coded and distributed, only to be rendered obsolete by new metal-working upgrades that spread virally along trade routes. The magic conjured by these powerful new ideas gave us yet more power over the world outside the Communiverse. This new technology was jealously guarded by the dominant few. They imported that mystique into their avatars and grew so colossal and convincing that they became nothing short of living gods: so richly overladen with meaning and significance in the connected hearts and minds of their subjects that they buckled the fabric of the Communiverse. Over time, these most intensely meaningful regions of the Communiverse would become the realm of the supernatural – an unknowable place beyond the reach of all but a chosen few.

With the internet of writing, ideas became more specific and less vulnerable to constant re-remembering and reinterpretation. Now you could start to have records of events, rather than shared memories. You could start to compare and contrast things and calculate outcomes. Ideas evolved into theories and theories into strategies. Years of saved records and calendars began to reveal repeating cycles, and the framework of the Communiverse became more expansive. The randomness that used to freak us out had turned into pretty patterns in the Communiverse. Suddenly we saw the future in HD.

The idea of agriculture germinated in this bigger, more expansive Communiverse; it grew and branched out, transforming things as it went. People settled down; they started harnessing the land and creating surplus for the first time, and this gave them more opportunity and energy to build new, revolutionary things in the Communiverse.

Around the same time, the internet of numbers came online. Now people were able to quantify their experiences and their surroundings precisely. They could share commodities, assess context, analyse data and agree value. They had invented the objectivity, and the Communiverse would never be the same again.

With extra time, plenty of food and the combined internets of language, art and numbers, humanity and the Communiverse went ballistic. The vast canvas of the online imagination was filled with plans, processes and systems. The powerful people harnessed the internet of numbers to create order and predictability. They infused the internet of language with objectivity, and the idea of law was born. The elites used this new power to enshrine their positions further; they wrapped it around themselves and across the fabric of the Communiverse, guaranteeing compliance from their followers through a rock-solid combination of emotional belief and rational agreement. Now even bigger forces of humanity could be controlled and motivated. Civilization had arrived.

And what an achievement civilization was. So many people doing things in concert, so great a level of coordination and combined firepower for progress. When we look back at the early civilizations, we often focus on the artefacts we can still see and handle – the poignant ruins jutting out of the past, the scars left by industry and infrastructure, the fragments of lives sketched in pottery and glass or vivid pinpoints of Technicolor mosaics and stubborn gold. But, just as with our own civilization, these physical markers are only the outward expression. The structures that held these vast civilizations together were in the Communiverse; their bricks and mortar were the shared beliefs and values of the people who made them.

While people believed in the framework of their civilizations, held to their mutual agreements and abided by their laws, they grew from strength to strength and their civilizations became truly fertile. The internets flowered.

Language, numbers and law blossomed into philosophy, mathematics and science, and the Communiverse evolved an elevated realm to match the supernatural. Somewhere between these two knots in the fabric, religion evolved, bringing reason and objectivity to the mystery of existence and shedding light on the workings of the Communiverse. In a few rarefied places the Communiverse became self-aware enough for the delicate flower of democracy to take root and for the power to build things to be shared out more evenly. However, even in the republics of Greece and Rome, the vast majority remained in harness, for better or for worse. In most cases, the powerful few continued to bend the Communiverse to their will. As their influence was stretched, they downloaded more awe and authority into their avatars. They built impenetrable battlements of tradition and fear around themselves so that, ironically, only their closest associates could pose a threat. When we look with 21st-century eyes at the oversized statues of late-Roman emperors, like the Colossus of Constantine (now only a dismembered marble head, hands and feet in a museum courtyard), we see monstrous vanity and laughable ego, but actually we're looking back through a window into the Communiverse as it was in AD 315 and we're seeing Constantine as he appeared to his people. That 40-foot figure, with godlike expression and larger-than-life eyes cast up towards heaven, is exactly what the emperor's avatar looked and felt like. He was not a five foot eight man with pretensions; he was that *thing*, just as surely as Stefani Joanne Angelina Germanotta is Lady Gaga.

And when people started to lose faith in the meaning and values of their civilizations, the cracks spread in the Communiverse decades before signs showed outside on the villas, temples and fortresses. Once the beliefs had been betrayed and the contracts broken, nothing the despots could do would stop the dominoes tumbling. No force of arms or shoring up could halt their decline and fall in that shared space between the hearts and minds of their disillusioned citizens.

So the outposts of the Communiverse set themselves on a cycle, first expanding into glorious civilizations and then, when the cat's cradle of beliefs could stretch no more, unravelling in chaos and recrimination. Empires rose and fell. Bits of the Communiverse crashed, their hard drives wiped as generations perished in wars and libraries burnt. In Europe the collapse of the Roman Empire was a catastrophic server failure. Our connectivity reduced, our collective memory fragmented, our view of reality diminished and our ability to mobilize in one direction evaporated. We tried for a millennium to get back online but, in the end, it took a download of original software to move us forward. By a stroke of luck someone had copied a corner of our old written internet and saved it in a nearby Communiverse. The ideas from these Greek and Roman books were uploaded back into our Communiverse in the 1400s and helped trigger the reboot of the Renaissance.

UPLOAD THE REVOLUTION

Throughout all this ebbing and flowing the status quo for people stayed largely the same. There were a few masters of the Communiverse who had learnt to build in it – aristocrats, monarchs, emperors and popes – and a vast helpless majority who were variously inspired and humbled by it. Most had little idea that the Communiverse even existed, and this suited the few very well indeed, thank you.

But then in Europe a radical new internet came to the rescue. When Johannes Gutenberg invented the printing press in the mid-15th century, he let rip the most disruptive and revolutionary internet since language itself. Here was an internet that could broadcast complex ideas over vast distances extremely quickly, but more importantly this internet allowed two new things. Firstly, anyone who could write now had the power to start building important structures in the Communiverse. You didn't have to be an aristocrat or a politician – now intellectuals, poets, writers, philosophers and monks could become architects too, and there was nothing the old elite could do about it. Secondly, anyone who could read could be influenced in the privacy of their homes – in the past, if you were interested in radical ideas, you'd have to go and put yourself in the firing line. Now you could pick up a copy of a controversial book and anonymously upload its anti-establishment memes into the Communiverse. It was a democratic revolution, and the Communiverse became a more exciting, volatile and honest place almost overnight.

One of the biggest changes this radical new internet created was the dismantling of the Catholic Church's controlling presence in the Communiverse. The printed word infected it with an unstoppable virus – Reformation.exe – forcing it to change its ways and setting in motion a revolution in self-awareness and individual freedom. Martin Luther was the figurehead, the person who had the thoughts and coded the virus, but he was not the first. There were many before him who tried to challenge the corrupted foundations of the Catholic Church. He succeeded where others failed because he spread his ideas on the new internet of the printed word. The battle for the fate of Christianity took place entirely in the Communiverse. Before this new internet, the establishment would act ruthlessly to undermine anyone who attacked it, stripping their avatar of its status, branding it 'heretic', piling on shame and leaving it isolated: the equivalent of being un-friended by everyone you know on Facebook and blocked by everyone you follow on Twitter in one go, and the definition of death in the Communiverse. But this time too many people had linked in to Luther. They'd read his books and they believed in him and his ideas. He just had too many followers and too many 'likes' for the pope's trolls to make an impact. He could not be isolated, and his ideas lived on.

With this democratic shift, more and more people became influential in shaping the Communiverse, and it grew in richness and fertility with all the fresh experiences and ideas. The modern idea of culture emerged as a kind of multi-internet Communiverse within a Communiverse. The educated middle classes evolved to became powerful sources of content. Enthused by their new-found influence, they contributed across science, engineering, technology and the arts.

The ancient institutions of monarchy and religion came under more pressure as challenging ideas spread across the internets and people began to see them for what they were. The light of reason had been turned on in the Communiverse, and any structures that didn't add up stuck out like sore thumbs. People began to be aware of how the Communiverse worked; the middle and then working classes felt the force of the beliefs that held them and questioned things. Europe was swept by revolution after revolution.

Freedom of thought and a growing access to the levers of the Communiverse escalated progress. The Enlightenment dawned and with it the internet of the scientific method. New technology was conceived. Global trade and exploration increased, connecting Communiverses and cross-fertilizing internets. As our shared worldview expanded beyond the planet, we started delving deeper into the interior. The internet of arts shifted focus from building avatars for the powerful to sharing the human condition. The novel, poetry, music, painting, theatre and ultimately philosophy and psychoanalysis were set free to map the inner space of the Communiverse. It's no coincidence that art at the turn of the 20th century started looking like cave paintings again.

CONTROL, ALT, DELETE

The modern age dawned and a tidal wave of new internets hit home. The telegraph was the first global internet that connected in real time. The internet of the telephone soon followed, and with it the first inkling of cyberspace. Then came radio, cinema and television, all internets that connected further, faster and in ways that enlarged and enriched the Communiverse. As with the printed word, people had high hopes that each subsequent internet would have the same unifying and liberating power but, while the telephone and telegraph were great connectors, the three that followed would prove to be as controlling as they were liberating. The thrilling emotional power and universal reach of radio, cinema and TV fell into the wrong hands and a new generation of tyrants used them to claw back the freedoms that the printed word had won. The fascists and communists of the early 20th century understood as well as any earlier warlord or decadent emperor exactly how to twist the Communiverse to their will. They waged war on the book and ruthlessly exploited the new internets to download their distorted worldviews directly into the souls of their subjects. Never before had the Communiverse been so rotten. Never had it been so coldly and thoroughly reprogrammed. In the Communiverse according to Hitler, Mussolini, Franco, Stalin and Mao, only one idea was allowed, and everyone had to log on to it at all times. In each case, the idea's hellish gravity was so intense that the operating system of the Communiverse failed and every fundamental human value lost its meaning. These Communiverses were unstable; the black hole at their hearts grew too massive and they imploded, leaving their people naked and out in the cold.

The world wars tore the Communiverse into tatters, and humanity faced another time of fragmentation. But the 1950s rebuilders were hopeful. They quickly invited the isolated to join their new model Communiverse and created internets like the United Nations to force a fusion between the splintered parts. But, as the Cold War proves, not everyone wanted to join and, for a while, the world was split between two super-Communiverses: two alternative social and political cyberspaces with almost the whole world logged on to one or the other.

While politicians were busy trying to cajole people on the other side to climb over the firewall and join their superior Communiverse, new manipulators came out of the woodwork and began to take control. This time it wasn't aristocrats, emperors or even popes – their meaning had been largely deleted. And it wasn't presidents, prime ministers or general secretaries either – they'd lost touch with what was happening inside. Our Communiverse was left open and unguarded, and it was global corporations that stepped in.

Big businesses became the new rulers of the Communiverse. They rolled their products out en masse in factories, but they built them first in the shared consciousness. Corporations used all the internets at their disposal to create powerful layers of meaning around their products, to make them magnetic in the mind. Their favourite by far was TV. Here was an internet that had all the reach and intimacy of the written word, more immediate gut impact and none of the frustrating return path. Advertising became a superfast fibre-optic link, perfect for uploading ideas and associations. In the in-fight between competing corporations, meaning-inflation hit the Communiverse again, and more and more powerful values and beliefs were uploaded. Companies, products and services morphed into brands and the consumer society was born.

As economies recovered and living standards improved, the Communiverse became overrun with brands determined to attract and persuade. Our shared mental space gradually turned into a marketplace, and our imagination and energy were channelled towards hankering after and acquiring. The Communiverse had never been more influential, and it was systematically harnessed by marketing departments and agencies. They invented market research to better understand its inner workings and created the focus group to look at slices of it under a microscope in laboratory conditions. The great brands became as permanent and unassailable as any movement or institution in the past. After over 120 years of selling carbonated soft drinks, Coca-Cola is still in charge, even though most people prefer Pepsi in blind tests. Coke just tastes too damn good in the Communiverse.

By the end of the 20th century, we found ourselves in a world overfilled with material things – products, goods and possessions. Never before in history had there been so much 'stuff', and the Communiverse was so busy helping us focus on which trainers to buy or which car to drive that we could barely tell it was there. We elevated the individual. We became sceptical about connecting. We became isolated. We couldn't see the wood for the trees, and it wasn't sustainable.

REALITY GOES OPEN-SOURCE

Thankfully, as the 21st century approached, our newest and bravest internet arrived to shake things up again. The internet of connected computers, with its roots in the 1950s and its heart in the 1960s, is the most radical and revolutionary yet. No internet in history has been more disruptive or more liberating, not even the printed word. Why? Firstly, because it was built that way by idealists, with community and democracy in its DNA. Secondly, because it contains and supersedes all the previous internets – it trumps TV and cinema for mobility and flexibility, it's richer than radio, it beats books for speed and simplicity, and it even finds ways around language gaps. And thirdly, because it hands out the power to build in the Communiverse to absolutely anyone. You don't need to be a tribal leader, an emperor, a politician or a pope. You don't need to be an intellectual, have a reputation or secure a publishing deal. All you need is a strong enough idea, a heartfelt opinion or an interesting experience to share and you have the bricks and mortar needed to make a mark.

Our newest internet is having a profound effect on the Communiverse. The more time we spend online – making connections, learning from each other's experience, uploading and downloading ideas – the more we see the Communiverse coming into focus around us. Our permanent virtual reality of shared feelings, meanings, values and beliefs is becoming tangible in cyberspace. We're beginning to see how it works.

Thanks to social networks, invisible objects from the Communiverse like 'friendships' now have a shape we can see and a journey and gallery of sensations we can share. A hashtag search on Twitter can give us a live snapshot of people's beliefs and opinions about almost anything. We can see the shapes in the Communiverse moving and evolving before our eyes. Thanks to the blogosphere, institutions, governments, organizations and brands can finally be seen for what they are. They can't get away with building monuments of lies and hypocrisy or hiding their true intent behind walls of soft-focus advertising, jargon or straplines. Their claims to our hearts and minds can be interrogated and tested. We can push at their foundations. We can ask what they stand for and, if their values don't add up, we can walk away or bring them crashing down.

At the same time, more and more of us are making stronger allegiances to the movements, organizations, brands and causes we believe in. Now we can see for ourselves how things are built in the Communiverse, we know far more clearly which ideas we want to support.

So what does this mean for the future? We all know we're living through challenging and uncertain times. Global warming, economic crisis, overpopulation, inequality, injustice, poverty, disease: these are our threats today. But being under threat is nothing new for us; it's only the scale that's different.

In the past, the Communiverse was our evolutionary advantage. In it, we found the answers to our problems and through it we created the means to overcome. Our threats and challenges may be bigger today, but so is the Communiverse and, what's more, it's never been more free or more fertile.

These days, it doesn't matter if you're a global brand, a public company or a private individual, if you're honest about your intent and inspiring about what you want to achieve you can harness the energy to make it happen. The internet of computers has created the biggest Communiverse in history and, just like our ancestors before us, we're using it to store information, to form movements and to solve problems. Mass online collaborations like *Wikipedia* are an old-fashioned blend of our big brains and our community spirit, and they show the way ahead. Human-based computation and 'games with a purpose' are being harnessed to tackle everything from mapping the human brain to mapping the known universe.

Whatever happens, whenever the next internet emerges, if we keep on imagining together, the answers and energy we need will always be there, in the folds of the Communiverse. What are you going to build?

ST
London

EPILOGUE

"I just loved the idea of producing *Digital State* as an anthology. The more I thought about the theme, the more I thought that it couldn't be done any other way."

> *The whole web had always been done by people who were very internationally-minded, very public-spirited, and very excited about the outcome.*
>
> TIM BERNERS-LEE, IN ANDREW EDGECLIFFE-JOHNSON, LUNCH WITH THE FT: TIM BERNERS-LEE, *FINANCIAL TIMES* (7 SEPTEMBER 2012)

I just loved the idea of producing *Digital State* as an anthology. The more I thought about the theme, the more I thought that it couldn't be done any other way. The approach had to reflect the subject matter. And it had to reflect the sentiment behind the subject matter, the true spirit of the internet. If the subject matter was all about how the internet creates open invitation, where multiple contributors with multiple ideas and viewpoints build our (Digital) State bottom up, and where its future is so speculative, unknown and unknowable, then how could the book's commentary justifiably involve just one guy, me, banging on for 70,000 words?

For *Digital State*, I wanted to go on a journey, with some friends (internationally-minded, public-spirited) and very smart people whom I've met on my journey so far, to canvass their opinions and perspectives, to *source* my own *crowd*. *Digital State* just *had* to be about collaboration, and had to take a wide angle, drawing upon compass points that drew in the likes of Los Angeles, New York, London, Manchester, Gothenburg, Berlin and Sydney.

Of course, collaborations can be tricky. They can collapse, can implode like garage bands, but they can also produce things of wonder, spark all kinds of originality and ideas that only gain and gain in momentum and potential force. I was shooting for the latter, ever jittery to the former.

In the final analysis, if this is it, I think *Digital State* certainly kept the right side of the collaborative line, and that happy outcome had everything to do with my collaborators. If we'd been a garage band, we'd have been able to rent our own apartment, maybe even afford our own tour bus.

*

> *The first day on the new world had begun.*
>
> SYDNEY BOEHM, 1908–90, US SCREENWRITER

I'll close on proceedings with a 'beginning', what feels like a first-day beginning for many, in the first-person experience sense. I joined the working world in September 1996. The office-scape had computers on everyone's desks, but running Word and Excel at the same time was an exercise in high risk, and double-clicking on PowerPoint with any other package already open was like purposefully flying into a mountain. Dinosaurs did not congregate by the water cooler, and people's wardrobes weren't so wildly different to today, but it was of course a very foreign country.

In the agency I joined, teams of 15 or so people shared one stand-alone PC that was 'connected to the internet', and that PC largely stood alone, drawing blank expressions, some dust, and representing little obvious utility. I remember sitting next to a colleague, who was on the phone to a client one average afternoon, where the conversation went along the lines: 'An *e-mail*? Sure, why not! Let's try it; send me one!' She then cupped her hand over the mouthpiece and asked, 'What the hell's my e-mail address?' Once it had been supplied, she delicately spelt out each vowel, consonant and 'full stop' of her address, explaining it also had 'one of those curly ats', and emphasizing the 'dot-com' suffix as though she was practising elocution with a mouth full of marbles. She then repeated the whole thing, for what was the second time ever in her life. I'll repeat the year: 1996.

Of course, Tim Berners-Lee had only invented the world wide web six years prior, sending the first successful HTTP missive on 25 December 1990.

While so many of us were tucking into our turkey, who knew that this was the first day of our new world?

At the Cannes 2012 ad festival, one speaker shared the anecdote of how his six-year-old daughter had recently asked him, 'Daddy, before computers, how did people get on the internet?'

Three dots in time, 1990 to 1996 to 2012. This is the distance we've come.

There's a second generation of Digital Natives entering our world. For anyone born around 2006 or any time thereafter, which applies to all three of my children, 'the internet' is a very seamless and interwoven *given*, where they drag and click on screens by finger-touch, and if the screens don't act like a tablet then the assumption is they must be broken.

The internet has, it seems, become as much an elemental part of our world as air and water, has physically integrated with our homes, places of work, our inner and outer lives. The internet has become a constant, an absolute given, an always-there and in-reach companion. It has become ubiquitous. Have wi-fi, will be omnipresent.

And each new generation will arrive into this world where the internet is simply *there*. We are borderline forgetful of when the internet happened and now almost blind to its novelty. *This* Digital State, *our* Digital State, will continue to open our eyes to the possibilities, and by a second heartbeat, the consequences will also be ours to bear.

SP
London

APPENDIX

So this is what everyone got. I wrote the book's outline, loved the idea of doing it as an anthology, recruited the people I figured could best help me storm the castle and slay the dragon, and then sent them the following: one diagram of circles, converging, 250 words, and two questions:

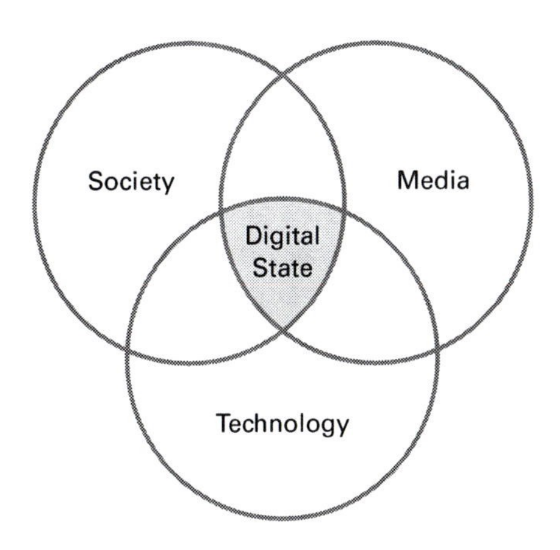

The Digital State

A nation state of the mind; a mental, emotional, conceptual geography, populated by very real people, and providing a stage for their practices and self-expression.

Is this land a Thomas More-style Utopia, an Orwellian Dystopia, a blend of both, or neither? And to better refine the question, what could this part-built land become? What is its potential? An empire with hegemonic possibilities? A rogue state? A nirvana, enlightened and illuminating? Or something much darker, bleaker and 'end of days'-like?

*

> *The Digital State has no fixed or physical borders. It is fluid, not demarcated by a bold black line in the understood Old World analogue sense. The Digital State is built brick by individually contributed brick, the collective endlessly adding new building blocks, generating, regenerating, editing, growing, redefining.*
>
> *The Digital State is self-governed, legitimized, regulated by the all and any that log on, 'like' or upload. The Digital State is everywhere and nowhere, not aspiring to be sexily enigmatic or paradoxically postmodern. Very simply, the Digital State is* made real *by the very real people who populate it, residents who meet their very real needs through digital interactions and encounters.*
>
> *It is both atomized and galvanized, rebellious and unified. It is egalitarian in its promotion of self and the means by which it gives anyone 'voice' and expression. It is a free state, open-source, laissez-faire.*
>
> *It is our future.*

*

And specifically, for you, *it is two questions: what is the Digital State? What is our Digital State of Mind?*

It's an open brief, clearly interpretive. That's the idea.

Please explore the directions that feel right, in much the way you've explored the world and the places and spaces your career has taken you. Then hit me with it. Don't hold back in putting it down and putting it out there. If the end product is 15 or so chapters brimming with personality and punch, then the final product will really be something.

Until soon,

Simon

CONTRIBUTORS

Hans Andersson has an MSc in civil engineering. He spent the 1980s designing ports and bridges around the world. He then went on to the theatre business (where he still fiddles as the chairman of a suburban, multi-ethnic theatre company). Hans jumped the fence to the advertising world, and specifically to Forsman & Bodenfors, in early 1996. In 2001 he became a senior partner, having worked with many of F&B's clients in Sweden and abroad, and was further appointed CEO and chairman for the companies in the group. At present, he also spends a fair share of his time with the world's largest ferry company, Stena Line. He sits on the board of Forsman & Bodenfors, but in real life he lives in Gothenburg, where he is married to Carolina and is a father of five.

Vicki Connerty had an early sojourn as a roving reporter for BBC local radio. She was ultimately lured away from the glitz and glamour of traffic reporting to join the bright lights of London's thriving media scene. This was in the late 1990s. Positions followed at Chrysalis Radio, Classic FM and Virgin Radio, the latter during the Chris Evans years, which remain something of a champagne-fuelled blur. She subsequently moved across into the media agency world, working all over the globe and with renowned global clients such as Diageo, Disney, Nestlé, Honda, Reckitt Benckiser and Qantas. In 2011, she was appointed to launch and run Newcast Australia, the branded content division of Publicis-owned global media agency ZenithOptimedia. Like many other fair-skinned, rain-weary Brits, she is currently based in Sydney and enjoying all that Australia has to offer.

Greg Grimmer has spent all his working life in the London advertising world, at a number of the biggest global agencies. He founded his own agency, HMDG, in 2008 and continues to be one of the sector's brightest, wittiest and most outspoken voices. He has won numerous awards in online, mobile and social networking (as well as more traditional media channels), and helped *Wired* successfully relaunch into the UK. An oft-quoted press figure, he also appears at many media, digital and creative events, and has trained and recruited a number of the best creative talents to be found in the communication planning fraternity. A natural networker, he is well connected to the London digerati as well as the Silicon Valley crowd, and when pushed can always be prompted to predict the next big thing (or more often prick the bubble of hubris).

Malcolm Hunter is a pioneer of international advertising and integrated communications planning. He has been chief strategy officer both at major international advertising agencies and at media companies. His most famous work includes 'The World's Local Bank' for HSBC and 'Dirt Is Good' for Persil. More recently he developed and implemented Aegis Media's integrated communications planning process. He believes that today, the more technology transforms marketing, the more we need to put humanity at the heart of everything we do. He helps his clients develop human brands for the Digital Age. He was born in Liverpool, educated at Oxford University, and lives in London with his wife and three children.

Christian Johnsen featured in Forbes USA's '30 under 30' (marketing and advertising) for 2012. It followed in recognition of a year where his knowledge and strategic insight proved instrumental in the development of innovative communication strategies that helped Carat USA to a record-breaking new business performance, winning Macy's domestic broadcast and digital media, and General Motors' $3-billion-a-year global media account, the largest single contract ever awarded in the industry. He is a strategist, activist, actor and storyteller, who currently resides in New York City and dreams of changing the world (for the better).

Austen Kay is co-founder and joint managing director of w00t! Media, a digital agency helping brands connect with young adults. He works with acclaimed youth publishers such as Pitchfork, Mixcloud, Drowned in Sound and SBTV, and has delivered media partnerships for clients including Sony, Intel and Kraft. Prior to w00t! Media, he worked both agency and client side, devising and implementing media strategies for Sainsbury's Bank, Scottish Widows and the Co-operative Group. He lives in Manchester with his wife and three children, supports Manchester City and tries to be a 'mensch' just as his grandmother always wanted.

Judd Labarthe is US-born and Berlin-based. He writes and speaks widely on the topic of creativity and effectiveness. A 25-year veteran of agency life, he has had three careers in the business (account handler, then copywriter, now planner), experienced diverse agency cultures (from DDB to Ogilvy to German digital hotshop Argonauten), and advised clients such as Volkswagen,

Leica, Pernod-Ricard, Nestlé, Westin, Anheuser-Busch, Deutsche Bahn, Disney and many local and regional brands across Europe and Asia. A member of the Effie Worldwide advisory board, he has also had a hand in some 50 Effie winners on three continents and serves regularly as a judge and moderator for Effie programmes worldwide.

Christopher Lockwood has been described as a brilliant misfit and media visionary. He is a 'content' polymath who has used his unusual combination of creative ability and entrepreneurial business acumen to constantly drive fresh thinking in the fields of brand communication and consumer editorial. His career has stretched from leading fashion and style magazines, and top-flight agencies, to his own branded content studio. His main job is now editorial director of social video agency Adjust Your Set, but he continues to involve himself in a variety of exciting and dynamic projects as designer, curator, illustrator, artist, film-maker, and platform and technology innovator. For a daily dose of creative inspiration, follow at: **www.pinterest.com/generationcreat**.

Nicholas Pont is a senior vice-president at PIMCO, one of the largest investment solutions providers in the world (to companies, central banks, educational institutions, financial advisers, foundations and endowments). He works with institutional clients and global financial institutions, and sits on the investment advisory committee for the PIMCO Europe Foundation. Previously, he was an associate with Julius Baer Investments and, before that, Western Asset Management Company (WAMCO). He has 10 years of investment experience, and holds an undergraduate degree in economics and politics from the University of Exeter. Before embarking on a career in asset management, he was a professional cricketer.

Tamara Quinn is a qualified barrister and practises as a solicitor in London, specializing in intellectual property law. She has had years of experience as a partner in a City law firm, as well as having worked in-house as head of intellectual property for a major retailer, and as head of legal for a publishing company. As an undergraduate, Tamara studied medicine, and then law and anthropology. She has a longstanding fascination with all things scientific and admits to an alarmingly extensive knowledge of James Bond trivia. She tweets @tamarajq.

Bettina Sherick is the SVP, Digital Strategic Marketing for 20th Century Fox International, where she is responsible for managing relationships with leading digital marketing and technology companies, and ensuring that digital is at the core of all marketing activity within the division. During her 12-year tenure, she has managed the launch of over 150 international digital marketing campaigns for titles such as *Avatar*, all films in the *Ice Age* franchise, and *The Simpsons Movie*, the latter of which won the Webby Award and People's Voice Webby Award in the movie and film category. She was named an Internationalist of the Year by the *Internationalist Magazine* in 2010, and was the recipient of the 2011 iMedia Visionary Entertainment Marketer Award. She's the proud mother of a digitally savvy nine-year-old, who keeps her on her toes.

Stefan Terry helps organizations and brands to define and present themselves. After studying music at King's College London, he moved into advertising, starting as a planner at Saatchi & Saatchi. In 2003 he co-founded branding agency Heavenly, where he worked with the BBC, the Royal Society, the British Library, the Wellcome Trust and BSkyB, and internationally with NBC Universal and Star India. He's now getting ready to launch a new branding agency with a mission to help clients succeed by harnessing the energy and creativity of their people. He thinks, he writes, he collaborates, and he lives just outside London with his wife, son and daughter.

Faris Yakob is a strategist, writer, public speaker, creative director and geek. Most recently he was chief innovation officer of MDC and founding partner of Spies & Assassins, the creative technology boutique. Previously, he was chief digital officer at McCann Erickson, and digital ninja at Naked Communications. He's won and judged numerous awards, strategic and creative, served as chairman of the content and contact and integrated juries for the Clios, and created the 'New' category for the London International Awards. He teaches at Miami Ad School. He was named one of the top 50 creatives in the world by the Clios, and one of 10 modern-day Mad Men by Fast Company. He writes and speaks on technology, media, brands and creativity, all over the world, and was featured in *The Greatest Movie Ever Sold*. If you want him to write, speak, think about things or have ideas for you, you can find him online @faris and farisyakob.com. He hopes you have a lovely day.

ACKNOWLEDGEMENTS

This is an anthology, so it's quite the cast of thank-yous.

First, foremost, of course, to the 13 contributors who 'came to the aid of the party' and helped build this 'body of thought'. You're a seriously smart lot, and I'm very fortunate and honoured for my life path to have crossed with each of yours. This was fun, and I hope for each of you too. Thank you to Hans Andersson, Vicki Connerty, Greg Grimmer, Malcolm Hunter, Christian Johnsen, Austen Kay, Judd Labarthe, Christopher Lockwood, Nicholas Pont, Tamara Quinn, Bettina Sherick, Stefan Terry and Faris Yakob.

To Christopher Lockwood (and yeah, it's a double-thanks) for turning words into illustrations that knocked me over with their sheer awesomeness.

To Matthew Smith. I keep owing you.

To Helen Kogan, and the rest of Kogan Page, for your ongoing support, drive, and genuine spirit of partnership.

To all the spouses and partners and friends who lent an ear and an idea, who inspired and indulged each of the contributors to go on the journey they did and ultimately write the chapters they delivered. A great idea has many mothers, no man is an island, the true power sits behind the throne... You get the idea and I'm sure you'll thank me for not going on.

I thank you all.

CPSIA information can be obtained at www.ICGtesting.com
Printed in the USA
BVOW011632210513

321301BV00002B/2/P

9 780749 468859